from GOATHERD to GOVERNOR

The Autobiography of

EDWIN MTEI

from GOATHERD to GOVERNOR

The Autobiography of

EDWIN MTEI

Mkuki na Nyota Publishers
P. O. Box 4246
Dar es Salaam, Tanzania
www.mkukinanyota.com

Published by:
Mkuki na Nyota Publishers
P. O. Box 4246
Dar es Salaam, Tanzania
www.mkukinanyota.com

© Edwin Mtei, 2009

ISBN 978-9987-08-030-4

All rights reserved. No part of this publication may be reproduced or transmitted in any form or by any means without the written permission of the copyright holder or publisher.

CONTENTS

Acronyms x

Acknowledgements xiii

Introduction xiv

CHAPTERS

CHAPTER 1 My Life in Summary 1

CHAPTER 2 Birth and Childhood 5

CHAPTER 3 Going to School 13

CHAPTER 4 High School and University 27

CHAPTER 5 Employment and Engagement 42

CHAPTER 6 Joining the Civil Service and Getting Married 49

CHAPTER 7 Promotion and Independence 61

CHAPTER 8 Secondment to EACSO 71

CHAPTER 9 Translation into Finance 78

CHAPTER 10 Appointment as Governor 89

CHAPTER 11 Launching and Nurturing a Central Bank 92

CHAPTER 12 The Arusha Declaration and Birth
of the Community 106

CHAPTER 13 International Finance
and Payments System 111

CHAPTER 14 Growing in the Bank 115

CHAPTER 15 Back to an EAC on the Brink of Collapse 123

CHAPTER 16 Back to Finance 135

CHAPTER 17 Events Leading to My Resignation 149

CHAPTER 18 Economic and Other Policies
   of the Nyerere Regime .158

CHAPTER 19 Public Financier Turned Farmer 167

CHAPTER 20 Appointment to Executive Board of IMF 174

CHAPTER 21 Mixing Farming with Public Service. 189

CHAPTER 22 Multiparty Politics and Nurturing a Political Party . .195

CHAPTER 23 The 1995 General Elections 202

CHAPTER 24 Subsequent General Elections. 209

CHAPTER 25 The Epilogue 222

Glossary of non-English words .228

ILLUSTRATIONS AND PHOTOGRAPHS

My earliest photo unearthed from my records 19

With my friend Wilfred Marealle, a studio photo we took before he left
Kampala for Kabete. 40

Johara Hassan Marealle at the time of our engagement 45

Outside the Ngaruma Lutheran Parish Church after the wedding
ceremony, 6 August 1960 58

Johara and me 'At Home' in our Marangu House after our wedding. . 59

East African Government, EACSO and private sector managers
at a seminar held at Marangu Hotel, 1963, sponsored
by the Ford Foundation 68

On secondment from the Tanganyika Civil Service to the Secretary
General's Office, EACSO. 74

Servicing the EACSO Authory as Clerk with Members signing an
agreement with the U.K. High Commissioner. 75

President Nyerere's all-African Permanent Secretaries,
December 1964 82

Welcoming First and Second Vice-Presidents (Karume and Kawawa)
at the inauguration of Bot Operations 98

The Bank of Tanzania Headquarters Building,
opened in July, 1969. 103

President Nyerere examines a Commemorative Coin, presented to him
at the formal opening of the Bank of Tanzania Building,
July 1969. 103

As Governor: at my desk, with the President's portrait
in the background 104

Being welcomed by Robert Ouko into the EALA Chambers, for
swearing in as a Member, 25 April 1974 124

At my desk as newly appointed EAC Secretary General, May 1974 . . .126

Presenting my budget in parliament as Minister of Finance in 1978 . .142

Paying a courtesy call on Indian President Sanjiva Reddy in New Delhi,
during my 1979 official visit to India as co-Chairman
of the Indo–Tanzanian Joint Commission on Co-operation 148

With President Sir Seretse Khama, after he had opened the Southern
African Conference of Ministers of Planning on Lessening Dependence
on apartheid South Africa, 1979 (precursor to SADC) With
President Sir Seretse Khama and M. Fawley of EEC at first SADCC
Meeting 1979 149

As Executive Director: leading an IMF Delegation to the ECA
Ministerial Meeting , Addis Ababa .187

Playing host to General Olusegun Obasanjo on his visit to Tanzania as
Chair of Africa Leadership Forum .191

Campaigning with Mary Kabigi, who headed the Women's Section, to recruit members for Chadema, 1994. 199

Campaigning in the Arusha Urban Constituency for a Parliamentary seat, October, 1995. 204

Opposition Party Leaders on tour in the Federal Republic of Germany. 206

CHADEMA presidential candidate, accompanied by his wife and two retired National Chairmen march to the site for the launch of the Campaign. 213

Retired founder Chairman Mtei greets the multitude at the launch in Shinyanga. 214

Freeman Mbowe, addressing the multitude at the launch of his presidential campaign, 2005 215

Mbowe continued to attract huge crowds right up to the end as seen here in Moshi. 216

Three Generations: a rare group photograph of ourselves, our children, their spouses and all our grandchildren, at the Ogaden Estate, December 2002. 226

ACRONYMS

AGM	Annual General Meeting
ALF	Africa Leadership Forum
ASP	Afro-Shirazi Party
AU	African Union
BoT	Bank of Tanzania
CCM	Chama cha Mapinduzi
CHADEMA	Chama cha Demokrasia na Maendeleo
CUF	Civic United Front
DP	Democratic Party
EA	East African
EAA	East African Airways (Corporation)
EAC	East African Community
EACB	East African Currency Board
EACSO	East African Common Services Organisation
EADB	East African Development Bank
EAH	East African Harbours (Corporation)
EAHC	East Africa High Commission
EALA	East African Legislative Assembly
EAP&T	East African Posts and Telecommunications (Corporation)
EAT	East African Tobacco Company
ECOSOC	UN Economic and Social Council
FAO	UN Food and Agricultural Organisation
KIA	Kilimanjaro International Airport
IMF	International Monetary Fund
I.Q	Intelligence Quotient
MECCO	Mwananchi Engineering and Construction Company
NBC	National Bank of Commerce
NDC	National Development Corporation
NEC	National Electoral Commission
NEC	National Executive Committee (of a political party)
OPEC	Organisation of Petroleum Exporting Countries

PAYE	Pay As You Earn (income tax)
RC	Regional Commissioner
SAP	Structural Adjustment Programme
SDRs	Speacial Drawing Rights
TaCRI	Tanzania Coffee Research Institute
TANROADS	Tanzania Roads Maintenance Agency
TAZARA	Tanzania-Zambia Railways Authority
TCB	Tanzania Coffee Board
TCCCO	Tanganyika Coffee Curing Company Limited
TCGA	Tanganyika Coffee Growers' Association
TDFL	Tanzania Development Finance Company Limited
TLP	Tanzania Labour Party
TRA	Tanzania Revenue Authority
TShs	Tanzania Shillings
UDETA	Union for Democracy in Tanzania
UDP	United Democratic Party
UMD	Union for Multiparty Democracy
UN	United Nations Organisation
VAT	Value Added Tax
WB	World Bank

Acknowledgements

Although I have written many articles, papers, reports and memoranda for years, the writing of this story of my times and life has been an arduous task; and I would not have completed it without the assistance and encouragement of many people. I can only mention a few.

Top on the list have been the latest: the editors Mary Jay, Penelope Ormerod and the publisher Mr. Walter Bgoya. They have not only made valuable comments and suggestions for improvement of the manuscript, but have encouraged me to complete it.

Above all, I want to acknowledge that this work has been a joint effort by all members of my family: my wife Johara commenting on every chapter or addition as I wrote, and the children criticizing and suggesting improvements as progress was made and especially, instructing me on how to use the computer. Even the older of the grandchildren read some parts and sought clarifications tp which I responded and sometimes incorporated in the work. I am most thankful to them all.

As indicated in most captions of the photos I have included, the Bank of Tanzania, the *Daily News*, the Information Department of the Government of Tanzania and the Archives Unit of State House proved most helpful in providing photographs of scenes I had myself lost because of the many unsettling movements I have had to undertake in my public service career. Recent snapshots of potical party campaign scenes have been generously supplied by the *Tanzania Daima* newspaper and others have been taken by my own children. I am obliged to all of them.

Lastly I want to record my appreciation of the elucidations and explanations by several relatives, friends and acquaintances of incidents of historical significance in Tanzania, especially in Marangu, my birth-place. I cannot mention all of them; but Mwitori Petro Itosi Marealle, my late uncle Eliab Mlyingi and my brother-in-law David Marealle serve as their representatives.

In conclusion, I want to state, however, that any ommissions of vital facts or their misrepresentations in this narrative, which I regret, are entirely my own responsibility.

Introduction

A number of people, who know my background and history well, have suggested that I should write an autobiography so that more members of the public may share in their knowledge. Although I feel honoured by these suggestions, I have hesitated, possibly because of a sense of humility. Recently, it has been suggested in newspaper articles, radio and television programmes that those who worked closely with and under President Mwalimu Julius Nyerere, should tell their part in the history of developments in this country. My name specifically has been included among the people who could put in writing what happened in those days, especially in their relationship with Mwalimu Nyerere. I feel it is an honour to do so.

Obviously, the most interesting part of my story is that relating to the events when I held senior positions in Nyerere's Government and in the public service generally. Subsequent participation in the evolution of economic and political history of Tanzania is touched upon in the narrative. However, in planning to write this story, I have felt that it is worthwhile starting right at the beginning of my life. In this way, I aim to give some idea as to what it was like growing up in my birthplace, Marangu, in the tribal and colonial environment of Tanganyika in the 1930s, 1940s and 1950s. I touch on some of the traditions and beliefs of those days and on some colonial laws that impacted on our lives and surroundings. My story will also reveal that it was possible to achieve high office even from a humble background: For mine was very humble indeed.

CHAPTER ONE

My Life in Summary

In the lounge of the house in which we presently live, there is a painting hanging on the wall by the artist John E. Lyimo. It is that of a Chagga traditional grass-thatched hut, conical in shape, with the goats' pen outside. Two Chagga ladies are outside, one seated on a log of firewood and the other standing near the entrance to the hut. This is a typical hut as it looked at the time I was growing up and going to primary school. At that time I actually lived in such a house and after returning from school in the afternoon, I used to take the goats to the grazing grounds or went to fetch feed for them if the grazing grounds happened to be unavailable. This was the case if they were planted with a crop such as maize, finger-millet or beans.

In our family we call this painting *Tumetoka Mbali*, meaning 'We have come from afar', and our children and grandchildren entirely agree. Our grandchildren who have only seen this type of hut at the Village Museum in Dar es Salaam, marvel at the fact that I lived in such a house; and they always pester me to show them the exact location of their great grandmother's house whenever we visit Marangu.

Additionally, there is another painting hanging on the wall in my study. This is by the famous East African artist, Elimo P. Njau. It is the scene of a few goats being herded by a boy who is actually hidden behind a huge shady tree. When Elimo Njau visited my home one day and discovered that I had bought his painting from one of his exhibitions, he was quite excited.

I took the opportunity of his visit to discuss some features of the painting with him. During this discussion I asked Elimo why he had not put the goatherd fully in the scene, and he explained that he would have had to show the true likeness of a person who was not, in any case, important in the painting. He said the boy could be himself or even Edwin Mtei, for that matter. I agreed with him for we were neighbours when we were growing up in

Marangu, and he and I used to take our respective family goats to graze. Elimo Njau now lives in Kenya.

One of the friends, who suggested that I should write this story, Dr. Anthony Bulengo, saw both these paintings. When I explained to him how dear they were to me as reflecting on my early life, he remarked: 'Why don't you write your story and call it "From Goatherd to Governor "or simply "From G To G". At the time this exchange took place, about early 1975, I had just completed my service as Governor of the Bank of Tanzania and was Secretary General of the then East African Community (EAC). So was conceived the title of this story, "From Goatherd to Governor".

The story could have ended at the end of my tenure as Governor but beginning in 1975 other, perhaps even more interesting parts were still to come. Neither Tony nor I knew that after my term as Secretary General and the collapse of the East African Community in early 1977, I would be appointed Minister for Finance and Planning. Other exciting times were in store, as I moved, rather dramatically, from the Ministry of Finance to become a coffee farmer at the beginning of 1980. Less than three years later, I found myself a nominee of Mwalimu Nyerere's Government as an Executive Director of the International Monetary Fund based in Washington DC and sitting on the Board of one of the most prestigious financial institutions in the world.

The stint in Washington for four years saw me as a real globetrotter, (another "G"), for in my capacity as Executive Director representing all English-speaking Africa, except the then apartheid South Africa, I visited practically all countries in Africa. Indeed, I even touched on apartheid South Africa several times when on my way to or from my constituent countries of Botswana, Lesotho, Swaziland and Mozambique. As a Tanzanian national, I could only at that time stay in the transit lounge of the Johannesburg International Airport when waiting for flight connections. My Tanzanian passport was specifically stamped that South Africa was excluded from the countries I could visit when using it. I was also able to tour most of the countries of Asia, Europe and South America. Those of North America are, of course, only a few, and I visited them all, or at least touched down on their international airports on my way to or from official visits in that hemisphere.

I returned home at the end of 1986, when President Ali Hassan Mwinyi who had succeeded Mwalimu Julius Nyerere was already in his second year of office. I resumed the management of my farm in Arusha, although Mwinyi's Government appointed me to serve on several boards and commissions on a part-time basis. The most notable of these were the Presidential Commission on Banking and Financial Restructuring, of which I was a member; and the Presidential Commission on Taxation, Government Revenue and Expenditures, which I chaired. My Commission handed in its Report in November 1991, just as the Nyalali Commission on Multiparty Democracy was completing its task.

Then came 1992 and I found myself in the throes of Tanzanian multiparty politics. As founder national chairman of *Chama cha Demokrasia na Maendeleo* (CHADEMA), literally translated as 'The Party for Democracy and Development', my background attracted a lot of attention. The new environment of enhanced open society and transparency enabled people, especially the media, to enquire as to what happened during many of the occasions I was connected with, in the recent history of our country. For example, they wanted to know what precisely happened when early in December 1979 I wrote to the President tendering my resignation as Minister. Why was I not detained as so many other dissidents before me had been? Why did I not go into exile or run abroad like others who had resigned before me? Why did I differ from Mwalimu to the extent of resigning, when my views and approach to public policy appeared so clearly egalitarian and therefore not so different from the basic approach of Mwalimu Nyerere?

Leadership of a new political party in the new Tanzanian environment, where the old pundits of power tenaciously hold on, by hook and crook, in order to retain their posts and, in many cases, literally in order to earn a living, has been an arduous and challenging task. What are the real prospects for the evolution of genuine democracy in our country under such circumstances?

As we hand over to the new generation leadership, what should we urge them to observe so that genuine democracy in Tanzania may not be aborted? Is there a way we can prevent Tanzania from being torn asunder in the light of the apparent unfathomable ambition and greed on the part of individual politicians who are determined, whatever the consequences, to retain or assume power? Above all, what policies should we advise the new generation leaders to adopt so that this country can extricate itself from the grinding poverty that has bedevilled its people during decades of futile doctrinaire socialist experimentation and protestations? Is there any hope of removing the rot engendered by corruption, currently eroding the very fabric of society? Is there a way of preventing the country from degenerating into chaos in the light of the yawning gap between the new filthy, mega-rich, in league with avaricious foreigners masquerading as development partners, and the masses of the poor, in a country of untapped vast natural resources?

Those are the highlights of my story and the questions I discuss. However, before going into detail, let me give some account of my personal background.

CHAPTER 2

Birth and Childhood

My mother, Ngianaeli Ngekalio Mtei (née Mlyingi), became a widow when her husband, Victor Shambari Mtei died in 1928. She was then only 32 years old and had been left with two children, Ismael and Cecilia to look after. She resolved that she would not re-marry and that she would continue to try, as best she could, to raise her two children. Indeed, in accordance with Chagga customs and tradition, a widow with a son was rarely re-married, especially if the son had inherited land *(kihamba)* adequate to live on. And it happened that Ismael had inherited from his father ample land on the basis of standards of Marangu in those days.

Eliapenda Ngapanyi Mtei, a younger cousin of Victor Shambari, lived in the adjoining *kihamba*, and was sympathetic, kind and helpful to the young widow; in contrast to the surviving brothers of Victor, who would have inherited his properties had he died without leaving a son. The inheriting of widows under Chagga custom is not automatic as in many other tribes. Even in those days, a widow had to be willing and consent to be considered as a wife of a surviving brother of her deceased husband. Indeed, at this time my mother suspected that one of these brothers of her late husband was planning to harm her son, and so for a long time, she arranged for Ismael to live at our maternal grandfather's home.

I was born on 12 July 1932 in a rather dramatic manner, my father being Eliapenda Ngapanyi Mtei: My mother had planted maize and beans in a plot of land located at Rawuya, about eight kilometres away from where she lived in central Marangu. July was the harvest month for beans and she had started harvesting early, anxious to finish this task as soon as possible because she knew she was heavy with child. Early in the morning of 12 July, accompanied by her neighbour, Ndeambiliasia, who was also harvesting beans in an adjoining plot at Rawuya, she walked those eight kilometres to continue with her task. They arrived at their destination and were each working in their respective *shamba* when later that morning my mother shouted for her friend to come for help. She was in labour! I was safely born soon afterwards in that field of beans and maize; and late that afternoon, my mother slowly walked back home with Ndeambiliasia assisting to carry me. So in that humble but unusual way, I began an exciting life.

Although my father knew I was his son and continued to assist materially, my mother initially adamantly refused to reveal my father's identity. Eliapenda had been baptised into the Lutheran Church in 1929, and early in 1932 had married Lucia Mawolle in a solemn Christian wedding ceremony, which was well publicised. The strict German missionaries who ran the Lutheran Church at the time, would immediately have excommunicated Eliapenda and nullified his marriage with Lucia had it become known that at the time of his wedding, he had already sired a child with his cousin's widow.

So I continued to live with my mother and my half-brother and sister, Ismael and Cecilia. At that time I was in fact referred to as the son of Victor, until my father was excommunicated from the Church for reasons quite unrelated to my being his son. The reason for this action by the Church authorities was that in 1940 Eliapenda formally and openly took a second wife, by the name of Kichacha, under Chagga customary law, because he had realised that Lucia could not bear him a child. The consummation of a marriage, in accordance with Chagga customs and tradition, is the birth of a child; and the Marangu community fully appreciated Eliapenda's decision regarding a second wife, in spite of the rules of the Church.

My mother initially gave me the name 'Kilasara', which in the local language denotes defiance, implying that she would not worry or be frightened despite the many problems which normally confronted a widow in the tribal environment. However, following a serious illness when I was three years old, my mother realised she had to look for doctors and my cure on her own; so she decided to change my name to 'Mbiliewi', meaning 'with whom shall I consult?' As I grew up, people who had known me as 'Kilasara' continued to call me by that name, and others called me 'Mbiliewi' in accordance with my mother's wish. However, when I was about six years old, I personally refused to be called 'Kilasara' because I discovered that the name was unisex, and that a girl who used to visit us frequently was also called by the name 'Kilasara'.

Records at Marangu Native Authority Primary School (now re-named Mengenyi Primary School) and at Old Moshi Secondary

School will show that my name was Mbiliewi Victory. I deliberately added the 'y' to distinguish that this was different from Ismael's father. I was baptised into the Lutheran Church on 28 December 1947, when I had already been at Old Moshi for three years, and it was then that I personally chose the name Edwin Isaac (the last being my maternal grandfather's Christian name). Thus began that long name of Edwin Isaac Mbiliewi Mtei.

I continued officially to be called 'Mbiliewi Victory' until 1949, when I was able to persuade the school authorities at Old Moshi to re-register me as a Christian by the name of Edwin Mtei. Unfortunately, my father Eliapenda had died in May 1945 when I had been at Old Moshi for only four months. He was a jolly man who loved singing and was a member of the church choir, playing the trumpet or the accordion. He was a loving father and very proud of me that I had started to show good performance at school. In public he was, however, very argumentative, and many of his contemporaries say that this is the trait I inherited from him.

I should explain that although my father was excommunicated from the Church in 1940, he continued to participate fully with other members of the congregation in all activities except in Holy Communion. When he realised that he was critically ill in May 1945, he requested the priest to come to his bedside in Ashira Hospital where he had been admitted. After the usual confessions and reconciliation, he declared he was re-taking Lucia as his only wedded wife. He and Lucia, joined by a few Christian members of the family, together participated in Holy Communion at the bedside. My father further declared at that prayer meeting that he would like Lucia henceforth to treat Mbiliewi as her adopted son. After my father died, Lucia stayed on at our home for a few years before she decided to go and re-marry.

I grew up in a family where my tough, hardworking mother was the breadwinner. The family lived in a traditional Chagga hut, all grass-thatched and conical in shape. I shared the bed with mother, my half-sister Cecilia and my little sister Happiness, who was born in 1937. For a bed, we used only the hard ground covered with dry banana stalks for a mattress, over which was laid the softened hide of a cow. Ismael had a wattle-and-daub hut, rectangular in shape (*mchalo*), adjacent to our mother's, in which he slept overnight; on many occasions, with friendly boys from the neighbourhood of the same age. He was eleven years my senior.

The first incident in my childhood which I vividly remember was a wedding procession, when a neighbour of ours got married. After the church ceremony the large procession, on the way to the bridegroom's home where the celebrations and traditional feast were to continue, passed along the wide footpath (*mraru*) bordering our homestead. I was at home with my *ayah* and the procession included a local brass band with loud trumpets and drummers (my father playing the accordion) and the rest of the procession singing, dancing and shouting in joy. We went near to watch them. I wanted to follow them to their destination but my ayah restrained me and I remember bitterly crying in protest. The man who got married is still alive (2007) and is in his late nineties. When I recently met him and asked him if he could remember the date of his marriage, he said that it was in July 1936. I was just four years old then.

Another incident I vividly remember, because I was very frightened, was when a number of aeroplanes came and flew over our area very low, almost touching the top of the banana trees with deafening noise. They circled around the whole area of Marangu. I had not seen an aeroplane so close before and everybody panicked and was running for shelter without knowing how or where.

I came to learn later that there had been organised riots in 1937 by the residents of Marangu who had ransacked the Co-operative Society's warehouse and coffee buying post, burning the warehoused coffee, destroying the weighing scales and other equipment, and threatening the lives of the employees, including the manager. The cause of these riots was the residents' dissatisfaction with the low prices being paid for their coffee by the Kilimanjaro Native Co-operative Union (KNCU). The colonial Government had therefore sent the aeroplanes to scare the people and prevent possible spread of riots to the whole of the coffee-growing area of the then Moshi District of the Northern Province of Tanganyika.

I came to learn later also that the Government had rounded up the ring-leaders and that in the Mshiri Village, where most of the culprits lived, the colonial authorities had ordered mass punishment of the whole population by arresting their cattle and confiscating them. The ringleaders were arrested and detained. A court trial, presided over by the District Officer who had ordered the arrests, summarily rusticated them to restriction in remote areas of Tanganyika for long periods. My own maternal uncle, Eliab Mlyingi, was among those rounded up and was banished to Iringa, where he was detained and restricted until after the outbreak of the Second World War in 1939. He himself told me later that he was only released because they wanted to enrol him into the King's African Rifles, but after medical examination when he was already in camp and had been given army uniforms, they discovered that he suffered from an ailment he had contracted whilst in detention and could not continue in the army. He used to envy his contemporary colleagues who were retained in the K.A.R. for they went all the way to Abyssinia and Burma, fighting with the British.

I remember that two or three days after the aeroplane incident, one of the residents of Mshiri Village, trying to avoid the mass punishment, brought two huge cows at night to our homestead. He tied them each with ropes in a grove in our farm, where no member of the public could see them. He tried to persuade my mother to mix his cows with our cattle to avoid identification, but she refused to be more involved in the man's efforts to mitigate the effects of the communal punishment. The only help she could offer was to allow the animals to remain in our area without reporting to the authorities. For a few days, Cecilia and I had fun trying to feed the cows in that hide-away place until the owner returned (again furtively at night) to take them away.

Thus in this incident, our family, including my maternal uncle, as well as the people of Marangu experienced and many suffered the impact of some of the obnoxious colonial laws: namely, indiscriminate mass punishment of whole communities, the arrest of suspected culprits and their prolonged detention and imprisonment without proper trial. It is sad and shameful that so many years after independence, some of these laws still remain on our Statute Book.

I should like to explain that as a result of having vigilant members, such as those who spear-headed the riots described above, the Kilimanjaro Native Co-operative Union (KNCU), which had been founded in 1932, at its heyday in the 1950s and

60s became one of the most successful in Africa. Initially run by a European General Manager, A. L. Bennett, who was succeeded by a local man, Andrea Shangarai, this co-operative union led and encouraged the growing of coffee on the slopes of the mountain and organised its marketing very successfully. In the late 1940s it was already sending its staff for training in the United Kingdom and used its surpluses for the building of a Secondary School at Lyamungu and a commercial training centre at its headquarters. It initiated the building of a college for the training of its inspectors, which initially was run in parnership with the Co-operative Alliance of Africa. Eventually this has grown into a university specialising in commerce.

I mention the KNCU, not only because it was partly due to its success that we were able to have fees waived for our secondary schooling, but to stress that it is possible to run a co-operative successfully if it is devoid of political interference and its membership freely ensures that its staff are honest and competent. It is recalled that at the time of Independence, the TANU government, trying to emmulate the KNCU and Bukoba examples of co-operative unions, established almost by decree regional co-operative unions throughout the country. A new law directed them all to be run by officers sent by the Government and soon incompetence, theft and corruption started to afflict the movement. By a twist of imagination, co-operatives were abolished when *Ujamaa* village shops were set up. Re-establishment of co-operatives has been attempted in recent years, but the trauma of political meddling still bedevils the movement.

One more incident I vividly remember, demonstrated another aspect of law enforcement in those days: a neighbour of ours, who was a notorious thief, accompanied by a number of fellow thieves had broken into a homestead and stolen a bull. They had driven the animal up the Moonjo River where in a thicket of bush, they had slaughtered it. They shared between themselves the choicest of the meats, leaving the remaining carcass including the head and offal to be eaten by stray dogs and vultures. When the owner raised the alarm on discovering the theft the next morning, he was joined by most of the adult male villagers, including the Headman, in the search for his bull. They followed the footprints and ultimately came to the grove in the river valley where they found the remains. The Headman gave permission for searching all suspected houses, and late that morning found a lot of the meats in the notorious thief's place. The thief was promptly arrested and thoroughly beaten up by the crowd.

It was about eleven thirty in the morning when they passed by our place on the way to the Chief's Court, and I was just returning from Ngaruma 'bush' School. So I joined the crowd. The thief had first been led to the site of the slaughter from where he was made to carry the remains of the bull as exhibits. The Headman made him wear these foul-smelling exhibits as a large necklace round his neck, with meats hanging on his back and front. On the way, they obtained a large, freshly cut bunch of green bananas and forced him to carry it on his head. If he slowed down with this heavy load, the Headman whipped him hard. The owner of the bull had a sharp knife and was walking beside the thief. He would cut a piece of the raw meat on which the trickling sap of the green banana had dropped. He would then instruct the thief to open his mouth and force him to chew and swallow the raw meat. If the thief resisted, he would threaten him with the knife and the Headman would whip him hard again. It was a humiliating spectacle and we children were heckling and booing the thief as he plodded on towards the Chief's Court.

At about midday the procession reached the market place, Kinyange, where there were hundreds of people – men and women – buying and selling their wares. The Headman decided to make the thief walk round the market and through the crowded lanes, whipping him; and the owner of the stolen bull feeding him with the dirty, almost putrefied raw meat soaked in green banana sap. He was telling the thief: "You stole my bull, you scoundrel! Eat it now so that everyone can watch how you enjoy the products of other people's sweat!" Women who saw this spectacle wept as it was so dehumanising. Women who knew the thief personally ran away crying because of the shame inflicted on him.

After going round the market several times, the Headman decided to proceed to the Chief's Court passing by the Native Authority Primary School. Here all the teachers and pupils got out of their classrooms to witness. The thief was booed and heckled as he was whipped and was forced to swallow the dirty, raw meat. He had a swollen face and eyes from the beatings he had sustained from fellows who enjoyed punching him. The whole school joined the procession and escorted him to the Chief's Court, where he was locked up in the remand room until the next day when he appeared in the primary magistrate's court. He was later sentenced to prison.

The treatment meted out to the thief that day and the public humiliation he suffered must have acted as a deterrent to others. Present day shooting and killing of thieves in hot pursuit or burning them to death whilst wearing "necklaces" of rubber tyres is a post-colonial development and was not part of the culture of those days. The killing of anyone, including a thief, would have resulted in thorough investigations by the colonial authorities and possibly even in mass arrests, and it rarely happened.

CHAPTER 3

Going to School

With the exception of Cecilia, no other member of our family in those early days was baptised. Indeed, Cecilia had been baptised as a child into the Roman Catholic Church in an emergency, when she fell ill. However, although we were non-Christians, we all went to church every Sunday, and when I was old enough and able to go on my own, I enrolled at the 'bush' school at Ngaruma Lutheran Parish Church. This was at the beginning of 1941. I was eight-and-a-half years old, but among the youngest boys in the class.

The 'bush' school was a sort of kindergarten where we played, learnt to pray and the Catechism in accordance with the teachings of Dr Martin Luther. Here at Ngaruma we started to learn the three 'Rs: namely, Reading, Writing and Arithmetic. There were no classrooms and we sat on the benches of the Church, nearest to the altar. These front benches were fixed with raised front boards and served as long desks. There was a movable blackboard placed on a tripod stand on which the teacher wrote with a chalk. In starting to learn how to write we used slates and slate-pencils which, like the blackboard, you could wipe off with your hand or with a piece of cloth. There were no classes as such at Ngaruma, but beginners came late in the morning at 11 a.m., whilst those who were in the second year or more advanced, reported early at 7.30 a.m. In 1942, when I witnessed the beating of that notorious thief, I was already in the second year.

I was very keen to learn when I went to school. Ismael gave me his old slate as he did not need it since at the school he was then attending, they used exercise books. By the end of 1941 I was able to read in Swahili and was gradually improving my handwriting on the slate. The side of the slate used for handwriting exercises had permanent parallel lines in which the pupil tried to write, and this made us get used to writing letters of equal sizes. The other side was ruled with squares and was used for arithmetic exercises. We also learnt the prayers and the Catechism by heart.

As a church school, Ngaruma, of course, placed a lot of emphasis on religious knowledge, and the stories of the Bible were intensively taught. As soon as a pupil was able to read, he or she was expected to have the Bible in Swahili. During "Advent", the month preceding Christmas, the teachers, who were also evangelists, would give me one or two excerpts from the Bible which I would cram and then recite to the congregation during the evening prayers. I remember reciting excerpts from The Old Testament, forewarning of the coming of the Messiah, shouting in Kichagga from "*Zechariah* Chapter 9, Verse 9".

The pupils attending the bush school were of different sizes and ages. Especially some of the girls were quite advanced in age, and they used to stop coming for classes as soon as they were able to read and write. Most parents then wanted their daughters only to be able to read the Bible and sign their names, and as soon as they were able to do so, they stopped coming to school. These girls would then learn at home how to attend to family chores and have the procedure of clitorisdoctomy (genital mutilation) performed on them before they got married. Although around Marangu this practice more or less lapsed in the 1960s because the educated leadership strongly objected, it is sad and shameful that female genital mutilation has not yet been nationally outlawed, despite more than forty years of enlightenment under an independent government.

Many boys were much older than I was, and those who found it difficult to learn as fast as we smaller boys, felt embarrassed or frustrated and became truants. The Church and the Native Authority, even in those days, strongly urged parents to send their children to school. Especially for boys, going to school was regarded more or less as compulsory. When the teacher during the morning roll-call discovered that a boy had not turned up, he would send a team of strong boys to the truant's home to trace him and bring him forcibly to school if he were not sick. Girls who played truant were not affected by this type of compulsion.

When I returned from school I would look after the goats, and afterwards Ismael, when he was back home from his own school, would teach me more reading or arithmetic. I was so fond of arithmetic that when I was able to add and subtract, I used to go into the farm during weekends to count all the banana trees, identifying which were mere suckers and which had borne fruit. Sometimes I would count the bananas by their varieties or species, and other times I would count the coffee trees. My neighbours of the same age thought I was crazy, but I enjoyed adding the figures when completing an exercise, since when counting I was frequently interrupted when my mother wanted me for other more urgent chores, such as looking for firewood or fetching water from the furrow.

At school I liked playing with other boys, although because I was rather a weakling, I was frequently bullied. One day in 1942, we were playing *"kijogoo"* (cockerel), a game whereby two boys each standing on one foot, folding their arms on their chests, would go to the centre of the ring and start pushing one another off balance until one of them fell down. On this occasion the boy I was playing with, Kaleb Yoshua, pushed me off balance and I fell down while laughing and broke one of my freshly grown front upper teeth. I also sustained a cut on my upper lip and another on my face.

As I bled profusely, an older boy, Gasper Ndeshiwesa Ndekao, was asked by our teacher to accompany me to the hospital at Ashira. At the hospital, Bibi Elisabeth, the German missionary doctor-in-charge, treated me very kindly. I returned home in the afternoon with a bandaged head but was soon better. Thus in that incident, I acquired the permanent distinguishing feature (Mtei's 'Trade Mark') of a chipped upper left molar tooth. Apart from this, I have been fortunate and the dentist has had no complaint from me ever since.

We played other traditional games too: we boys played the Chagga version of the Swahili *Bao* by making 36 small holes in a smooth hard ground, mostly in an abandoned pathway. For the round pebbles we used the hard fruit of *ndulele*, the fruit of a wild shrub with short thorns and rough leaves, which grows in grazing land areas. The scoring was similar to that of the Swahili Bao and one had to be fast and good at counting in order to win.

When herding calves and goats, boys would play *ORO* if the grazing ground was large enough and flat. We would make a big ring the size of a bicycle wheel out of twigs and small bendable tree branches by tying them with soft dry banana stalks. One boy would stand at one end of the playing ground with the large ring, whilst his team mate with an improvised javelin or spear would stand at the side of the playground, halfway down towards the other end of the ground. The boy with the ring would throw it to roll fast towards the other end of the playground, and his colleague would throw the javelin in such a manner as to stop and catch the ring in the middle of the playground whilst still rolling. If the ring were caught by the javelin sticking into the ground upright, then the couple would win that round. Another couple would then take the ring and javelin and try to carry out the same exercise. The couple with most wins at the end of the game would be entitled to an *ORO*, namely a billygoat. To win, you had to be good at throwing the javelin and accurate at estimating the speed of the rolling ring to catch it whilst in the middle of the field. I guess this was the game of our forefathers when training as soldiers during those encounters with the Maasai warriors in the eighteenth and nineteenth centuries.

Wrestling is an international game and we boys used to play it too. The game was, however, less rough than what appears on television these days. The referee of our type of wrestling would have promptly disqualified any participant who kicked his competitor below the belt or trampled on him after throwing him down. The modern type of wrestling would be rated sadistic by the Chaggas of those days.

I left Ngaruma for the Native Authority (NA) Primary School, Marangu, in January 1943. I was registered by Mwalimu Philemon Salakana, the head teacher and, after an entry test, was admitted into Standard III. There had been some argument at home whether I should go to the Practising Primary School run by the Marangu Lutheran Teachers' Training Centre rather than the NA Primary School. Teachers at the NA Primary School were notorious for flogging and caning pupils who misbehaved or did not perform well. So my mother preferred the Practising Primary School. In the end I was asked to decide myself and I chose the NA Primary School because most boys from the neighbourhood were attending that school and I wanted to continue with company I was used to. Our class teacher in Standard III was Mwalimu Godwin Nakara. One of my classmates was John Jacob Lyimo, the radiologist consultant and my lifelong friend.

When I had completed only a month at the NA Primary School, my class teacher, Mwalimu Godwin, had a personal confrontation or quarrel with Ismael, my half-brother, for reasons quite unrelated to me. When he entered the classroom the morning after this quarrel, he ordered me out of the classroom, saying that my parents had not bothered to bring me to the school for formal registration. This was an unusual requirement, but I went home to report to my mother. Ismael at this time was a trainee teacher, boarding at the Marangu Lutheran Teachers' Training Centre. My mother could not therefore contact him immediately to find out what had transpired between him and Mwalimu Godwin.

The next day my mother and I went to the school but Mwalimu Godwin refused to discuss any subject with her, saying he could not engage in a serious discussion with a woman! My mother shed tears with shock and humiliation, and we returned home. She was shocked because Mwalimu Godwin was a neighbour of ours and a distant relation, who knew us very well. When a few days later Ismael came home, he would not discuss the cause of his quarrel with Godwin but suggested that I should transfer to the Practising Primary School. When I went to that school, this time accompanied by Ismael, I found that their Standard III was already full and they could not admit me.

My mother tried to approach Mwalimu Philemon, the headteacher of the NA school, pleading with him to intervene so that I could be re-admitted;but he insisted that he was unable to compel any teacher to admit a pupil into his classroom. I therefore remained at home for more than three months. I had nothing useful to do at home at that tender age of only eleven years. So my mother gave me some money and I resorted to buying chicken and eggs from neighbours and re-selling them at Kibo Hotel, a kilometre away from our home.

However, one Saturday morning when I was returning from Kibo Hotel carrying a chicken I had been unable to sell, I met Mwalimu Godwin. He asked me what I was doing and I replied in tears that I was only trying to buy chicken and eggs and re-sell them at Kibo Hotel. As I was describing this, I actually broke down sobbing and weeping. Mwalimu Godwin felt sorry for me and told me that if I was still interested in going to school, I should report to his class the following Monday. So I happily hurried home, washed and ironed my school uniform and resumed schooling the next Monday, as directed. I was delighted.

On returning to school, and in spite of having missed classes for more than three months, I performed very well in all subjects. Instead of being caned, I was being used by Mwalimu Godwin as the pupil to go out to look for canes for beating up pupils who made silly mistakes or misbehaved. If I brought a cane which easily broke when in use, Mwalimu Godwin would call me, beat me up with the part of cane remaining, and then instruct me to go back for a better one. As I did not want to continue suffering in this way, I learnt to bring strong, unbreakable canes. This, however, did not make me a popular pupil in the class.

At the end of the school year 1944 we sat the Standard IV examinations for Northern Province, the passing of which would qualify us for entry into Old Moshi Junior Secondary School, the only Government secondary school in the province. Other options for pupils completing Standard IV at that time were to enter the junior seminary at Singa Chini run by the Roman Catholic Church or to continue to Standards V and VI at the NA School. After Standard VI, pupils were selected, depending on their performance or aptitude, for Teacher Training or for vocational training in trade schools, where they were trained in carpentry, masonry, tailoring, plumbing, motor or electrical mechanics. Pupils who in previous years had not succeeded in the very competitive examination to enter Old Moshi and had proceeded to Standard V or VI were allowed to re-sit the examination with us in Standard IV if they looked small or were 16 years old or younger.

The results of the Standard IV examinations were announced in January, 1945, when the Headmaster of Old Moshi Secondary School, an Englishman by the name of G.W. Ginner, came to the NA School, Marangu, where the pupils had been specifically assembled to meet him. Mr Ginner read the list of those who had passed. The exhilaration and pleasure I felt when my name was on top of the list of successful pupils going to Old Moshi almost overwhelmed me. After we had been given admittance instructions for Old Moshi School, I literally ran the one kilometre to our home to tell my mother.

The earliest photo I have been able to recover from my documents, taken in 1946

On hearing this good news, she hugged me screaming with joy, until my father joined us to inquire as to what was going on. He was also very pleased and congratulated me, stressing that I should always work hard, however good the results were, or whatever difficulties I faced at school.

So on 31 January 1945, I left for Old Moshi accompanied by my lifelong friend Wilfred Marealle who had also passed the entrance examination. We boarded a bus at Marangu (actually a converted box-body lorry with fixed benches for seats), bound for Moshi town. At that time the currency used in Tanganyika, the East African Shilling, was very strong, and the fare to Moshi was only Sh 0.50 (sumuni). We alighted from the bus at Kiborloni, three or four kilometres from the centre of Moshi town. From Kiborloni we walked up the steep ten kilometre road to Old Moshi Secondary School.

Wilfred, being the son of the Chief, had a wooden box for a suitcase, in which he put all his belongings, and he carried it on his head. In my case, I had wrapped all my clothes and some books Ismael had given me, in a sheet of cloth (actually my mother's head scarf), which I strapped on my shoulder as we walked up the hill. We had never been in this part of the country before, but we knew the route from descriptions of those who had been students at Old Moshi before us.

When we reached Old Moshi School, we found that Mbulu and Arusha fresh boys had arrived by train the previous night. The head teacher, Mr Erasto Mbwana (Mang'enya), was there to receive us. After all new arrivals had identified themselves to the head teacher we were instructed to follow him to the store where each of us was issued with utensils, a bedsheet and two blankets. The utensils consisted of a spoon, enamel plate and bowl. We newcomers were given old enamel plates and bowls with chipped rusted patches having fallen and broken off their enamel cover. New and other un-chipped plates and bowls were reserved for pupils in higher classes. These senior pupils were not in residence at the time of our arrival as they were still on their end-of-year holidays and were expected to return the following week. We had gone a week earlier for orientation.

I should add that during the British colonial days, there was discrimination even in the terms used for describing the teaching staff at school. A teacher or rather 'a school teacher' was an African who taught at school. A 'school master or mistress' was a European who taught at school. This description was applicable whether the person concerned had a degree, diploma or a simple certificate to teach. So the Headmaster was the European head of a school. The Headteacher was the most senior African in the teaching staff.

All fresh boys were initially accommodated in a long single dormitory called Majengo. There were no beds in Majengo, but each boy was given two planks of wood joined together like a door, which was used as a bed. The leg end of this plank rested on two bricks cemented into the floor of the dormitory six feet from the wall. The head end of the plank rested on the protruding basement foundation of the wall. One blanket was placed on the plank to serve as mattress and a boy would cover himself during the night with the other blanket and bedsheet. Pillows and pillow cases were not provided by the school authorities and students had to buy them in Moshi town if they had money and needed any. Even if they could afford it, pupils were not allowed to purchase mattresses for using on their planks. Fortunately, there were no malaria-carrying mosquitoes in Old Moshi and so we were not issued with nets, although some boys returning from areas where malaria was endemic, suffered attacks of the disease at times.

For purposes of residence, students at Old Moshi were organised in six 'Houses'. These were named after the main mountain peaks of the three major districts of Northern Tanganyika from which most students emanated. These peaks were Kibo and Mawenzi for Moshi district, Meru for Arusha district, Hanang for Mbulu District, and Kindoroko and Shengena for Pare district. I was placed in Kibo House, whose house prefect was Ainamensa E. Mbuya, who was to become one of the first African professional civil engineers in Tanganyika and the first African Permanent Secretary in the Ministry of Public Works and Communications after Independence. Ainamensa treated me very leniently as I was the smallest boy in his House, and nicknamed me *kimana* for 'the baby'.

Kibo House had three dormitories and each dormitory had ten students. My dormitory initially was No.14, and the other nine students included a classmate of mine, Herman Sarwatt from Mbulu, who later became famous as the sole Independent (non-TANU) Member of Parliament in the first National Assembly of independent Tanganyika. Sarwatt went on to become the Speaker of the East African Legislative Assembly at the time I was Secretary General of the East African Community (1974-77). Herman Sarwatt came to Washington D.C. at the time I was serving as an Executive Director of the International Monetary Fund, but by this time he was critically ill and needed dialysis. He died when I was at his bedside in a Washington hospital and we had to arrange to send his remains home.

One of our leaders in Dormitory No.14 was Abdulrahman S. Msangi who was to become the first African Director of the East African Research Institute for Malaria and Vector-Borne Diseases at Amani. He was later appointed Professor of Zoology at the University of Dar es Salaam and subsequently was founder Executive Director of the Tanzania Organisation for Science and Technology.

Another contemporary at Old Moshi Secondary School was Cleopa David Msuya, who was to hold various ministerial posts culminating with the prime ministership and vice-presidency. He had joined the school a year before me and was in Meru House. We became acquainted, but our friendship deepened when I followed him to Tabora High School in 1951, where we lived in the same house (Biscoe). At Makerere University College, where I followed him in 1953, we also stayed in the same Hall of Residence.

It was in Standard V at Old Moshi that I started learning the English language as a subject in the classroom. Prior to this period, all my teachers had been Grade II teachers or of lower qualification who did not know enough English to be able to teach it. Indeed, the medium of instruction in all subjects at the bush school or at the NA Primary School had been the vernaculars, namely Kichagga or Kiswahili.

The medium of instruction in Standards V and VI at Old Moshi continued to be Kiswahili, but the teaching of the English language, as a subject, was very rigorous. Even the teaching of the other subjects, such as History, Geography, Mathematics (Arithmetic, Algebra and Geometry), Science (Physics, Chemistry and Biology), Civics and Kiswahili, was also very intensive. Because of this medium of instruction, all our teachers in Standards V and VI were Africans as they were conversant (indeed very proficient) in Kiswahili. Each one had either a Diploma in Education from Makerere College or was a Grade I teacher. The European masters/mistresses taught in Standard VII and above, where the medium of instruction was English.

As noted previously, Old Moshi Secondary School was the only Government secondary school in the Northern Province. There were seven other Government secondary schools in the whole of Tanganyika Territory, one in each of the other provinces, except that Southern Province had none and the Lake Province had two such schools. There was a Government High School for boys at Tabora, where those qualifying after Standard X in the eight Government secondary schools went for higher academic studies. There were a few other secondary schools in Tanganyika run by Voluntary Agencies (the missionary churches) and these also trained pupils up to Standard X. At this time, there were two other High Schools for boys run by voluntary agencies preparing them for the Cambridge School Certificate Examinations. These were St Mary's Secondary School at Tabora (Catholic) and St. Andrew's Secondary School at Minaki (Anglican). The Asian community also had a number of secondary schools, but because of the colour bar these were strictly for their own children, who went on to pursue further studies in India or Pakistan after completing Standard XII.

Regarding girls, the Government had at this time only one secondary school taking them up to Standard X and this was at Tabora. Tabora Girls' Secondary School also started to take pupils up to Standard XII in 1952. So some girls attended Standards V and VI in schools like Old Moshi, if their parents permitted them. But these were day pupils, not boarders. I remember we had Hadija Solo (later Mrs Kilumanga) and Eileen Chitenje as classmates at Old Moshi. Bertha Lucas (later Mrs Reading) was also a day pupil at Old Moshi, but she was a year behind me.

Pupils completing Standard VI sat examinations standardised for the whole country on the basis of which they were selected for entry into Standard VII or for teacher training (for Grade II teachers) or trades schools. The teacher training centres and trades schools also admitted ex-Standard VI pupils from Native Authority and voluntary agency primary schools, depending on their performance and aptitude.

At the time I sat for the Standard VI examination in 1946, I was still in a state of shock, having lost my father the previous year. I opted to go for training in tailoring, as I feared I would not get remission in school fees to proceed to Standard VII. However, my performance in the examinations was so good that the headmaster undertook to write to the Chief of Marangu to urge him to recommend me for remission of fees. Fortunately, at this time the Chagga Council was re-organised with the introduction of Divisional Chiefs (Mangi Mwitori), and one of their first innovations was that the Native Authority Council should take over the payment of all fees for all Chagga pupils in secondary schools. The question of remission of fees from 1947 did not therefore arise.

Life at Old Moshi School was very tough at this time. Even at primary schools it was really like leading a spartan life. In spite of the fact that many pupils were of very tender age, classes at the NA Primary School Marangu, for example, started at 7.30 in the morning. Some pupils had to walk ten kilometres from their homes to the only Native Authority primary school in East Vunjo. (East Vunjo included Mwika, Mamba and Marangu). I was fortunate in that my home was only one kilometre from the NA school, but I remember one of my schoolmates, Wilbert Kleruu (at that time his name was Ndechumia Ndefuno) used to walk more than ten kilometres from his home in Mwika. Whether it rained or however cold it was, these pupils used to be even more punctual than those, like myself, who resided nearby.

At Old Moshi, students from less well-to-do families organised themselves so that they marched on foot all the way to and from Marangu. Many pupils from Machame too marched all the way to Old Moshi. Even Wilbert Kleruu used to join us in the march to Old Moshi. The upper route passing along the edge of the Kilimanjaro Forest Reserve is shorter than the route through Himo. But it goes through deep valleys and precipitous ravines, crossing many streams and rivers originating from the foot of the mountain. We used to walk those thirty-five kilometres from Marangu, starting just about 11 o'clock in the morning and we would reach Old Moshi School about six o'clock ready for the evening roll-call. In the case of Wilbert Kleruu, there were, of course the extra ten kilometres he had to cover between his home in Mwika and Marangu before he could join us in the march.

As events demonstrated later, Kleruu proved a tough man throughout his life. After Old Moshi, Tabora and Makerere University College, he went to the University of California (L.A.) for postgraduate studies. He returned home with a PhD in Political Science and straight away joined TANU as Publicity Secretary on very meagre emoluments during the fight for independence. He was Regional Commissioner for Iringa at the time he was tragically gunned down in December 1971 by an irate farmer dissatisfied with the Tanzania Government's policy regarding communal farming and the re-allocation of land. This assassination was the first in Tanzania's history.

Old Moshi teaching staff in the years 1945-50 included a number of the people who were later to play prominent roles in the early years of Tanganyika's independence. Besides Erasto Mbwana Mangenya, to whom I have already referred and who became Minister, Speaker of the National Assembly and Ambassador to the United Nations, there were Stephen Mhando, Eliufoo Solomon, Daniel Lucas Mfinanga and Charles Ley. Stephen Mhando became Organising Secretary at TANU headquarters prior to Uhuru and also served as an MP. Eliufoo served briefly as President of the Wachagga before he joined the national Government as Minister of Health, and later Education. Mfinanga served as Ambassador to a number of countries, and Charles Ley was a Member of Parliament.

Among the students who were my contemporaries at Old Moshi who later figured prominently in national affairs, I have already mentioned Herman Sarwatt, Cleopa Msuya, Abdulrahman Msangi, Ainamensa Mbuya and Wilbert Kleruu. My friend and companion Wilfred Marealle was to become one of our first African Veterinary Surgeons, and later Regional Development Director. There was also Professor Arnold J. Temu, the historian, with whom we marched those miles through the edge of the primeval forest to and from Old Moshi. At this time we also had Isaeli Elinewinga, who later served as Minister of Education in the Nyerere Government. People who were to figure as first African consultants in their branches of medicine were schooling at Old Moshi during this period. Doctors Tito Andrew (Gynaecology), John J. Lyimo (Radiology) and Widmel Pendaeli (Psychiatry) were my contemporaries. So were Professors Alfred Meena and John Pendaeli, who were actually my classmates and with whom I went to Tabora High School and on to Makerere University College. So Old Moshi Secondary School ranked high in preparing people who featured prominently in the history of Tanzania.

It is significant that until 1950 there were only ten Government secondary schools in the whole of Tanganyika. Tanganyikans who had gone to university and obtained degrees could be counted on your finger nails: they were not more than ten, and we knew them all. Looking back, just over fifty-five years later, when the Marangu Division of the Moshi Rural District alone has ten secondary schools, one feels that we have made rapid strides and that it has been worthwhile to rid ourselves of foreign domination.

CHAPTER 4

High School and University College

I was over eighteen years old and so no longer a child when we embarked on the train at Moshi Railway Station in January 1951, on our way to Tabora High School after successfully passing the Standard X Territorial Examination we sat in October 1950. It was an overnight train to Korogwe, where we boarded a Tanganyika Railways Bus to Morogoro through Handeni and Mziha. This bus ride took a whole day. The road was of rough *murram* with potholes all the way, and the driver was so rough in the humps and bumps that many of us who had not travelled continuously for such long distances suffered nausea and threw up most of the day. The two hundred miles took more than twelve hours, and we arrived at Morogoro Railway Station at 9 o'clock, thoroughly exhausted.

The train from Dar es Salaam for Tabora was expected at one o'clock in the morning and we had to sleep on the benches at the Railway station, with mosquitoes biting and stinging all over. Those of us who had money went to the near-by Community Development hostel, where they got rooms and were able to lie in bed with mosquito-net cover. I did not have much pocket money and so I had to wait for the train lying on those benches, praying that I would not catch malaria before arriving at Tabora School.

The passenger train bound for Tabora was on schedule at 1.00 a.m., but the Third Class coach allocated to Tabora High School pupils was already almost full of students who had boarded it at Dar es Salaam. We had to squeeze ourselves in, and since the earlier occupants were strangers to us, they were reluctant to rise up from the seats they were lying on to give us space to sit. Like the Moshi/Korogwe train, the Central Railway train was slow and after approximately every fifty miles, it would stop in the bush to load firewood for the steam locomotive engines. At Dodoma, which we reached at about nine in the morning, more Tabora-bound pupils, especially emanating from Iringa, Kondoa and Arusha, joined us and the Railways staff allocated us an additional coach. More students joined us at Itigi, late that night. Most of them were from Rungwe/Tukuyu and Mbeya and together we made our last lap to Tabora, which we reached at 5 o'clock in the afternoon. It was a three-day gruelling experience.

John Crabbe, who had been a mathematics lecturer at Makerere University College for many years, had just taken over as Headmaster for Tabora School and received us the following morning. Tabora Boys' School was actually two schools in one: there was the Lower School, which had pupils from Standards V to X and occupied the old buildings erected early in the 1920s, and had served as the élite school for sons of Tanganyika chiefs. This is where people such as Adam Sapi Mkwawa, Abdallah Said Fundikira, Humbi Ziota, Harun Lugusha, David Kidaha Makwaia, Thomas Lenana Marealle, Patrick Kunambi, John Ndaskoi Maruma, Vedasto Kyaruzi and, their star, Julius Kambarage Nyerere went in the late 1920s and 1930s.

The other school was the Upper School, built in the late 1940s to take students who had successfully completed Standard X and prepare them for the Cambridge Overseas School Certificate Examinations. Entrants into the Upper School came from all other secondary schools that taught up to Standard X in Tanganyika, as noted in the previous chapter. Prominent personalities in our history such as Rashidi Mfaume Kawawa, Oscar Kambona and Job Lusinde had just left Upper School Tabora when I joined in 1951. Geoffrey V. Mmari, who was to become Vice-Chancellor of the University of Dar es Salaam and later of the Sokoine University of Agriculture, joined Tabora with me in 1951. He had been at Ilboru Lutheran Secondary School.

Although the teaching facilities at Upper School Tabora were excellent and the teachers very highly qualified, the climate and the other amenities were not very congenial, especially to me personally. I suffered frequent bouts of malaria and on several occasions during the two years I was at Tabora was admitted at the infirmary suffering from malaria or dysentery. The food did not agree with me at all. Even drinking water was bad. This problem did not affect me alone. Several students, especially those from Kilimanjaro, also suffered, although probably not as often as I did. In the end we called Tabora 'Taabu bora', meaning 'suffering worth having'. In spite of these handicaps, I continued to do well academically and in those two years (1951 and 1952) won the

Form Prizes for the best student. I also maintained my interest in drama and debating.

During my period at Tabora I tried, as much as my limited pocket money could carry me, to know as much as possible of our country, Tanganyika. When proceeding on the half-yearly holidays, I used to opt to go home either by the Dodoma, Kondoa, Arusha, Moshi route; or by the Morogoro, Handeni, Korogwe Moshi route. I then had a chance to break the journey several times and stay with relatives or friends in those areas. These relatives or friends would be people working there and when they went to their chores, I would just explore the areas around. In this way I came to know Dodoma, Kondoa, Babati, Arusha, Morogoro and Korogwe and their environs fairly well.

The Dodoma-Arusha route at this time was serviced by a private bus company, Harchand Singh Bus Service. The bus took us from the Arusha Railway Station all the way to Dodoma Railway Station. During this period the Government school authorities issued warrants for travel only for the Railways and the associated Railway Buses if such services were operating between the towns concerned. Because the train service between Moshi and Arusha was very inconvenient for those students in Moshi town and Moshi District, we never used the Moshi-Arusha portion of the railway warrant. We used to travel by bus between Moshi and Arusha by paying for the fare ourselves. It was at any rate, only fifty miles and took just about one-and-a-half hours. The train journey would have taken five hours and boarding the train at Moshi was almost invariably at two o'clock in the morning.

There were very frequent breakdowns in the buses ploughing between Arusha and Dodoma. I recall one occasion when we spent more than twenty hours at one spot on the road between Kondoa and Babati, waiting for our broken-down bus to be repaired. A spare part had to be brought all the way from Dodoma and, since there were no mobile telephones, it was the assistant driver who got into a lorry bound for Dodoma to fetch the spare part. Our packed lunches and other vitals were exhausted, and we had to contribute money to buy a huge billy-goat, which we slaughtered and barbecued Maasai-style. We ate the meat with roasted sweet potatoes we obtained from the same people who sold us the goat. Incidentally, this whole meal cost us only 3 Shillings, showing how strong the East African currency was. At that time (1952), the EA Pound was equal to the British Pound and, as it may be recalled; 4 US Dollars were equal to one Pound Sterling at this time.

There used to be very lively debates at Tabora School. Politics in Tanganyika was getting heated up following the independence of India and Pakistan in 1947 and the Mau Mau uprising in Kenya in 1951. Movements for self-government or independence were gathering momentum in various colonial territories all over the world. Tanganyika, which was administered by Britain as a Trust Territory under the Trusteeship Council of the United Nations Organisation, could not remain immune to such movements. So we talked a lot of politics at Tabora and most of the organised debates were on subjects related to the timing for self-government or independence.

I recall one evening when the subject for debate was 'Tanganyika should get Self-Government Now'. I was to lead as the proposer and a member of staff, Mr Kingsbury was the seconder of the motion. The opposer of the motion was my classmate Mark Bomani, who was also an eminent debater. Bomani was seconded by no less a person than Mr Crabbe, the Headmaster.

That evening, the Upper School Assembly Hall was packed to the full. Every seat was occupied and extra seats and benches had to be brought from the dining hall and the Lower School, as many Standard X and IX pupils from the Lower School were attending. Mr Kingsbury was our English Language master and, as I mentioned before, Mr Crabbe was not only Headmaster, but he also taught Mathematics in Standard XII.

Prior to the commencement of the Debate, I consulted with Mr Kingsbury and we agreed how to handle the issues. He expressed his confidence that I would be able to drive the various points home in my usual pungent style. He added, however, that since as proposer for the motion I would also be entitled to be the last speaker in the winding up of the debate, I should be cautious and avoid being too rough in analysing Mr Crabbe's contribution. After all, Kingsbury said, he was the Headmaster and good debaters should always be civil and respectful to everybody in their audience, especially those in authority. I thanked Mr Kingsbury for his encouragement and advice. So before I went into the Assembly Hall I jotted down a note to praise Mr Crabbe for condescending so generously and coming to discuss with 'youngsters like us' this important subject. This demonstrated how concerned he was for our future and that of our beloved Tanganyika, and also how he loved his profession. He was a loving father for us all and he cared about our development to the extent of giving us practical lessons on how to prepare for self-government.

During the debate, there was the usual talk of caution by some students who said we were not yet ready and that we needed more educated people with degrees in every subject required for the running of a country. At that time only a handful of Tanganyika Africans had such qualifications. Others talked of the necessity to have a university of our own before we even thought of self-government. Mark Bomani, in particular, made a strong argument by pointing out that it was laughable to demand self-government now instead of pressing for a second High School to be built and run by the Government. First things must be done first, he and others stressed. Expanding education and training Tanganyika Africans not only in administration and law, but in all other subjects, were absolutely necessary before we make demands for self-government. It was premature to demand self-government now, and so Mark argued that the motion should be rejected.

As I indicated above, in my concluding remarks I used my notes and complimented Mr Crabbe, the Headmaster for accepting the invitation to participate. After referring to his generosity in agreeing to come and argue with youngsters such as ourselves, in spite of his other important tasks, I stressed that this demonstrated his concern for our people's welfare and his love of the teaching profession. I praised him as a loving and caring father who wished his children a good and prosperous future. I concluded this part of my reference to the Headmaster by asking the audience to stand up and give him three cheers. I was leading the cheers by 'Hip, Hip' and the audience would shout 'Hurrah, Bwana Crabbe'. Before the audience sat down I started singing:

'For He is a jolly good fellow,
For He is a jolly good fellow (etc.)
And so say all of us'

And the whole audience joined in the refrain. It was a good and dramatic turn of events, and I was enjoying myself.

After the shouting and singing, the Chairman of the proceedings, Mr Partner, who was also a member of the teaching staff, called for order so that I could resume my concluding statement. I then had the chance to drive my points home. I said that those who hesitated lacked the essential knowledge of history, particularly of independence movements and struggles. I reminded them that Liberia was granted independence in 1847. There were no schools or universities in that country at the time. The Liberians then had only been freed from slavery in America and shipped back to Africa! I referred to Ethiopia. This was a proud and dignified country with people walking with their chests forward, proudly representing Africa in the United Nations. I argued that if there were good patriotic citizens in Tanganyika (and I knew there were thousands and thousands of them), with goodwill and commitment, they would be able to advance us faster than the British had done for decades and decades. I stressed that a Government controlled by Tanganyikans would hasten the building of high schools, and develop one of them into a university in a matter of a few years.

I drew the attention of those who were proud of being British that their best Prime Minister, Winston Churchill, only completed Standard XII at Harrow School. Churchill did not go to any university! To me, I said, to press for self-government now was a holy mission and that this must be achieved peacefully at the earliest moment possible. I stressed that it was only committed and patriotic Tanganyikans who could lead us out of the poverty and backwardness that confronted our people. Such commitment and patriotism was not necessarily imparted by university degrees.

Using my knowledge of the Bible, I called those who doubted our ability to undertake self-government now 'Doubting Thomases', and expressed my disappointment that of the disciples of Jesus it appeared that here in Tanganyika even disciples John and Mark were joining Thomas in doubting. (This evoked laughter as the audience understood I was referring to Mr John Crabbe and Mark Bomani). I added that they should repent and ask God for forgiveness through Jesus Christ in whom they apparently believed.

I ended by asking the audience that, as present and future leaders of Tanganyika, they should support the motion for the immediate granting of self-government. Secondly as good citizens, we should resolve that since the 'powers that be' may not act soon, we must organise ourselves to freely, publicly debate this subject forcefully in order to convince them to act promptly. Not only in schools, but in our homes, in the social halls, in bars and any possible gathering, as well as in newspapers, there should be this debate. I ended by stating that I believed that unless the authorities acted promptly and granted self-government, Tanganyika could not avoid degenerating into a conflagration similar to the then current Mau Mau in Kenya.

The motion was carried with an overwhelming majority of the audience. Usually all debates at Tabora School were followed by a secret ballot to determine ranks for the four lead speakers. After the counting I was rated number one, followed by Mark, Kingsbury and Crabbe. No wonder in the Testimonial for Completing Tabora School at the end of 1952, Mr Crabbe, the Headmaster, wrote among other things, that I was 'an Excellent Debater'.

We sat for the Cambridge Overseas School Certificate Examinations in October 1952. These were examinations for all secondary schools in Tanganyika, Kenya and Uganda. They were set and later marked in the United Kingdom. I believe even in Nyasaland (now Malawi) and Northern Rhodesia (now Zambia), students simultaneously sat for examinations of the same standard designed for those territories, as on passing they also qualified to be admitted into Makerere University College.

After the examinations we had end-of-year activities, which included prize-giving for good performers in various school vocations, and activities including sports and academia. In November we left for home to await the examination results. Many of the finalists sought and obtained temporary employment in Government departments, in most cases as clerks. In my case, I returned home where I worked in my *shamba* which had an acre planted with coffee during my grandfather's days. It was harvesting time, and after picking and preparing the coffee for delivery at the Co-operative Society's warehouse, I started pruning the coffee under the training and guidance of my uncle, Aminieli Mtei. There was a part of the land without coffee and I arranged to have seedlings from the Co-operative Society's Nursery for planting. I recall that Wilfred Marealle was also planting coffee seedlings at that time and, indeed, it was he who introduced me to the Nursery attendant in order to get my seedlings.

Before we left Tabora, Wilfred and I had arranged so that all correspondence, including that in respect of the results of our examinations would be sent to us via Kibo Hotel, Marangu. We informed the manager of the Hotel about this and requested him to pass on to us any letters addressed to us coming through his post office box. He readily agreed to this and arranged to place such letters in a special box near the Hotel Reception Desk. After Christmas 1952, when we knew the results would be out anytime, we started to check at the hotel every morning and evening.

By mid-January we were getting tired of this routine checking. Without checking that morning, Wilfred and I decided to go and visit a mutual friend in Kilema. Our friend received and entertained us very well so that we stayed on until late afternoon, when we started walking back home those seven kilometres. We passed at my home first where my mother gave us a verbal message that a friend of mine had brought news about the results of our examinations. From her description we knew that it was our classmate Alfred Meena from Lekura, Mamba. She said he had letters, but he would not leave them with her as he thought he might find us in Wilfred's home. So we left for Wilfred's with haste, anxious to know what Alfred had reported.

By the time we reached Wilfred's home it was six-thirty and getting dark. We found no news of Alfred's visit and so we decided to try to go to his home. We would have to walk about eight kilometres and back, and so we decided to go to request Chief Petro Itosi Marealle, who was Wilfred's uncle, to allow his son to drive us in his car to Alfred's place. His son, Geoffrey, had in fact already suggested that we approach his father and so we boldly went up to the Chief, explained our anxiety to know the results of the examinations, and pleaded that he allow us to use his car. He had been very supportive in our efforts for higher education and realising how anxious we were, agreed to allow Geoffrey to drive us to Mamba.

By eight o'clock we were in Alfred's place, riding for the first time a posh Vauxhall saloon car. But Alfred was not at home. Apparently he had gone out with friends and relatives to celebrate his pass, enabling him to go to Makerere University College. This was good news to us and we felt we too must have passed; otherwise Alfred would not have come all the way to Marangu to tell us of his own passing. At this time, it occurred to us that we had not checked at the Kibo Hotel that day. We returned, passed by the Hotel, and there in the special box by the Reception Desk were the letters from the Headmaster, Tabora High School. With our hands trembling, we opened them, saw the contents, started hugging one another and began celebrating there and then. Whatever little money we had in our pockets we spent at the Hotel's Bar with Geoffrey and other acquaintances we met there that evening.

I had passed the examination and obtained a First Division Certificate (actually placed top of all candidates who sat in Tanganyika). The letter informed me that I would be admitted into Makerere University College with the option of pursuing either an Arts or Science Degree course. As I had already decided that I must start earning a living as soon as possible, and was keen to be an Administrative Officer, I opted for the Arts Degree course.

The arrangements for entry into Makerere involved getting a bursary from the Government of Tanganyika, and for first year undergraduates, these were made by the Tabora School authorities. We received all the necessary documents and in February we travelled to Kampala by train from Moshi via Voi on the Kenya-Uganda Railway. It was a journey that took more than two and half days, but as we were travelling Second Class, which had sleeping facilities, it was enjoyable, unlike the gruelling experience of going to Tabora in a Third Class coach.

At the time we were admitted, Makerere University College was the University College of East Africa (Tanganyika, Zanzibar, Kenya and Uganda), having attained university status in 1950. It had a special affiliated relationship with the University of London. Graduates of Makerere were actually granted degrees of the University of London as external students. An East African University Grants Committee determined what each of the four territorial governments paid for the running of the University College, depending on the number of students and the type of course being pursued by each student.

All students at Makerere were accommodated in the halls of residence, with full board and lodging. As a first year student, I was accommodated in Northcote Hall. In the case of Tanganyika students, each of us also received an additional bursary to meet our expenses for books and stationery as well as pocket money. However, at the beginning of every academic year, each student was assessed by his respective District Commissioner as to what fee his parent or guardian would pay to partly defray the cost of his education. The procedure for assessment of fees varied from district to district.

In the Moshi District (which comprised the present Siha, Hai, Moshi Urban, Moshi Rural and Rombo Districts), the procedure for assessment of fees required that each student, accompanied by his parent or guardian, went to his *Mangi* (Chief) for initial assessment and determination of the family's capacity to pay. The Mangi would ascertain what earnings the family had, what other responsibilities for maintenance and fees the parents had to fulfil, and give his opinion regarding the amount of fees for Makerere. With this initial assessment, the student would then go to his *Mangi Mwitori* (Divisional Chief). The Divisional Chief had councillors from the respective students' wards, with whom he critically examined the Mangi's assessment and decided what to recommend. The student would take this recommendation to the *Mangi Mkuu* (Paramount Chief) who considered it and made his recommendation to the District Commissioner. The District Commissioner would then decide finally what fees, if any, the student would pay.

As both the Mangi Mkuu and the District Commissioner were busy people and were frequently on duty outside their offices, students made many trips to Moshi before they were able to get their fees determined. For some, this entailed staying overnight in Moshi several times, either to try to see the Mangi Mkuu or the District Commissioner. When they were on the end-of-year leave in December 1954, they therefore decided to write a letter to the Mangi Mkuu and the District Commissioner requesting that the procedure be shortened by the students taking the Divisional Chief's recommendation direct to the District Commissioner. This request greatly angered the Mangi Mkuu, who considered it as insubordination.

The Mangi Mkuu therefore summoned all Makerere students in the Moshi District, together with their parents, to a meeting in the Chagga Council Chamber where all councillors were also assembled. When he entered the Chamber everyone rose up and bowed in homage and respect to the Mangi Mkuu. The Council Secretary then said a prayer and, after we had resumed our seats, he announced that the meeting had been called to discuss the question of fees for Makerere students emanating from Moshi District, and a letter the students had addressed to the Mangi Mkuu. He then asked the Mangi Mkuu to open the deliberations.

Before his address, the Mangi Mkuu directed the Council Secretary to ascertain that all the Makerere students concerned were in attendance. After checking this, the Mangi Mkuu explained the procedure for assessment and remission of fees for Makerere College students. He then read the letter requesting a change in the procedure, which the students had addressed to him and the District Commissioner. He stated that he considered this letter lacked respect for his office and showed that the students were arrogant and big-headed. He referred to the fact that when on leave none of the students had ever paid any courtesy call on him. After asserting that the letter was an insubordination to the office and person of the Mangi Mkuu, he said he would not recommend any remission of fees for students from his district unless there was an appropriate abject apology from each student. He further stated that he would recommend non-readmission into Makerere College of any student who did not properly apologise.

The Council clapped hands when the Mangi Mkuu concluded his statement. The students, who were in a state of shock as a result of this tough chastisement, were not asked if they had anything to say. Then one of Mangi Mkuu's personal assistants (Tarishi Msabaa) brought in a bundle of graciaenna leaves (*masalle*) which had been specially prepared and came to the area where we were seated. He spoke to us loudly so that all the councillors could hear. He stated that if we wanted to apologise, each one of us should take some leaves and go to offer them to the Mangi Mkuu to demonstrate our utter and unreserved apology and plead for forgiveness. This was a rare traditional ceremony of abject apology, but my uncle Aminieli, with whom I had gone to the meeting and who was seated in a chair behind, touched me on the shoulder and whispered to me. He advised that there was no harm for me to offer this traditional remorseful apology as required, as he feared that my course at Makerere could be terminated if I refused. I could not argue with him at that time, and so I followed my colleagues and all of us went up to Msabaa, took some masalle leaves, bowed low to the Mangi Mkuu and offered him those leaves as an apology.

It is significant to recall that this humiliating ceremony for these students took place at a time when the climate for political change in the country and East Africa generally was getting very hot. At Makerere, some Tanganyika students had just established a TANU branch, although we as individuals were careful not to declare publicly such membership since the Tanganyika colonial administration could have denied us scholarship or even eventual employment. Nevertheless, the Mangi Mkuu did not endear himself to these prospective future political leaders of Tanganyika. Rather, in fact, he sewed seeds for his eventual dethronement.

His friendship with Kenyan settlers such as Lord Portsmouth, who was guest of honour at the following annual Chagga Day celebrations, made many of us shudder. Especially since we were aware of the sufferings being inflicted on Kikuyu tribesmen by the settler-backed Kenyan Government as a result of the Mau Mau rebellion, we felt that the Mangi Mkuu was out of touch with current nationalist realities.

To give credit where it is due, Thomas Lenana Marealle, the Mangi Mkuu, was otherwise a very progressive leader and spearheaded the launching of many infrastructural, environmental and social development projects in his area of domain. His good rapport with the colonial authorities made it easy for projects sponsored by his administration to receive central government funding as subsidies. At the same time, the Chagga Council under his leadership provided financial support for and encouraged self-help projects, such as the building of feeder-roads, their maintenance and repair. New middle and primary schools and dispensaries were built, partly by organised self-help labour and partly by funds from the Chagga Council. The co-operative movement in Kilimanjaro was strong and effective during this period, providing leadership and example for the whole of Tanganyika; and surpluses from KNCU. operations, at Mangi Mkuu's behest, even built a secondary school at Lyamungo and opened a commercial school at its headquarters. With Mangi

Mkuu's encouragement, the KNCU. at this period also sponsored several members of its staff for training in the United Kingdom.

At the time we were admitted into Makerere University College, those seeking an Arts Degree had to pursue, in the first two years, a course in English Language and Literature, History, Geography and Social Sciences, at the end of which they sat for what was called the University of London Intermediate Examinations. After the ceremony at the Chagga Council, I returned to Makerere in January 1955, having passed these examinations and it was then that the actual degree course in Political Science, History and Geography began. As I explained earlier, I chose this short Bachelor of Arts Degree course because I wanted to graduate early and start earning a living. I thought that with a qualification in these subjects, I might be appointed to a position in the Tanganyika colonial administration, initially as a District Officer (Cadet).

My academic performance at Makerere continued to be good. For example, in 1956 I entered a History Essay Competition sponsored by the British Council for Commonwealth University undergraduate students, and won the top prize. I was informed of this as we were preparing for our final examinations in December 1956. The prize was in the form of books worth 200 Pounds Sterling, a lot of money in those days. The British Council sent me almost a whole shelf of books on the constitutional history of the Commonwealth, including *The Statute of Westminster* and Winston Churchill's history of *The Second World War!*, which I have only been able to complete reading recently, after I retired from active public service.

In 1956 the academic staff at Makerere University College, who were mostly European, Canadian and American, managed to persuade the authorities to change the academic year to start in July, so that the long holidays would be between April and July. This was so that they would be able to take holidays during the northern summer when their own children, schooling mainly in Europe and North America, would be able to accompany them. Our stay at Makerere was therefore prolonged and we were only able to sit our final examinations in March/April 1957 rather than the previous November.

With my friend, Wilfred Marealle: we had this studio photo before he left Kampala for Kabete (I am the one seated)

After the examinations, we had the usual end-of-academic-year festivities, parties and ceremonies throughout the University College and in the halls of residence, when those completing their studies bade farewell to those remaining. It was also the time to say goodbye to colleagues with whom we had been in class for those four-and-a-half years, some of whom had become very intimate friends. Makerere, as noted previously, had students from the four East African British dependencies of Tanganyika, Kenya, Uganda and Zanzibar, as well as from Northern Rhodesia (Zambia) and Nyasaland (Malawi). We expressed hope that we might meet again, but in any case wished each other good luck. With these ceremonies, I ended my formal academic education. I would be twenty-five years old on my next birthday.

CHAPTER 5

Employment and Engagement

Before leaving Makerere University College, students in their final years were interviewed by prospective employers. Indeed, prior to the beginning of the end-of-year vacation in December 1956, the Government of Tanganyika had arranged for all students whose final year would end in April 1957 to travel to Dar es Salaam for interviews with various Heads of Departments. So for the first time I visited my capital city, Dar es Salaam, where I was subsequently to spend more than twenty-five years of my working life. We were accommodated in the Rex Hotel. The Mnazi Mmoja recreational grounds formed a front view for the hotel, and we newcomers ,mainly from rural Tanganyika, marvelled at the façade. The Arnatoglu Hall stood alone to the north of the recreational grounds. We were able to walk in there that weekend evening and bull-danced to the local jazz band music. That is where I first met Ally Sykes, who led the band, playing the guitar.

For the interviews, we were taken to the Central Secretariat where we met the Member for Local Government, a Mr Page-Jones, and other officials, including one who was later to become a personal friend, by the name of George Bernard Gordon. In the form we were asked to fill, I indicated that my first choice for a job was District Officer. It was understood that, if successful one would go for a year's course in public administration at Cambridge University, the so-called 'Devonshire Course'. The Tanganyika Broadcasting Service also wanted to interview us and we went there, toured the studios and talked with the Director, who assessed our voices and whether we would be suitable for reading the news. The Department of Commerce also interviewed us and took down our details.

After these interviews, we were made to understand that the University College authorities would forward the results of our final examinations direct to the Government, on the basis of which decisions on our employment applications would be made. We returned home for the end-of-year holidays and in January 1957 went back to College for our final semister. During that semister, commercial firms desirous of recruiting graduates also sent representatives to Makerere to interview us. In this connection, Royal Dutch Shell Company, Standard Vacuum Oil Company and East African Tobacco (EAT), a subsidiary of British-American Tobacco) on different occasions interviewed me. The interview with EAT was somewhat sophisticated, with aptitude and I.Q. tests. Before I had completed the final examinations, EAT sent me a letter offering me an appointment as a Manager Trainee. I was therefore a very happy and confident man during the last days of the examinations.

The offer by East African Tobacco stipulated that I would initially be based in Nairobi, where their largest factory was located. I would first train and observe operations in the cigarette manufacturing factory, and later move to other departments, including the sales districts and then the head office. The salary for the job was much more attractive than I envisaged getting if I were offered the District Officer post by the Government. Therefore I promptly replied to EAT accepting the offer, with the expectation that if the Tanganyika Government offered me the job of my heart's desire, I could resign. Indeed, at that time it was rather difficult to work in rural Kenya because of the State of Emergency declared by the British colonial administration in order to fight and contain the Mau Mau Rebellion.

On completing my studies at Makerere University College, I therefore travelled to my home in Marangu, Moshi where I spent a few weeks before I joined the East African Tobacco Company in Nairobi as an employee on 1 May 1957. Two other contemporaries of mine at College, Stephen Ngoloma and Migire Alila, both Kenyans, were also offered Manager Trainee jobs by the company and reported for duty on the same date. We found a recent graduate, Andrew John Omanga, already on the management of the company. Omanga had left Makerere only three years before us, and so we had hopes that soon we might also complete the training and start rising.

On reflection, however, those few weeks I spent at home in Marangu were among the most crucial in my life, for it was then that I plucked courage and formally proposed to Johara, and she accepted!

I had known Johara's parents since I was a small boy and, as I was senior to her by almost ten years, I had watched her grow into a girl I greatly admired and adored. She was then in her last years at secondary school and since under Chagga customs, the period of betrothal could be as long as four years, I was determined to wait for her to finish.

I say that I had to be bold to propose to Johara because there were two main hurdles to surmount: the first related to her schooling. I knew her father, Hassan Marealle, was keen that she should pursue higher education and professional training, and so he would object to my 'meddling in her future'. The second hurdle was the fact that all members of her family were practising Muslims, and her father, in particular, would strongly resent any attempt to convert her to Christianity before getting married to me.

Nevertheless, immediately she accepted, I arranged for my family to proceed with the initial customary steps to demonstrate that I was a serious and committed suitor. My mother was especially excited by the prospects of Johara being her daughter-in-law, for she had feared that my sojourn in far-off Uganda could have brought her a Muganda girl. Indeed, my mother, as a child, had grown up as a neighbour of the Marealles. She knew them intimately, and was very friendly with J's mother.

As noted before, the period of betrothal under Chagga traditions could be quite a prolonged one. So I avoided touching on the question of precisely when we would get married, whenever I was able to talk with my future father-in-law. In the following months, whenever I was at home, I only talked with him about education for my fiancée'. At this time I also decided to start building a small modern house at home to replace the wattle-and-daub hut *(mchalo)* I had built in 1949. Therefore, almost every end-of-month weekend, I would visit Marangu to check on the progress of the construction and pay the contractor, a German-trained builder by the name of Ndesanjo Kessy.

During the 1957/58 Christmas/New Year celebrations, I managed to get two-weeks leave from my employers and spent it in Marangu. It was then that I was able to have enough time with Johara to be able to persuade her to go for Bible lessons prior to being baptised into the Lutheran Church before our marriage.

Johara Hassan Marealle at the time of our engagement.

After persuading her, I politely requested her father to give me an audience. During our conversation, I pleaded with him that it would be best for Johara and I to have a Christian marriage. He himself had been baptised into the Lutheran Church in the late 1920s, but on getting employment in Mombasa, Kenya for a prolonged period in the 1930s, had converted into the Muslim faith. In the end, for the sake of our future happiness, he agreed with me, and so Johara was baptised in late 1959, just as she completed her final examinations at Machame Girls' Secondary School.

Returning to my employment with East African Tobacco, as I said above, we were first attached to the factory where cigarettes were being made. We put on overalls and were even trained how to 'receive' cigarettes, pick out damaged ones and ensure that they were packed correctly. We spent about four weeks in the making department. Another week was spent in the leaf department, and another in the Engineering Department. Finally we spent a week with the Excise Department, which was actually an extension of the East African Customs and Excise revenue collection machinery. Here we were co-ordinating with the tax officers posted to the factory, and agreed with them the amount of money that would be remitted to Government as excise duty on the cigarettes being sold. In this connection, I had the first contact with the revenue collection machinery of government, noting the very vigilant manner the Excise Department officer handled our packing, stacking and record keeping.

All factory workers, including management, had lunch at the factory at the company's expense. Management trainees lunched 'upstairs' with the departmental managers, who were all white except the Welfare Officer, a Mr Benjamin Wandera. If Mr Omanga from Head Office Personnel Department was on tour, he also joined us for lunch. I should explain that these arrangements for lunch were novel at that time, especially in Kenya where racial discrimination was widespread and still officially practised. It was only in a very progressive company like EAT that discrimination on the grounds of colour was not seriously observed. And so, even in this arrangement for our having lunch with the European staff, we were pioneers.

After about two months at the factory, I was assigned to Head Office Sales Department, whilst my colleagues went to other departments. The Sales Department, in addition to co-ordinating the marketing of tobacco products in all East Africa, handled the import of brands manufactured abroad by the British American Tobacco group of companies. Indeed, EAT enjoyed almost a monopoly of the tobacco market in East Africa, with a small company which manufactured pipe tobacco, packed in plastic sachets, based in Iringa being the only competitor at the time. Even the Iringa pipe tobacco company used EAT depots and distribution outlets to market its product.

I should recall that it was in June 1957 that the results of our final examinations at the University College were announced. My performance was again good and I had obtained a Bachelor of

Arts Degree in the First Division, winning the Shell Company Prize for the best student in the Faculty of Arts for 1957. Because of this performance, I was expecting at any time to receive a letter from the Government of Tanganyika, probably offering me the job of my heart's desire, namely District Officer (Cadet). Since by August 1957 I had not received anything from them, I decided to write a letter to the Director of Establishment in the Chief Secretary's Office, Dar es Salaam. I reminded him of our interview the previous December and gave my new address in case he wanted to contact me. In the letter I mentioned my performance in the final examinations.

In October 1957 I transferred to the Nairobi District Sales Office, which handled sales in Nairobi City and its environs. The District Office was also responsible for the organisation of the EAT Pavilion at the Nairobi Agricultural and Trade Fair, and so this was an opportunity for me to participate in collaboration with the Public Relations and Advertising Section of Head Office in a promotional and sales effort. After about a month, I was attached to what EAT called Greater Nairobi Sales District to understudy the District Sales Representative, a Mr N.U. Bhatt. Greater Nairobi sales district comprised all the surrounding government administrative districts of Kiambu, Thika, Ukambani and Masai-Narok.

With Mr Bhatt, in a Land Rover van carrying cigarettes and other tobacco products, I toured all the markets and shopping centres in these districts. He was showing me how to promote sales, supervise and check our distributors and other stockists handling tobacco products. In selling tobacco products one has to make sure that the stacking and ongoing sales facilitate no accumulation of stale or old stock. If a shopkeeper had stale stock, we would replace it by stock carried in our van. If the reason for having stale stock was because of bad stacking, namely selling new stock whilst old stock was still unsold, we would penalise the stockist by reducing his sales bonus. The bonus was based on quarterly turnover, which encouraged stockists to maximise sales. It is sad to note that this simple rule in retail sales is not being observed in departments such as government pharmacies where expired stocks of medicines can turn poisonous to patients.

When Mr Bhatt proceeded to India on two months leave, I found myself acting as District Sales Representative. In this capacity, I was responsible for promotion and co-ordination of sales in the area, supervising four salesmen, each with his own van and driver. Some of our stockists took delivery of products from our depot in Nairobi, and others had to be supplied by our own vans. Controlling stock at the depot, ensuring the timely placing of orders from the factories and following up payments by buyers, as well as ensuring that the team of salesmen and their vehicles were properly catered for and serviced, became my duty. I had very good co-operation from the staff and matters ran smoothly until I was able to hand over to Mr Bhatt on his return from leave.

In March 1958 I was transferred to Nyeri, which handled the Mount Kenya Sales District. Again here I accompanied the District Sales Representative, a European named Malone, on visits and inspection tours of distributors and stockists in the area. I was in this part of Kenya for the first time, and was able to visit and stay for a few days in towns including Embu, Meru, Nanyuki, and went all the way to Isiollo near the Ethiopian border, and Garissa near the border with Somalia. It was a difficult time to travel in that area because the Mau Mau Rebellion was still ongoing, and there were occasional raids and skirmishes here and there in the area around Mount Kenya. A number of my colleagues at Makerere lived or worked, mostly as teachers, in these towns and it was a great pleasure and sometimes a surprise for me to be their guest.

My stay in Nyeri was only for three months, the last two of which I was again acting as District Sales Representative when Mr Malone went on overseas leave. On his return, I was transferred to Eldoret where I was given orientation similar to that I had experienced in Greater Nairobi and Nyeri. By the beginning of September I found myself in Kisumu, where I spent another three months before I returned to Head Office in Nairobi at the end of November 1958.

CHAPTER 6

Joining the Civil Service and Getting Married

In the meantime, when I was in Nyeri, about January 1958, I had received a letter signed by G.B. Gordon of the Central Establishments Department of the Tanganyika Government offering me an appointment as an auditor in the Controller and Auditor General's Department. I had been rather taken aback by this offer because I had not studied accounts at college, and my last contact with matters remotely related to this profession, was when I did mathematics for the Cambridge Overseas School Certificate Examinations at Tabora High School. As I said earlier, I had studied only History, Geography and Political Science at Makerere College for my Bachelor's Degree.

Nevertheless, I had a difficult decision to make: I was working in a country which I could not call my own, although EAT could easily post me to Tanganyika on completion of my familiarisation with the sales activities of the company. I was not greatly enjoying the job at hand, but the salary was good and I needed to save money in order to complete the building of my house at Marangu. I hesitated, but in the end I politely replied to the letter saying that I was unable to accept the offer. I said that I felt I was not qualified to be an auditor and that I would take rather too long to learn to be competent. Here I was being quite candid because I did not want to do a job where I would be rated mediocre. I stated that my first choice for a job in government was still that of an Administrative Officer, either based at the Central Government Secretariat, or in any up-country provincial or district office.

However, when I returned to Nairobi from Kisumu eleven months later, I had been asking myself if I were really cut out to be a salesman in tobacco products, even if I were to be a senior sales manager in the company. For more than a year, I had been participating in the organisation and running of the EAT pavilions in many of the agricultural and trade shows of the districts I had been posted to. I had participated with substantive District Sales Representatives in promotional activities relating to the marketing of cigarettes and other tobacco products, and several times had been incharge of such district sales offices. In some of the towns, such as Nyeri and Kisumu, I was even popularly called "Mr Clipper", the most popular brand of cigarette then on the East African market. However, in spite of the much more attractive emoluments than any I would be able to expect from the Government for any post I qualified for, I felt uncomfortable marketing tobacco. I therefore looked for the letter I had received from the Government earlier in the year, and decided to write demi-officially to Mr George Gordon.

I had met George Gordon during the interviews we had in December 1956 at the Central Secretariat in Dar es Salaam. In my letter to him I referred to the offer I had received regarding the Auditor post, and my reply of January 1958 in which I had explained the reasons for not accepting it. I stated that I had since then realised that I was employed in a job I did not much enjoy, in spite of its attractive emoluments. I sought his assistance in identifying a suitable job I could do in Government, reiterating that my first preference would still be that of an administrative officer at the Central Secretariat or in any up-country district or provincial office.

At this time I was aware of a new policy of the Government of Tanganyika regarding the hastening of the localisation of the Civil Service. Sir Richard Turnbull had taken over as Governor in July 1958 from Sir Edward Twining. In spite of his having been previously Chief Secretary in Kenya Colony and the official behind the tough suppression of the Mau Mau Rebellion, Sir Richard appeared more receptive to the demands of the nationalist leaders under Mwalimu Julius Nyerere and the Tanganyika African National Union (TANU). One of the main policies, which the new Governor publicly enunciated, was to increase the number of Tanganyikan citizens holding senior positions in the Civil Service in preparation for self-government and independence, and I thought I should take the opportunity to apply for one.

It did not take long for Gordon to respond. He wrote back in the third week of December 1958 to say that there were many posts in Government, but the best he could suggest for me was that of an Establishment Officer in his own Establishments Division of the Chief Secretary's Office. He explained that the duty of an Establishment Officer was mainly the interpretation and implementation of Government Personnel policy and regulations.

He added that, as I was not fully conversant with Government Personnel Policy, Regulations and Procedures, I would have to be in the Training Grade for a period of at least six months if I accepted such an appointment. By way of encouragement, he further pointed out that the Central Secretariat where most Establishment Officers were stationed was the hub of Government. As such, a young officer with talent would come into contact with challenging situations and senior government officials who could make his prospects in the Civil Service quite bright. He alluded to my poor health whilst at Tabora High School and Makerere College, which apparently made them hesitate to place me in the Provincial Administration where District officers led a somewhat hectic and strenuous life.

I made up my mind at once on receipt of that letter, and telephoned Mr Gordon from Nairobi to say that I would be glad to accept the appointment to the post of Establishment Officer (Training Grade), if formally offered. He said the written offer would be issued immediately, and we discussed over the phone the earliest date I would be able to report for duty. That day was 4 January 1959, and I said I had to give one month's notice of resignation from the company, which I could give immediately. I added that, once I received the offer, I would be able to travel and be in Dar es Salaam by mid-February 1959.

I was able to give a month's notice of resignation to my Sales Director on 5 January 1959. The company fully understood my decision and as I had two weeks of earned leave to my credit, I left Nairobi on 20 January for my home in Marangu, Moshi. Thereafter, I was in contact with the Establishments Division and travelled to Dar es Salaam on 9 February 1959 to take up my formal appointment with the Government.

My friend, Roland Mwanjisi, met me at the Dar es Salaam Railway Station. Roland and I first met in 1951 at Tabora High School, where we were classmates. Together we had gone to Makerere and on graduating in 1957, he had been offered a Government job as a Commercial Officer, whilst I had gone to EAT. He was still a bachelor and was living alone in a three-bedroom flat at Shariff Shamba, Ilala. He took me to his flat and offered to accommodate me pending my being able to rent my own house.

At the same block of flats I found another college mate, Dr Anthony Bulengo, who was working at the Sewa Haji Hospital, the main Government hospital in the country. Tony had recently married Martha, and they received me very warmly. Many other friends and former college- and schoolmates, as well as relatives, were working in Dar es Salaam and so, unlike in Kenya, I had good and familiar company. Among close relatives then residing in Dar es Salaam was my first cousin, Obed Aminieli Mtei, who was in the Police Force and had only recently got married. As I mentioned earlier, his father, Aminieli, acted as my guardian after my father's death. We had grown up very close together and some people even thought Obed was my young brother. Indeed, in Chagga the custom makes no distinction between cousins, half-brothers or half-sisters. They are all brothers or sisters.

My new job at the Central Establishment was unfamiliar, but I was able to learn quickly. Although all senior officers in the department were European and Asian, they helped me and co-operated in my efforts to learn and familiarise myself with the tasks I had to perform. I was taken to see the Director of Establishments, Mr Brian Hodgson in the first few days. Mr Hodgson had only recently been promoted Director of Establishments, having been District Commissioner of my own district of Moshi, where I had only heard of him. At the District Commissioner's Office, students' problems were handled by District Officers or by the District Education Officer.

Mr Hodgson told me that he was very pleased to welcome me to his department. He briefly described its functions. These included recruitment for the whole Civil Service, Personnel Policy and Regulations, and liaison with the Civil Service Commission. He further said that he knew that I had done very well at Makerere and hoped that in his department I would be able to complete the training grade period even before the stipulated six months. I would then become a fully-fledged establishment officer to take charge of one of the various sections. I thanked him for welcoming me, promising to do my best to learn quickly so that I could make myself useful in the Department.

For about four months following the interview with the Director, I was attached to heads of sections, seeing what they did and in many cases drafting letters or minutes relating to questions they were dealing with. Besides Mr Gordon, who was very keen to train me up and told me to feel free to walk into his office whenever I was in any difficulty, I found a Mr M.K. Nayar, an elderly Indian who had served in the Department for over twenty years, very helpful. Mr Nayar also had the title of Chief Establishment Officer, but he acted as the reference book of all precedents, and if any officer needed advice he would go to him. Mr Newman, the Deputy Director and Mr C.J. Chohan, another Chief Establishment Officer, were also most helpful in ensuring that I settled down properly in my new job.

Although I was not head of Section, I was given my own room for an office. In this room I kept books, papers and files I wanted to read. Soon I was drafting letters and minutes for the heads of sections to which I was attached. My main reading materials whilst in the office were what were called 'flimsy' files, which contained third or fourth carbon copies of all letters and memoranda issued by the Department the previous day. In this way, I became aware of what decisions were being made by the heads of sections, and also noted their styles of replying. If I felt I needed to know more about the background to a decision, I would call for the subject file and read it. I was attending the weekly Departmental Heads of Sections meetings where I met all of them, under the chairmanship of the Deputy Director. As the only Tanganyika African attending the meetings, the heads of sections soon found me useful and were seeking my views on various issues under discussion.

In July 1959 I became a full Establishment Officer, having completed the Training Grade period, and was assigned the Overseas Recruitment and Training Section. My section liased with Heads of Departments who had obtained Public Service Commission approval to recruit staff from abroad. On ascertaining the number of posts to be filled which had to be confirmed by the Treasury, I would forward the draft advertisements to the Government's recruiting agents in London or in India for publication. I was in correspondence with the Colonial Office as well as the Crown Agents in London almost every day regarding progress in recruitment of several different officers for the Government. Agricultural officers, vets, doctors and engineers were being recruited from abroad during that period. Sometimes the correspondence would be in respect of confirmation of Government acceptance of variation of the terms of appointment to take account of individual special qualifications or experience. Other times it would relate to the travel and passage arrangements for the newly appointed staff and their families. In other cases, it would be to agree to re-advertise after the failure to get suitable candidates. Similarly, I was in correspondence with the Government agent in Bombay, as recruitment from India and Pakistan was handled through that agent. Recruitment from India and Pakistan was mainly in respect of accountants and auditors.

In terms of the training, my section was responsible for the co-ordination of overseas in-service training for African staff. Heads of departments normally made the initial contacts with the training institutes and, in consultation with the Public Service Commission, would select deserving officers for such training. Training courses were, in most cases, financed by the Government and sometime by donors, either fully or partly. It was the responsibility of the Central Secretariat to liaise with donors and the training institutes and this was my section's role. I remember having correspondence with the Colonial Office regarding Administrative Officers attending the so-called Devonshire Course at Cambridge University; Loughborough College regarding co-operative inspector courses; and the Police College, Hendon in connection with police training. I had two Assistant Establishment Officers and a number of Establishment Assistants, who were all Asian. Africans were only at the clerical and typist levels.

Very soon after I took charge, I requested that senior African Officers be assigned to my section, as we handled rather sensitive issues. Indeed, when later this section was redesignated 'Africanisation and Training Division', I found myself being summoned almost every day by the Minister Without Portfolio in the Prime Minister's Office or the Assistant Minister to explain what we were doing or to get directives on matters relating to Africanisation.

As mentioned above, all letters issued from the Department had their carbon copies circulated as 'flimsies' in order to keep all the senior officers and Ministers (when they were appointed) informed. The Minister Without Portfolio, Hon. Saidi Maswanya, was very keen to follow up what was happening in the Department, and he used to summon me for long sessions with him to explain what we were doing. The Assistant Minister was Bhoke Munanka, and I recall one incident when he objected strongly to a letter we had issued and summoned me to explain. He got rather excited during the discussion and stood up pulling the flimsy file on which I had placed the cup of tea he had offered me. The tea was spilt on to the desk and dripped on to my white short trousers and shirt (the standard dress for civil servants in Dar those days) so that I was really dirty walking back to the Establishments Department from the Prime Minister's Office.

Soon after I joined the Civil Service, my friend and colleague Roland Mwanjisi, decided to resign so that he could work at TANU headquarters full-time as publicity secretary. He took me one weekend to Mwalimu Nyerere's house at Magomeni, where I was introduced. Mwalimu, who was soon to become Chief Minister, was very interested to know that I was at the Central Secretariat and remarked that I should stay on there and work hard to learn from those expatriates. Subsequently, I used to meet Mwalimu fairly frequently at the Cosy Café' in Mkwepu Street, where I regularly had my lunch. Other people I met at this popular rendezvous during the lunch hour were George Starley, a resident of Mtoni and Randal Sadleir, a former district commissioner who had been transferred to the Department of Information Services. In later years, I found myself a neighbour of Randal Sadleir in Mzinga Way, Oyster Bay, when we moved into the house I had built under the mortgage arrangements administered by the Ministry of Health and Housing. After his retirement, Randal wrote a book, 'TANZANIA, Journey to Republic', and I envy him that Mwalimu Nyerere was able to write a *Foreword* to it, before his passing.

I should explain that after sharing Roland's flat for a few months, the Bulengos vacated theirs and I was able to rent it, and so continued to live with my friend in the same block. Soon after Roland resigned from the Civil Service, he vacated his also, and moved to Magomeni where many politicians, including Oscar Kambona, the TANU Secretary General, lived. However, before Roland left, Oscar Kambona had been a frequent visitor to his flat, and so I came to know him then.

At this time, about March 1960, Johara and her best friend, Flora Jason Uriyo, had obtained employment in Dar es Salaam, and I had offered them one of my extra rooms, which they preferred to the Lady Twining Hostel, where they were initially accommodated. Flora was later to be married to Kambona in a well publicised and elegant wedding in St. Paul's Cathedral, London, where Mwalimu Nyerere actually acted as their best man. Other prominent politicians with whom I had close relations at this period included A.Z. Nsilo-Swai, who had served as warden in our Hall of Residence at Makerere. He had left Uganda at the same time as I did to join the Tanganyika Co-operative movement, and then TANU as National Treasurer. Another was Solomon Eliufoo, who had taught us at Old Moshi Secondary School. All these were elected Members of Parliament and became members of the Cabinet at the time of Independence.

The period between October 1959 and Independence (December 1961) was a very exciting one for me and, I believe, for many public servants in Tanganyika, including politicians. As I said earlier, I had got engaged to Johara at the end of 1957, and she had been baptised into the Lutheran Church in December 1959. After secondary school, she had sought employment immediately, and from February 1960 was employed in Dar es Salaam. We therefore began to plan our wedding seriously from the time she came to Dar es Salaam.

The house I was building in Marangu was completed about May 1960, and after consultation with our families, Johara and I agreed that the date for our wedding would be 6 August 1960.

The ceremony was to be at Ngaruma Lutheran Church, where I had learnt the three 'R's. It would be followed by the traditional reception at my home. You can, therefore, imagine the hustle and bustle of organising such a crucial event at the same time as settling into a new job, with very exciting decisions to make almost everyday.

On my completing the Training Grade period in July 1959, I had become eligible for a car loan from the Government and with this I bought a small saloon car, a Fiat 1100. I was rather clumsy in learning how to drive and took a long time to qualify. However, I managed to obtain a driver's licence in January 1960. So in mid-July 1960, Johara and I, accompanied by Obed's wife, Eudora, started driving from Dar es Salaam in the little Fiat, to go to Marangu for the final arrangements for our wedding.

The main route from Dar to the North was still through Morogoro. We reached Mziha, halfway between Morogoro and Korogwe, at about 3.00 p.m. We estimated that we would cover the eighty-eight miles to Korogwe in another three hours; and as the Korogwe-Himo road was also *murram*, we planned to spend the night in Korogwe. I had covered another thirty miles towards Handeni when I lost control of the vehicle, veered to the left, and hit the embankment, smashing the left front mudguard. Fortunately, none of us was hurt since I was not driving fast. The only thing we could do after this accident was to unload our luggage, and look for someone to guard the wrecked vehicle for the night, before we got a lift in a bus to Handeni.

At Handeni we got accommodation in the Government Guest House. In the morning, I managed to telephone the insurance company in Dar es Salaam, who knew me well. They gave me the telephone number of a garage in Morogoro who would be able to arrange for a breakdown vehicle to go to the site of the accident and tow the vehicle. The insurance company also undertook to talk with the garage in Morogoro to confirm their readiness to pay for the expenses, including those of the subsequent repairs since my car was comprehensively insured. I then telephoned the garage in Morogoro, and after a lengthy explanation as to where the accident had occurred, they agreed to send the breakdown vehicle to the site. After these arrangements were completed, we boarded a bus for Korogwe where we were able to get the evening train from Tanga and travelled to Moshi.

We were three days late in arriving at home in Marangu. There were no telephone facilities in Marangu those days and so our families had started to get worried about our whereabouts. The superstitious told us that Johara and I ought not to have travelled together in the same vehicle, let alone a vehicle driven by one of us. People planning to get married, they insisted, must travel separately. Anyway, we thanked God, for it could have been worse.

The preparations for the wedding meant a very hectic time for me for the next three weeks. I was moving into my new house and had to travel to Moshi town several times to pick up furniture I had despatched from Dar es Salaam, as well as obtain other items, such as curtains for the house. In addition, Johara and I had to attend traditional counselling on marriage (mapfundo) at the church. An elderly retired evangelist, Philipo Njau, talked to us on these matters, which I found very interesting and revealing. We attended about four sessions with this old man, who happened to be Elimo's father.

Outside the Ngaruma Lutheran Parish Church after the wedding ceremony, 6 August 1960

The wedding was quite an event in our village, and the Mtei clan put on a magnificent show. A lot of the traditional local beer was brewed for the occasion. On Saturday, 6 August 1960 we were married. There was no hitch, and many of my friends, former school and college mates working in the Kilimanjaro and Arusha areas, turned up as guests. All our relatives came, of course, and the celebration and feasting lasted until late into the night. The next day we went to church, as it was a Sunday, and returned home for more feasting and boozing. My paternal uncle, acting as my guardian father, and my mother had a special brew for the occasion (irutsa mana); a brew meant to resuscitate me after the nuptial night). The feasting, in fact, continued until the following Tuesday.

We had to stay at Marangu for at least two weeks after the wedding because several other relatives and close friends were expected to arrange to 'receive' us at their homes. My father-in-law was the first, and his function took place a week after the wedding day. My maternal uncle, Eliab Mlyingi, followed a day later. Another major function 'to receive us' was arranged by an uncle who was husband to my father's sister. He had acted as the main witness, *(mkara o shima),* at our wedding for purposes of the dowry, or bride price, which under our customs is paid by the groom.

Johara and I 'At Home' in our Marangu House after our wedding.

At all these functions, I attended with my new bride, and we both gave locally brewed beer and food to the leading guests present.

I have given this account of the festivities connected with our wedding because it appears that, of late, Chagga partners and many other Tanzanians, who can afford it, have resorted to parties which are actually pompous extravaganzas, expensive by any standards. Ours was a series of community functions where many people shared the expenses by contributions in kind and in labour. Those who cannot afford the expensive weddings nowadays are embarrassed, and resort to eloping with their girlfriends, or simply deciding to live together without any formal or legal recognition. The only legal recognition comes by the lapse of time provided in the Marriages Act, which stipulates that a couple who continuously live together as man and wife for more than three years are considered to be legally married!

After the festivities, we were anxious to return to Dar es Salaam. Not only did I want to be close during the momentous events preceding the granting of Independence, but we were also aware that en-route we would have to spend a few days in Morogoro to follow up the repair of our car. We travelled by train and bus to Morogoro in the last week of August, and were received by Wilfred Marealle who was then working in Morogoro as a Veterinary Officer with the Government. Wilfred had already married Helen Mchaki in 1957, and although he had been unable to attend the wedding, as first cousin to Johara and my friend since childhood, he was keen to play host to us. Helen was a superb hostess, and we had a most relaxing four days in Morogoro.

The day after our arrival in Morogoro, I was able to go to the garage where our car was being repaired. I discussed and agreed with them on the cost of repairs and made the necessary down-payment before the insurance company could authorise completion. The few days that followed, with the company of Wilfred and Helen, were the genuine holiday we had, for it had been very hectic for us for the previous two months. We travelled by train to Dar es Salaam at the end of August.

Just before we had left Dar es Salaam in July, I rented a house in Kurasini and vacated the flat at Sharrif Shamba, Ilala. So, on returning from leave, we lived in Kurasini. We found ourselves neighbours to Paul Sozigwa, who had been my classmate at Tabora and all the way to Makerere and Cleopa Msuya. Paul was then working with the Tanganyika Broadcasting Corporation, whilst Cleopa was a Community Development Officer in the Government. They were both already married and so J. had good company in Rhoda Msuya and Monica Sozigwa. Another neighbour was the Reverend Father Joseph Sipendi, a Roman Catholic priest who was Secretary to the Tanganyika Episcopal Conference, and was later to become Bishop of the Catholic Diocese of Moshi.

CHAPTER 7

Promotion and Independence

At the time I reported for duty at the office, after my leave, the political atmosphere in Tanganyika, especially in the capital, was heating up. As I said earlier, Sir Richard Turnbull, the Governor was much more receptive to the nationalists' demands for early independence than his predecessor. His good rapport with Mwalimu Julius Nyerere made negotiations for orderly constitutional changes easier, and many of the terms for change and pace of progress were now acceptable even to many of the senior civil servants, all of them British, who worked under the Governor.

Elections into the Legislative Council, which had been approved and prepared by Sir Edward Twining, the previous Governor, were scheduled to be held in phases, in early 1959 and in 1960. Sir Richard decided to bring the second phase forward, so that these elections were held in September 1959. Prior to that, in July 1959, a number of Ministers had been appointed from among the elected Members of the Legislative Council. In the New Year, it was announced that the system of parity of the three racial groups in the Council would end in the following elections which, depending on the progress of the constitutional negotiations, would be held later in 1960 or early the following year.

Soon after my reporting for duty, a Salaries Commission was appointed on the insistence of the new Chief Minister, Mwalimu Julius Nyerere, who considered that the Lidbury Salaries Commission, which had reviewed salaries for the whole of British East Africa, had pegged its salaries on European standards of pay and were, therefore, too generous for the Tanganyika Government to be able to pay. The chairman of the new Commission was Mr A.L. Adu, who was then Head of the Ghanaian Civil Service. It was expected to recommend salaries more in line with the ability of Tanganyika to pay, and Mr C.J. Chohan, the Chief Establishment Officer, was appointed Secretary to the Commission. In order to be able to follow up the many verbal and sometimes vociferous representations to the Commission by the Swahili-speaking trade unionists, Mr Chohan requested that I be attached to the Adu Commission as Assistant Secretary. In this capacity I came to know Mr Adu well.

Immediately after the Adu Commission Report had been accepted and implemented by the Government, the Recruitment and Training Section of the Establishment Department was redesignated 'Africanisation and Training Division'. This was in March 1961, and I was promoted to Chief Establishment Officer to head it. My new post was graded in the Lower Super scale. This promotion meant that my annual salary jumped from 792 Pounds Sterling per annum to 1,660 Pounds Sterling . To be promoted in this way, just as I completed my formal probationary service of two years, was an outstanding achievement. Of course, this was an unusual period in the history of the Tanganyika Civil Service, and a number of other local officers were also moving fast. It was a period when 'jobs were applying for local staff' rather than the other way round.

At this time, another ex-Ghanaian civil servant, David Anderson, joined the Establishments Department as Staff Development Advisor. David Anderson was sponsored and paid for by the Ford Foundation. I understood that he had been recommended to Mwalimu Nyerere, the Chief Minister, by President Kwame Nkrumah himself. From then on I was to work very closely with Anderson.

David Anderson arranged for me to make a study tour of public administration training institutes in India, Pakistan, Thailand and South Vietnam from June to August 1961. This was my first trip outside East Africa and my Tanganyika colleague on the tour was Mr Brayne, the Principal of the Mzumbe Institute of Local Government Administration. The study tour was paid for by the US International Co-operation Administration (later renamed U.S.A.I.D) and included Ugandan officials, one of whom was Mr Y.K. Lule, the then Chairman of the Uganda Public Service Commission. I had known Lule as a Lecturer in the Faculty of Education at the time I was at Makerere University College. Later, he was President of Uganda for a brief period, following the ousting of Idi Amin.

Presumably the American sponsors wanted us to see how they were handling training in South Vietnam, but Saigon was a very tense city at the time of our visit because of the war between the Vietcoms and the Americans. The Saigon part of the tour, although memorable, was not very useful. But the rest of the tour gave us great insights into the organisation and running of crash training programmes for civil servants in emerging administrations. Our discussions in Lahore, Pakistan, in New Delhi, India and in Bangkok, Thailand, were most instructive. I made copious notes and obtained many documents which proved most valuable as references later at my desk. On our way home we spent a few days in newly independent Singapore, putting up at the Raffles' Hotel.

On returning from South East Asia, I found Dar es Salaam busily preparing for the Independence celebrations. The negotiations for the compensation of the British expatriate civil servants for their loss of career were completed about this time, and a lot of them were opting to retire. At first, the exodus mainly affected the younger and middle grade staff, who saw no long-term career in Tanganyika and thought that they had better prospects of employment elsewhere. Senior grades or those at the top of their careers were elderly, and had to be given notice to retire when Tanganyikan citizens to fill their posts were identified. It was the task of my Division to organise training for these identified individuals, and David Anderson, as Staff Development Advisor, who had had similar experience in Ghana, was most useful to me as my mentor and counsellor in this connection.

As it turned out, the compensation arrangements were very generous to those expatriates retiring prematurely, and the British Government gave a loan to the Government of Tanganyika to make the "golden handshake" possible. The negotiations for this package had taken place between the Tanganyikan politicians led by Mwalimu Julius Nyerere and the British Government, which was claiming that contracts between the employees and Tanganyika as a dependency were being breached. It might be argued that the British, as the responsible sovereign state, should have compensated these expatriates. But the offer of a loan, combined with the great desire to be free at the earliest moment, encouraged the nationalists to accept the compensation arrangements. Ultimately, the British, of course, cancelled this debt and took over the payment of pensions to these expatriate retirees when we were able to review and properly argue the case.

Although my main official preoccupation during this period was connected with arranging courses for African staff and other Tanganyikan students going abroad for short as well as long periods, the excitement in the air was the impending independence. Ever since November 1960, when the Colonial Secretary, Mr Ian Macleod, signed an agreement with Julius Nyerere at Karimjee Hall that independence would be granted on 9 December, 1961, the mood in Dar es Salaam especially, had been of great anticipation. Julius and Macleod became household names, and I know friends who named their newborn sons Ian, Macleod or Julius. Everyone was looking forward to that day of days.

The preparations for the actual celebrations were carried out partly in the Prime Minister's Office and partly in TANU Headquarters. Eventually, 8 December came, and State Guests from many parts of the world were assembled in Dar es Salaam. These included His Royal Highness Prince Philip, The Duke of Edinburgh, who was to represent Queen Elizabeth II in handing over the Instruments of Sovereignty to Prime Minister Julius Kambarage Nyerere. Many Tanganyikans felt that they were lucky to be alive to witness this one act symbolising the birth of their nation. Dar es Salaam had the largest number of visitors from up-country. All hotels and guesthouses were full, and most residents had guests in large numbers.

As I said earlier, we were living in Kurasini at this time. Our house was only one kilometre from the new National Stadium, where the midnight symbolic handover was scheduled to take place. My parents-in-law had specifically travelled from Marangu in order to participate with us in the celebrations, and they were our guests. As I was not senior enough to receive an invitation card to attend the midnight function, we got into our little Fiat 1100 at 7.00 o'clock and drove to the National Stadium to try to get good seats in the general public stand. We found that we were already late for parking. Even at that comparatively early hour, we had to park our car almost half a kilometre from the entrance. We might as well have walked from our house. We stood in the long queue and slowly moved on for almost two hours before were able to get seats in the open stand. Fortunately, it was a dry night and not too cold. We had come prepared, with jackets and sweaters on, just in case it became chilly.

By the time we were able to get seated, the military and police bands were already in full swing, playing music at opposite ends of the stadium. Many other dancing groups were drumming, dancing and loudly singing; so much so that we could hardly talk or understand one another. It was only after 9.30, when the VIPs started to enter the stadium in their cars, that the noise subsided as people started clapping and cheering famous personalities going up to their seats on the main stand.

The whole stadium was floodlit, and from the vantage position where we were seated, we could see the VIP stand and the floor of the stadium very well. The flagpole with the Union Jack flying in Tanganyika for the last time was on the left of the podium from which the Duke of Edinburgh, the Governor and the Prime Minister would be speaking. Members of the Cabinet started arriving at about 10.30 and the cheering and clapping were almost deafening. Our beloved Prime Minister, Mwalimu Julius Kambarage Nyerere, was expected at any moment now and our hearts were pounding with expectation. The bands were playing when the sirens of the Prime Minister's motorcade were faintly heard from afar. There was a momentary silence, followed by a burst of tremendous, thunderous applause shaking the whole stadium almost to pieces. When the motorcade entered, the whole stadium was uproarious: Everybody stood up, jumped and danced in their place, shouting and hugging each other. Those seated near the floor of the stadium broke the cordon, entered the grounds spontaneously singing, clapping, dancing and jumping. You could see that people were blissfully, triumphantly and wonderfully happy.

After almost an hour, the police were able to calm people down who returned to their places to sit. The moment of history was drawing near, and so at about 11.30 the Governor, Sir Richard Turnbull, with his motorcade came in, followed soon by the motorcade of His Royal Highness, The Duke of Edinburgh, who was riding in the State Rolls Royce. Both these were received with thunderous applause and rejoicing, but nothing like that accorded to our beloved Mwalimu. This was partly because everyone was now so anxious to reach that historic moment of Freedom, and partly because Mwalimu's struggle was our struggle, and his achievement was our achievement.

Very few of the Tanganyikans who attended that function paid much attention to the speeches that were given on that occasion. The Governor, who immediately assumed the title of Governor General, spoke. The Duke of Edinburgh spoke, delivering a congratulatory message from the Queen. Our beloved Prime Minister spoke, not only thanking those who had made possible this happy day and welcoming the state guests, but stressing that freedom and independence (*uhuru*) were worthless without hard work on the part of the people of Tanganyika. But almost everybody was too excited to follow seriously what was being said.

Nevertheless, we did not miss much, for these speeches were all fully reported in the newspapers later. They can also be read in the history books relating to our independence. What most people wanted to witness at that moment was the physical lowering of the Union Jack and the raising of the National Flag of Tanganyika in its place. It was a breath-taking moment: The British national anthem, "*God Save our Gracious Queen*" was solemnly played by all the bands in attendance as the Union Jack was coming down. Exactly at midnight, the Union Jack touched down; and the same bands started to play the Tanganyika National anthem, with a tremendous thud, as our own Tanganyika National Flag (the Yellow, Green and Black Ensign) was being raised to replace it. It was fantastic. Some people even shed tears with pleasure. It was excitement beyond measure. Other than the leaders at the podium and a few people on the main stand, nobody bothered to observe the exchange of formal documents conferring sovereignty on Tanganyika. We knew it. We saw the Union Jack down on the ground, and we saw our National Flag up flying high! That was enough.

The formal festivities and garden parties were, of course, held on 9 December 1961. There was a huge garden party at Government House renamed, State House. Even officers of my grade got invitation cards to attend. There we met many people we knew, and some started describing how excited and delighted they were to see the British flag come down. We all felt excited and happy to have lived in an historic moment; to have been metamorphosed from the subjects of an alien power into citizens of an independent sovereign nation. I am proud and glad to have experienced, emotionally and physically, that transitional moment.

After the celebrations, it was all work. There was, however, one sensational incident that took most people by shock and surprise, and that was the resignation of Julius Nyerere as Prime Minister less than a month after independence. Many did not fully understand when he explained that he wanted to devote his time to re-organising and strengthening TANU as a political party. Rashidi Mfaume Kawawa took over as the new Prime Minister. It was, however, obvious that Nyerere was the man behind the scenes, and that he was being consulted and had to approve and agree on any major national decision.

During the period of the reorganisation of TANU by Nyerere, the constitution for a Tanganyika Republic was also being prepared. This was to culminate in the election of Julius Nyerere as President, early in December 1962, and the declaration of the Republic on the first anniversary of independence; and the departure of Sir Richard Turnbull, our first and only Governor General.

The year 1962 was a very eventful and exciting period for the Civil Service in Tanganyika. Drastic changes were made in the top posts of the service. I recall the stunning announcement of the appointment of the first African to head the Police Force. Mr Elangwa Shaidi, who was only an Assistant Commissioner of Police, was promoted to the post of Commissioner of Police, taking over from the British incumbent, who immediately went into premature retirement. Many other top posts, such as Permanent Secretaries in ministries, were similarly Africanised: Home Affairs, Communications and Works, Commerce and Industry, Local Government, Health and Housing were all taken over by African staff. Even Brian Hodgson, the Director of Establishments, was replaced by Mr M. Chande Othman, previously a District Commissioner from up-country. The most senior African Administrative Officer, Mr Dunstan Omari, who at Independence had initially been appointed Tanganyika High Commissioner in London, was recalled and took over from Kim Meek as Secretary to the Cabinet and Head of the Civil Service.

Expatriate Heads of Departments were replaced almost overnight by those senior African officers in the Departments who had professional qualifications. Some were actually ready for such promotion, but had been ignored by the system because of the inherent discrimination in the colonial administration.

East African Government, EACSO and private sector managers at a seminar held at Marangu Hotel, 1963, sponsored by the Ford Foundation. I organised the seminar and I am second from left in the back row. Notice the heavy snow ladden summit of Kilimanjaro mountain before global warming reduced it to what it is today and to the threat of all of the snow disappearing in the not-too-distant future.

Others needed further experience, and arrangements were made to have temporary consultants to work with them. A number of these freshly appointed officers needed more confidence in their assignments and special crash training courses were organised by consultants secured through various foundations. Seminars were also arranged, so that those involved could exchange views and experiences. The Ford Foundation, the Rockefeller Foundation and many others either gave us consultants or sponsored the courses and seminars for our staff. USAID also financed local, East African and foreign seminars or courses in which these officers took part. Many of these contacts were initiated by Anderson following his experience in Ghana, but I, as Chief Establishment Officer responsible for Africanisation and Training, had to make the request formally on behalf of the Department, and in the process gained confidence and made very valuable contacts.

I was working very closely with the Staff Development Advisor in the arrangements for the courses and seminars. David Anderson was in contact with Heads of Departments to identify suitable candidates for accelerated promotion. In many cases, I brought to Anderson names of officers I knew and we arranged to meet them to make preliminary assessments before broaching the possibility of their consideration to the respective heads of departments. If heads of departments appeared conservative or unwilling to try out a candidate we thought was suitable, Anderson would write a Minute to the Prime Minister, and in many cases decisions were made in favour of the bold move forward. From David Anderson I learnt that in preparing officers for new jobs, one has to be bold and take some risk to absorb those skills available and then to develop them well and as speedily as possible. No institution is perfect, and employees have to be prepared to learn continuously. A similar boldness has, however, to be exercised in reverting a mistaken choice to their previous position.

Particularly at these times of rapid change, it was necessary to instil and build confidence in newly promoted staff. In my own case, it was arranged that I attend a Seminar of Senior Administrative Officers from Commonwealth countries at Cambridge University in the summer of 1962. I met a number of Nigerian, Ghanaian. Sierra Leonian and Ugandan officers in similar positions, and it was most useful comparing notes. It was my first visit to the United Kingdom.

It was further arranged, again at David Anderson's initiative, that on my return journey I should pass through Ghana and Nigeria to see and discuss with senior officers in the Personnel and Training Departments, as well as to tour their institutes of public administration. I therefore visited Accra for discussion with the Director of Establishments, the Public Service Commission and also went to the Legon and Achimota Institute of Public Administration. In Nigeria, I saw the Federal Ministry in Lagos who gave me manuals on training before my visiting Ibadan, the capital of Western Region. Thereafter, I took a flight to Kaduna, where at Zaria I visited the very impressive Institute of Public Administration then under the leadership of Ian Livingstone.

The Ford Foundation was sponsoring my West African study tour, and I recall driving with the Foundation's Assistant

Representative in Nigeria from Zaria all the way to Kano Airport to catch the Ethiopian Airlines plane for Khartoum. From Khartoum, I caught a British Overseas Airways Corporation flight to Nairobi, and onward to Dar es Salaam. My trip to England and West Africa had lasted for two months. I was glad to be back at my desk, and I believe I was better equipped and more confident in carrying out the tasks entrusted to my Division.

The clarion call for all the people of Tanganyika was *Uhuru Ni Kazi* meaning 'freedom is hard work', and we really applied ourselves at this time. Local institutions for specialist training were being strengthened or being established *de novo*, and my Division spear-headed such activities. I recall that soon after I was back, I took the Ford Foundation local Representative to the Mweka Wildlife Training Institute and the Ol Motonyi Forestry Training Centre, as these were then being established and receiving assistance from the Foundation.

CHAPTER 8

Secondment to the East African Common Services Organisation (EACSO)

Regarding other events impacting on my own career at this period, I should mention that Mr A.L.Adu, who had headed the Salaries Commission, returned to East Africa early in 1962. This time he was appointed Secretary General of the new East African Common Services Organisation by the EACSO Authority.

At the time Tanganyika attained independence, it was agreed to maintain the common services run under the East Africa High Commission, on condition that the Organisation be led by the Prime Minister of Tanganyika, the Chief Minister of Uganda and one of the most senior Ministers of Kenya, which at that time had what was called 'responsible government'. Nyerere had therefore been joined by Milton Obote and Jomo Kenyatta (alternating with Ronald Ngala) in the appointment of A. L. Adu.

As Secretary General of EACSO, Adu was trying at this time to recruit East Africans for his office in Nairobi, and generally for the Organisation. I met him when he came to Tanganyika for this purpose in about October 1962, and after discussing the vacancy he urgently wanted to fill in his own office, he persuaded me that I should take up the appointment, if necessary, for a brief period. He undertook to discuss this with my immediate boss, the Director of Establishments, who was then Mr M.C. Othman. Before Mr Adu returned to Nairobi, I was informed that he had made a strong case for the early localisation of EACSO personnel, and that the Director had agreed to my being transferred on secondment to EACSO for a maximum period of two years.

Immediately after Mr Adu returned to his office in Nairobi, I received a letter offering me an appointment on secondment to EACSO as a Deputy Secretary in the Secretary General's Office. The letter was addressed to me through my Head of Department, of course, and was endorsed by him that the Government was prepared to release me for a period of not more than two years. The post carried an annual salary of more than 500 Pounds Sterling higher than that attached to my post at the Establishments Department. In addition, EACSO offered free housing for staff at this level. I therefore accepted the offer with real pleasure.

I was due to take my annual leave in December and therefore requested that the transfer to Nairobi should be in January 1963. Immediately after the celebrations of Tanganyika becoming a republic on 9 December 1962, we packed all our belongings and arranged for them to be railed to Nairobi in the New Year. We then drove to Marangu for our leave; this time in a convoy of three cars, as David Anderson and his family and another friend all wanted to tour the North during their Christmas holidays. I had acquired a new Ford Zephyr saloon car by trading in the old Fiat 1100, and we had the pleasure of driving with Nora, our first daughter, to our ancestral home. Nora was then only four months old.

Anderson and his family spent about a week at Marangu Hotel and I was able to show them our ancestral home and some tourist attractions in Marangu, and also to return their frequent hospitalities to us in a traditional Chagga manner. Afterwards, they drove to Arusha as they were planning to spend the Christmas holiday period in Ngorongoro and Lake Manyara and Serengeti National Parks. For us, it was a good time to arrange for the baptism of our daughter, which we accomplished on Christmas Day at Ngaruma Lutheran Church, the place where we had solemnised our marriage in August 1960. We christened her Nora Ngianaeli, and my mother was delighted by this apparent immortalisation.

After a further exchange of letters with EACSO head office, regarding travel and accommodation arrangements, we drove to Nairobi in the third week of January 1963. This was almost exactly four years from the date I left Nairobi after resigning from East African Tobacco Company. I was allocated a house in the Kileleshwa sub-urban area, but initially we were booked in the New Stanley Hotel for a few days while arrangements for moving in were completed. We found our equipment and furniture railed from Dar es Salaam had already arrived at Nairobi Railway Station, and with the assistance of EACSO staff, they were cleared and moved into our new residence.

I reported for duty immediately on arrival, of course, whilst my wife was supervising the move into our house, including attending to the making of window curtains and shopping for other requisites. As Deputy Secretary in the Secretary General's Office, I was personal assistant to Mr Adu: my office was adjacent to his and had a door opening directly into his. His Personal

Secretary was on the other side of the office, and the waiting room for his visitors was beside her. As Personal Assistant to the Secretary General, I co-ordinated his appointments, especially ensuring that Heads of Departments provided proper briefs for him when meeting with senior Government officials or other VIPs. I also dealt with official correspondence addressed to him personally, replying on his behalf where possible, or providing him with draft replies if necessary. He liked my work and complimented me frequently for lightening his own workload. Adu was the best civil service boss I ever worked with and I learnt a great deal under him.

The Secretary General (SG) was officially the Secretary to the EACSO Authority as well as for all the EACSO Ministerial Councils. When Ministerial Councils met, the respective departmental heads acted as clerks to the meetings, and prepared the Minutes for the SG to clear before circulation to participating ministers. When the Authority met, I acted as clerk, prepared the Minutes of the meeting and cleared them with the SG before circulating them to Members of the Authority. Prior to these meetings, I co-ordinated with Heads of Departments in preparing the Memoranda on the various subjects for consideration. I obtained drafts from them, which we edited with the SG, sometimes inserting his views before despatching them to Members. Memoranda were normally brief, but had large attachments or addenda consisting of special or annual reports on the Departments or Corporations concerned.

At this stage, for the sake of record and elaboration, it may be worthwhile to give more background to the East African Common Services Organisation. Prior to the independence of Tanganyika, the British East African dependencies of Tanganyika, Kenya, Uganda and Zanzibar had a Common Market and many common departments and services, some dating back to the end of the First World War. These were administered under the East Africa High Commission (EAHC). There was even an East African Central Legislative Council which enacted legislation relating to the subjects earmarked as common services.

These were the Railways and Harbours, the Posts and Telecommunications, the East African Airways, the Civil Aviation and Meteorological Services, the Customs and Excise Department, the Income Tax Department and most of the scientific research services.

On secondment from the Tanganyika Civil Service to the Secretary General's Office, EACSO.

There was a common currency, administered by the East African Currency Board: the East African Shilling, which was legal tender in the four dependencies, as well as in the Aden Protectorate (now South Yemen). There was also the East African Court of Appeal, to which all cases were finally appealed from the territorial High Courts, before resort to the Privy Council in London.

Julius Nyerere, as leader of the independence movement in Tanganyika, highly valued the co-operation between these territories. He even expressed his willingness to delay the independence of his own country, Tanganyika, if the British would hasten that of Kenya and Uganda so that the three could form a Federation at the time they simultaneously got independence. The British Government did not take Nyerere seriously on this point. So at the time of the final negotiations for Tanganyika's

Serving the EACSO Authority as clerk: Kenyatta, Kawawa and Obote (not in the picture) signing an agreement with the UK High Commissioner. *(I am standing at end of the table sorting out papers. Mr. Adu not in the picture, sat opposite facing Members of the Authority)*

independence, it was agreed that most of the common services under the EAHC would remain as common services provided that they be under the control of an Authority headed by the nationalist leaders of the three territories. Nyerere refused to sit with the British Governors of Kenya and Uganda to lead the organisation.

The Administrator of the EAHC, who headed the Central Secretariat and led the official side of the East African Central Legislative Assembly, was to be replaced by a Secretary General. When the EACSO Authority met for the first time, they decided to appoint as Secretary General, Mr A. L. Adu, who was then retiring as Permanent Secretary to President Kwame Nkrumah and Head of the Ghanaian Civil Service. As I said earlier, he had made his mark in East Africa when he led the Salaries Commission for the Tanganyika Civil Service in 1960/61. He knew me then, as I had acted as Assistant Secretary to his Commission, and on returning to East Africa, traced me for the job.

On returning to Nairobi, I was able to re-establish contact with my friends and acquaintances of the late 1950s. Kenya was at last firmly on the road to independence, and many of these people were climbing up fast on the ladder of their careers, whether in the Government or the private sector. My classmate at Makerere, who also was my neighbour in New Hall, Peter Kabibi Kinyanjui, was already a senior manager with ESSO and lived in his own house at Riruta on the outskirts of Nairobi. Habel Nyamu, also a classmate at Makerere, who had been a very kind host during my brief stay in Nyeri, was now principal of the Institute of Public Administration at Kabete. Elimo and Rebecca Njau were in Nairobi already, and it was a marvellous reunion for all of us. Elimo was curator of the Sorsbey Gallery, whilst Rebecca was teaching and writing her first novel.

As I have said above, working with Adu was an enjoyable interlude for me. He also thought highly of me, and in August 1963, when the expatriate Secretary for Administration opted to retire, I was promoted to the post whilst continuing to serve as his Personal Assistant and Clerk to the Authority. This was a post equivalent to that of Permanent Secretary in the national governments. I was travelling with Mr Adu to the capitals whenever he wanted a senior officer to accompany him. He even preferred to ask me to represent him whenever he was unable to attend functions relating to his job. I was addressing the Trade unions on his behalf, and this I found very tricky.

One morning, for example, I found myself, on behalf of the Secretary General, meeting the newly appointed President of the Court of Appeal for Eastern Africa at the Nairobi International Airport. Apparently this eminent West African jurist had not met Adu for a long time, and mistook me for the Secretary General as I was leading him to the VIP lounge to await his luggage and immigration clearance! I was so much younger than Adu that I was embarrassed. As we were being served coffee in the lounge, I kept explaining that I was only the Secretary for Administration. However, as the judge was either hard of hearing or had only had little sleep during the overnight flight from London, we could only understand one another once we were in the limousine on the way to the hotel.

In retrospect, I suspect that Mr Adu was at this time trying to make me practise taking on important tasks in preparation for the future. Indeed, when he visited the successor East African Community in Arusha ten years later, and found me in the pivotal post of Secretary General, he confessed to me that he had wanted me to be his successor when he left EACSO in June 1964. I was then, of course, too young and he had been succeded by Dunstan Omari.

CHAPTER 9

Translation into Finance

After the Secretary General, the second most senior officer in EACSO was the Financial Secretary, who at that time was John Hinchey. I presume that another reason for Adu giving me the assignments I have referred to, was because he felt uneasy about asking Hinchey to represent him at such functions, because Hinchey was an expatriate. At any rate, before Adu completed his contract with EACSO, he again promoted me in May 1964, to understudy Mr Hinchey. I therefore moved from the Secretary General's Office to the EACSO Treasury as a 'Supernumerary' Financial Secretary. I ceased to be Adu's personal assistant at this point.

The following month, June 1964, Mr Adu was succeeded by Mr Dunstan Omari as Secretary General. Mr Omari had just retired as Permanent Secretary to the President and Head of the Tanzania Civil Service. (It should be noted that following the union between Tanganyika and Zanzibar in April 1964 "Tanzania" came into existence and from then on this name applies).

The East African Central Legislative Council had started rotating its sittings in the three capitals, and its next session was held in Dar es Salaam in July and August 1964. All senior EACSO officers, including Hinchey and myself, therefore moved to Dar es Salaam. It was a marathon meeting, and I got tired of the hotel I was booked in. Light relief came when I could get an officer to sit for me in the gallery to take notes of what Honourable Members were saying, and I made a point of visiting Tanzanian civil service colleagues in their offices. Most of them had only recently been promoted and were excited in their new jobs. Osija Mwambungu was Permanent Secretary, Commerce and Industry; Cleopa Msuya was in Lands; Bernard Mulokozi in Foreign Affairs; Dickson Nkembo in Development Planning; and Ainamensa Mbuya in Works and Communications. All were former school or college mates.

One morning I paid a courtesy call on Joseph Namata, the new Permanent Secretary to the President and Head of the Tanzania Civil Service. I had sent him a congratulatory letter on his appointment, but had not been able to meet him personally to shake hands. Joe also congratulated me on my promotion to the EACSO Treasury post.

During our conversation, Joe enquired as to when my secondment to EACSO would end. I replied that I was due to complete the two years approved by the Government in January 1965. I added that I might write officially to him to request for an extension because I had only been promoted to understudy the Financial Secretary and would prefer to perform as substantive Financial Secretary for a longer period before reverting to the Tanzania Civil Service. I intimated to him that the expatriate Financial Secretary was in fact planning to retire towards the end of October, and I might take over substantively about that time. A day after I returned to Nairobi, Mr Hinchey confirmed his plans to leave in early November and I started preparing to move into his very elegant mansion in Lower Kileleshwa.

However, only a week after I returned to Nairobi, Joe Namata telephoned. He informed me that President Nyerere had decided to appoint me Permanent Secretary to the Treasury, and that therefore my secondment to EACSO was to end. He stressed that I had to report in September so that I could take over from the incumbent Permanent Secretary, Jacob Namfua, who was due to leave for a long-term course overseas.

Mr Namfua, a trade unionist-cum-politician, was a personal friend of mine. He had served as a Junior Minister for Finance but had been translated into the Civil Service post of Permanent Secretary to the Treasury recently on the expatriate incumbent, Colin de Hill, suddenly opting to retire. Apparently, Namfua was determined to leave early as he did not want to miss beginning his studies at Oxford University in the autumn semester.

I was in a quandary: I was a pensionable officer of the Government of Tanzania and EACSO was remitting to that Government the required contribution to sustain my pensionable status during the period of secondment. I was occupying a post in EACSO with much higher remuneration and benefits than I would ever get in my own country. My immediate boss in EACSO was a loyal, patriotic Tanzanian, who would not defy the Government in order to retain me in my current job. The job I was being offered at home had greater responsibilities and prestige, and indeed was second only to that held by Joe Namata himself, and previously by Dunstan Omari. Above all, the appointment was being offered by a Head of State I loved and admired. In any case, I was only 32 years old, had a small family and we would survive on reduced earnings. After a long discussion with Johara, which involved all these points, we decided that I should not even hesitate. I telephoned Joe Namata the next day to confirm my acceptance.

It was late August when we started packing again. But I soon realised that I would not be able to complete all the necessary arrangements, including the renting out of the house I had recently acquired in Muthaiga (financed by a mortgage), before mid-September. I again telephoned Joe Namata, explained all my problems and we agreed that I would report in the third week of September.

Johara was pregnant, the baby expected in late September. We knew that East African Airways observed an international aviation regulation which would not allow her to board their plane for Dar in the last two weeks of September. I therefore arranged for her and Nora to precede me in flying to Dar es Salaam. David Marealle, her brother, received and accommodated them in his house, pending my arrival.

After Johara and Nora left for Dar, I continued with the packing, assisted by EACSO staff. Following an advert I placed in one of the Nairobi daily newspapers, I got the Ford Foundation to rent my house in Muthaiga for one of its newly arrived staff. By mid-September my Ford Zephyr saloon car was on a covered goods wagon to be transported direct to Dar es Salaam: the construction of the Ruvu-Mnyusi rail link between the Central Line and the Tanga Line having been completed. Other items, such as furniture and domestic appliances, were included in the same covered wagon, and I had to move into a hotel for the last few days in order to attend parties to bid me farewell. I flew into Dar on 20 September 1964 to take up my new appointment.

The Minister for Finance was then Mr Paul Bomani. I was only able to talk with him briefly when I reported for duty because he was leaving for the Annual Meetings of the World Bank and the International Monetary Fund, which were being held in Tokyo. I found on my desk handover notes written by Mr Namfua, who had left to bid farewell to his family in Rombo before his departure for Ruskin College, Oxford. The notes were very comprehensive and useful to me, and included an attachment of a copy of the notes similarly prepared by Colin de Hill earlier in the year. Mr Mahon, the Accountant General, had been acting as Permanent Secretary since Namfua's departure, and I also found him very helpful in running me in. Another official I had to deal with frequently was the Junior Minister for Finance, Mr Salum Rashid, who enlightened me on the Zanzibar political and financial situation.

The next day I went to the State House to report to and talk with Joe Namata. He was able to arrange for me to call on the President immediately. The President was jovial, made me very relaxed as I thanked him for the honour of the confidence he had shown in me. He stressed that the Permanent Secretary to the Treasury occupied a crucial position in the Government machinery. He commended me to study the relevant laws, especially the role of the Paymaster General under the Finance Act. He pulled out, from among his papers on a bookshelf, a spare copy of the Exchequer and Audit Ordinance and gave it to me, saying that he suspected that Treasury officials might not bring it to my attention early enough. I thanked him again and promised him that I would always try to do my best, and would count on his guidance and direction.

Resettling in Dar es Salaam after those twenty-two months was fairly smooth. After all, I was returning as a very senior officer of the Government, and the Ministry of Finance was expected to assist in making matters easy for me. In a matter of days we moved into a house on SeaView Road, which had previously been the residence of an expatriate Permanent Secretary, who had gone on leave pending retirement. It was a large, spacious bungalow, not quite on the sea front, but near enough for us to hear the sea waves pounding on the rocks on the beach. We did not like the smell of the seaweed coming with the evening breeze, but eventually got used to it. For a number of days, friends and relatives were coming or inviting us to their homes to wish us a warm welcome and congratulate me on my promotion.

These celebrations and congratulations were heightened by the birth of our second daughter, Lillian, at the Ocean Road Maternity Hospital on 29 September. A few days after I took Johara and Lillian home from the hospital, my own mother and Johara's mother arrived from Marangu. They had come not only to join those wishing us well in our home-coming, but also to give a helping hand, in the tradition of the Wachagga, to the young mother.

President Nyerere's all-African Permanent Secretaries, December 1964. From left to right - *back row*: P. A. Sozigwa, E. I. M. Mtei, D. Nkembo, C. D. Msuya, G. Rugarabamu, G. Nhigula, B. Mulokozi, I. Mwajasho, B. Maggidi.
Front row: Bhoke Munanka, C. Mtawali, C. Kallaghe, J. Namata, The President, F. Burengelo, O. Mwambungu, M. C. Othman.

Work at the office was hectic, especially when the Minister returned from Tokyo. We were preparing a Supplementary Budget for submission to the National Assembly due to meet in November, and so there were seemingly endless discussions and arguments with the Departments concerned. Papers for Parliament had to be placed with Honourable Members two weeks before the session started, and so we did not have much time.

On a more personal note, I decided at this time that I should make use of the Revolving Housing Loan Fund, which in my capacity as Permanent Secretary to the Treasury, I was administering. I had already secured a Right of Occupancy for 99 years on a plot of land in Mzinga Way, in the Oyster Bay area whilst I was in Nairobi. I took the opportunity to brief an architect, Mr H.L. Shah (Sukhi), who soon produced designs which Johara and I were able to accept after modifications. We obtained a Building Permit from the Dar es Salaam City Council, and the Contractor, UNICO, moved to the site. UNICO were constructing other similarly financed houses in the neighbourhood. My house was slightly more costly than the maximum of 100,000 Shillings allowed under the Revolving Housing Loan Fund, but I was able to pay the difference prior to drawing on the Fund by using savings from the rent I was receiving for my house in Muthaiga, Nairobi.

Officially, another matter of importance which I had to attend to, and to be properly briefed on by my advisers, and indeed be instructed by my bosses, was regarding the future of the East African Currency Board. As Permanent Secretary to the Treasury, I was automatically the Tanzania Member of the Board. The other Members were my counterparts in Kenya and Uganda. The Chairman was Mr Dunstan Omari, the Secretary General of the EACSO. There was a Technical Adviser and Member from the Bank of England, Mr John de Loynes, who for all intents and purposes, was 'general manager' of the Board. At this time the East African Shilling also circulated in the British Aden Protectorate, and the civil service head of the Aden Ministry of Finance also participated as a Member of the Board.

The Board was due to hold a meeting late in October, and I had to study a Report on the Future of the Board prepared by a German central banker, Erwin Blumenthal, at the request of the Government of Tanzania. Apparently, this Report had already been made available to the other two Governments. The gist of its contents was that the continuation of the common currency after Tanzania attained independence in 1961 was on the assumption that a political Federation of the three countries would be established immediately on Kenya attaining independence. The Government of such a Federation would then have transformed the Board into a federal central bank.

Since in 1964 the prospects for a federation in the foreseeable future were no longer apparent, the urgent task of establishing a central bank required that each country go it alone. Blumenthal considered that the operation of a central bank serving three countries, pursuing different and sometimes conflicting economic and financial policies, was too novel to contemplate. The East African Currency Board (EACB) would therefore have to be wound up, and co-operation among the three countries on monetary and other related central banking issues would have to be the conventional type between neighbours.

At the EACB meeting late in October, I therefore asked if my colleagues from Kenya and Uganda had considered the Blumenthal Report and what their Governments' reactions were. The Kenya Permanent Secretary, Mr John Butter, an expatriate, stated that he had not been able to sound out his Minister on the subject. But his view was that East Africa could continue with the common currency, like the former French West African countries. Mr Butter was supported strongly by Mr de Loynes, the Technical Adviser/Member from the Bank of England. Jack Ssentongo, the Uganda Member, suggested that the subject should be discussed by the Ministers themselves as it had such serious political overtones. The Aden Member remarked that his Government had already taken steps to withdraw as a member of the Board, and so he had no comments to make. We agreed to refer the matter to the Finance Ministers who, in subsequent correspondence, agreed to meet specifically to discuss the subject in Entebbe in February 1965.

The Entebbe meeting was held in mid-February. The Tanzania delegation was led by Mr Nsilo-Swai, the Minister for Development Planning, who was acting Minister for Finance because Mr Bomani was unwell. Another member of our delegation was the Chief Economist, Mr John Scott. I remember that I travelled a day or so prior to the meeting, and spent the night as a guest of Mr John Butter in Nairobi since I wanted to sort out a problem with my tenant in the Muthaiga house. Mr Butter and I took the early EAA morning flight to Entebbe, and we were at the meeting venue even before the Tanzanian and Kenyan Ministers had arrived from their hotels in Kampala.

The meeting was a heated one. In the end, a communiqué was issued on 15 February 1965, saying that the future of the Currency Board had been discussed by the three Finance Ministers, but that a statement detailing their decision would be issued later. Actually the Ministers had agreed that it was not possible to continue with the Board, but they would assess the implications of the timing for a public announcement between then and the date of the next budget. At a subsequent meeting of the Ministers, it was agreed that the announcement regarding the winding up of the Currency Board would be made on Budget day, and that the target date for the launching of the successor central banks would be a year later around June/July 1966. It will be recalled that in those days the budgets of the three Governments, because of their membership of the East African Common Market, were co-ordinated and read simultaneously in the three parliaments.

I have given these details on the events leading to the demise of the Currency Board not only in order to put matters clearly within an historical perspective, but because they impacted a great deal on my own career. As I said earlier, Mr Nsilo-Swai led the Tanzania delegation at that crucial meeting in Entebbe. On our return, the President decided that we must quickly but quietly pursue the setting up of a central bank for Tanzania. Mr Bomani and Mr Nsilo-Swai were instructed by the President to work together on this project, with me as their civil service assistant. Subsequently, the three of us agreed that I should contact the Royal Mint in the U.K. and also banknote manufacturers to design the national currency, after which we would place firm orders. At the same time, I was to recruit experts to prepare the necessary legislation and organisation for the establishment of a central bank.

The President asked Mr Nsilo-Swai to prepare himself to

be the Governor of the Bank, and he and I were in constant contact in handling the replies regarding detailed designs of the new currency and following up the experts being recruited. We lined up local staff for training in central banking. Some were sent abroad (including Daniel Yona, whom I sent to the Bank of England for a special course), and some were attached with the local commercial banks. We selected the banknote manufacturers, Messrs Thomas de la Rue, and they quickly brought us banknote designs which we approved: Mr Bomani and Mr Nsilo-Swai being assigned to inscribe their signatures on them as Minister of Finance and Governor respectively.

I should mention here also that we had quite an argument as to which portrait of President Nyerere should figure on the banknotes. At that time there used to be an official portrait of Mwalimu clothed in a *mgolole* (long garment worn by passing it over the shoulder) like Kwame Nkrumah; and this was chosen in preference to a portrait in which he was wearing a Western jacket and tie. As to the coins, he himself agreed to a portrait created from photographs by the Dar es Salaam artist/painter, Raithatha. Mwalimu also insisted that instead of inscribing on the coins *Rais Julius K. Nyerere* we should only have the words *Rais wa Kwanza* without his name, followed by the year when the coin was struck. Just after the announcement was made in the Budget statement on 11 June 1965, I was able to despatch to the Royal Mint and Thomas De La Rue, the approved portraits and inscriptions, as well as the specimen signatures of Paul Bomani as Minister of Finance and Nsilo-Swai as Governor.

The Budget Session of Parliament had many other issues to discuss besides the future of the East African Currency Board, of course. For those of us from the Treasury, we had to follow up all the arguments for and against the taxation measures and the expenditure allocations to various Ministries. We had to prepare replies for the Minister in detail, and this entailed a continuous vigil at the Assembly Hall. Eventually, the session was completed, towards the end of August.

The Presidential, Parliamentary and Civic Elections were due to be held in October, and so immediately after the Budget session of the National Assembly all Ministers went to their respective constituencies to seek nomination by the Party and to campaign to be re-elected. Mr Bomani left for Mwanza, and Mr Nsilo-Swai left for Arusha. There was stiff opposition to Mr Bomani in Mwanza, particularly because his opponent was dwelling on the new Development Levy he had introduced, and other aspects of the preceding Budget not popular with the masses.

At that time, no elections were being held in Zanzibar and so at the end of September, Mr Salum Rashid, the Junior Minister for Finance, and I left for Washington for the International Monetary Fund (IMF) and the World Bank Annual meetings. We had to pass through Kingston, Jamaica, where the Commonwealth Finance Ministers were holding their annual meeting prior to proceeding to Washington. The Elections in Tanzania were held on the day we landed in Jamaica. Two days later, just as the Commonwealth Finance Ministers Meeting was ending, we received a telephone call from Dar es Salaam informing us that Mr Paul Bomani had lost his Parliamentary seat. We were confused because we were expecting that immediately after the results of the election were known, Mr Bomani would have flown to join us in Washington to lead the Tanzania Delegation.

As Alternate Governor for Tanzania on the Boards of Governors of the IMF and the World Bank, I found myself acting as leader of the Delegation, since Mr Bomani did not turn up. There was a problem of protocol, since officers from the Ministries on the Delegation regarded Hon. Salum Rashid as senior to the Permanent Secretary. But since he could not immediately be designated Governor for Tanzania, I had to talk on behalf of the Delegation as the Alternate Governor. Rashid was very understanding, and since I had all the briefs, some of which I had prepared myself, negotiations with the IMF and the World Bank were carried out without a hitch.

Besides attending the plenary session and meetings of the African Caucus, our Delegation was expected to negotiate with World Bank officials an International Development Association (IDA) credit. We were also to make arrangements with the IMF to provide technical assistance for the Drafting of the Central Banking Legislation, as well as secure their agreement to part-finance the recruitment and salaries for a number of experts who were to assist in the launching and initial management of the central bank. The IDA credit negotiations were handled by the line Ministry officials, after I had made the initial introductions in my capacity as Alternate Governor. I handled the negotiations with the IMF.

Whilst in Washington we were receiving news of Cabinet changes back at home, and some of us were getting anxious to return early to be at the scene of crucial events. I was informed that the new Minister for Finance was Mr Amir Jamal. Although I would have liked to meet my new boss at an early opportunity, I had an appointment in London with the Bank of England about an officer who was to join the new central bank. Whilst in London I was also expected to see Thomas de la Rue, the banknote manufacturers and the Royal Mint regarding the coins and their shipment. I managed to telephone Mr Jamal from the Tanzania Embassy in Washington to congratulate him on his election victory and appointment as Minister for Finance, assuring him of my support and co-operation in running the Ministry. I referred to the appointments I had in London, and he urged me to follow them up closely before returning home.

Chapter 10

Appointment as Governor

I arrived back in Dar es Salaam after my appointments in London, four or five days later than the other members of the Tanzania Delegation to the Washington meetings. Immediately I reported at the office, my personal secretary told me that State House had been looking for me. Apparently, the President wanted to see me urgently. Before I went to the State House, I thought I should sort out some crucial papers to take with me in order to brief the President properly about my trip. I then knocked at the Minister's door, but Mr Jamal was not in, and so I could not even greet him before going to see the President.

I went straight to the President's suite of offices. His Personal Assistant, Ackland Mhina, offered me tea, as the President had a visitor. As we were chatting informally about *calypso* and my trip to the West Indies, the visitor left and I was ushered in.

I do not recall to have congratulated the President on his re-election during my absence from the country, with a landslide victory of over 99% of the valid votes cast. Possibly this lapse on my part was because it was a foregone conclusion in our one-Party system. In any case, he himself immediately started the conversation by asking about the negotiations we were supposed to have undertaken in Washington. I briefed him on the IDA credit negotiations and also about the IMF team of experts scheduled to come to assist us in the drafting of the Central Banking Legislation. I touched on the lining up of three or four potential management staff from Sweden, the United Kingdom, Norway and Denmark to help in the launching of the proposed Bank of Tanzania. I also informed him that I had visited the currency manufacturers in the United Kingdom, and that I had seen the coins actually being struck. I informed him that I had reached some tentative agreements with the Mint regarding shipping. The commencement of the printing of the banknotes would be delayed since, because of storage problems, they would be required in the country only a month or so before the opening of the Bank to public business.

The President listened attentively and commended me for the preparatory work I had so far done for the Central Bank project. Then he told me rather slowly that he had decided that I should work full-time on the project as the future Governor of the Bank of Tanzania. He said that he had been advised that, since the Bank did not yet legally exist, as GovernorDesignate, I would continue to be Permanent Secretary to the Treasury (Special Duty). He added that he would immediately appoint another officer to carry out the other functions of Permanent Secretary to the Ministry of Finance.

I was taken aback, as I had not expected this decision. The President noticed that I was surprised, and told me that he was confident that I would be able to do the job because I had already demonstrated my organisatonal skills, my capacity to seek and follow expert advice, and to work closely with political policy decision-makers.

I composed myself and thanked the President for this expression of confidence in me, and added that I would try to do my best. Before I left his office, I raised the question of the banknotes, and the fact that we had to urgently instruct the manufacturers to await changes in the signatures before starting to print them. He responded by saying that I should arrange with Mr Jamal for his signature to replace that of Bomani, and mine to replace Nsilo-Swai's. Immediately I got back to my office, I sent a telex message to Thomas de la Rue, instructing them to await changes in the signatures before final engraving and printing.

My appointment as GovernorDesignate for the future central bank was announced that evening on the Radio, and figured as main news in the newspapers the next day. Mr Amon Nsekela was transferred from the Ministry of Development Planning to take over from me as Permanent Secretary to the Treasury. (At this time, Permanent Secretaries at one of their fortnightly meetings had actually recommended to the Government that they be redesignated "Principal" Secretaries, as they were by no means permanent. This designation was to last until 2002, when it reverted to the old title in order to be in line with designations of similarly placed officials in other Commonwealth countries).

I had officially worked as Permanent Secretary for only about one year and two months. From this point, and for a period of nine years, I carried the title of "Governor". Indeed, President Nyerere continued to call me "Governor" even after he transferred me to other jobs, saying "once Governor, always Governor".

The Swedish expert, Gunnar Akermalm, who was to be the Director General of the future central bank, arrived around the end of October 1965. Mr Akermalm had long experience in the Swedish Central Bank, holding the third most senior position in the Rigsbank. He had served as an Executive Director on the Board of the IMF, representing the Scandinavian countries for a number of years. He was recommended to the Government of Tanzania for the appointment as Director General by the Fund, and was coming to us under their technical assistance arrangements. Immediately after my assignment as Governor-Designate, I had telephoned the IMF and requested that he should come early, in order to work with me in the drafting of the legislation and on the technical preparation of the procedures for the operations of the Bank. Hence, his early arrival.

A Team of Experts from the IMF, led by Mr Jan Mladek, the Director of Central Banking Services, arrived a fortnight later, to work with the Parliamentary Draftsman, Akermalm and myself on the actual draft legislation. They brought with them their own preliminary or provisional draft, and by using other Central Banking laws as comparison, we were able to finalise ours for discussion with the Minister for Finance in another week. Mr Mladek and his team returned to Washington whilst I was drafting a Cabinet Paper with which to submit the Draft Bill for the Bank of Tanzania Act to the Cabinet. The Minister approved the draft paper, and before the fourth week of November, the Cabinet had formally approved our proposals. The Bill was published for the December Session of the National Assembly. It passed through all its stages in the Assembly before its adjournment, after which Members left for the Christmas holidays.

Chapter 11

Launching and Nurturing a Central Bank

Whilst the Minister for Finance, with our assistance and advice, was piloting the Bill for the Establishment of the Bank of Tanzania through the National Assembly, I received an invitation to attend a Senior Central Bankers' Seminar, which the IMF Institute was organising. The Seminar was to start on 2 January and last for three weeks. The Government agreed that it would be beneficial for me and the Bank, and I accepted the invitation.

Before I left for the Seminar on New Year's Eve, Akermalm and I had negotiated with landlords to rent premises from which to operate, pending the construction of the Headquarters building. At this time, both of us had offices in the Treasury building. I left Akermalm consulting with the architect regarding how to partition and remodel the rented premises. The only local architect I knew well was Sukhi Shah, who was supervising the construction of my own house at Mzinga Way, and he worked well with Akermalm on the remodelling of the premises we rented. We also had to order furniture for the offices, install telephones and related equipment, and line up rented residential accommodation for the managing staff we expected to start arriving about March 1966.

Akermalm's other preoccupation at this time was to finalise the Banking Regulations and Procedures, now that a clear outline of the Bank of Tanzania Act was known. The President was absent from Dar es Salaam for his Chrismas and New Year holiday, and it was expected that he would give his formal assent to the Bill to make it law on his return. Until the Act became law, all agreements reached between us and other parties were tentative, and I only operated an imprest account, allowed by the Treasury, whenever I had to spend money in relation to the establishment of the Bank. Indeed, even after the Bank of Tanzania Act became effective, we relied on the capital contribution made available to the Bank by Government, as sole shareholder, since the Bank itself was not yet earning any income.

The Seminar in Washington brought together senior officers of newly established central banks from many English-speaking countries. There were Deputy Governors from Trinidad and Tobago, Nepal, Cyprus and Malta; General Managers of central banks, or the equivalent currency boards from Malaysia, Singapore, The Gambia, Sierra Leone, Nigeria, Mauritius and Botswana. I was the only participant who was Governor Designate of a central bank-in-the-making. However, I received a cable from Dar es Salaam on 7 January 1966, reporting that the President had assented to the Bank of Tanzania Act the previous day, thus formally making me Governor from that date. Most of the other participants were later similarly appointed Governors of their central banks. I recall especially Victor Bruce of Trinidad and Tobago, and Sha of Nepal, with whom I continued to correspond for many years.

The Seminar was very illuminating on the role of central banks. There were speakers from the Federal Reserve Board of the United States, the Federal Reserve Bank of New York, the Bank of England, the Bank for International Settlements and, of course, from the IMF itself. We had opportunity to discuss matters such as fiscal policies, deficit financing and inflation, exchange rate policies, the international payments system, the role of gold and reserve currencies, including the US, Dollar and the Sterling Area arrangements. It will be recalled that in those days there was a fixed rate for gold in terms of the Dollar and the other so-called convertible currencies; and settlements between central banks were normally effected by the transfers of gold, which most central banks deposited in the Federal Reserve Bank of New York or the Bank of England. (One Troy Ounce of Gold was equal to US$ 35.00). The Seminar was also very useful in establishing contacts for me. I found myself later not only exchanging seasonal greetings with these eminent bankers, but also getting their annual and other reports for comparison with ours.

I returned home in the last week of January, and very soon afterwards moved my office from the Treasury Building into the rented premises of the Bank of Tanzania. At this time, the Exchange Control Division of the Treasury was formally transferred to the Bank and became our first fully operational department. There were no exchange controls against countries in the Sterling Area at this time. You could write a cheque in Dar es Salaam and post it to London, or to Sydney, Australia; Auckland, New Zealand;

Hong Kong or Kingston, Jamaica and the payee there would get his money without your being further bothered by your bank. The exchange controls our new Department administered were in relation to transactions with non-sterling area countries, such as those on continental Europe, America and the Far East.

The unit of currency we used, the East African Shilling, was equal to an English Shilling (one twentieth of the Pound Sterling). The East African Currency Board kept all its foreign exchange reserves in sterling with the Bank of England. Indeed, until about 1960, the Board had only issued its currency against its equivalent in Pound Sterling, although as the pressure for independence and economic development gathered momentum, it started to accept and purchase East African Government Stocks and Treasury Bills. Towards the end, the Board also made advances to East African based commercial banks against Crop Finance Bills, all the time ensuring that it acted evenly in all member states. These arrangements subsequently made it easy for Members of the Board to agree on how to apportion the EACB assets to the successor central banks.

It was the newly appointed central bank Governors and the Permanent Secretaries to the Ministries of Finance who participated in the negotiations for the winding up of the Board. This meant that Mr Amon Nsekela and I represented Tanzania. Governor Joseph Mubiru and Jack Ssentongo represented Uganda. Kenya was represented by an expatriate Governor, Dr Leon Baranski, who was sponsored by the IMF like my main advisor, Akermalm. As I said earlier, John Butter headed the Treasury and was the Kenya Member of the Board.

In the discussions, we noted first that the Board operated as a very lean organisation, with only an Executive Secretary and a few assistants, from rented accommodation in Nairobi. It owned no strong-rooms anywhere in East Africa, and for physical storage of currency, it used the facilities of the main commercial banks. Its currency centres were in rented strong-rooms in commercial banks in a few main towns; and commercial banks requiring currency collected it at their own risk and expense. We noted further that each unit of currency issued by the Board was backed by an equivalent equal amount of foreign exchange or the face value of East African Government stocks and bonds held by the Board. The foreign exchange, as stated earlier, was held in Pound Sterling in the Bank of England.

We agreed that, first and foremost, the new national currencies, whatever their respective names, would initially be at par with the East African Shilling. This arrangement was necessary in order to allow easy conversion from East African to national currency by members of the public. When converting from East African Shillings into a national currency, a central bank would issue the equivalent if its currency to members of the public. It would then present the EACB curreny so received from the public to the Board. On receipt, the Board would transfer to that central bank the equivalent in assets held by EACB. The assets to be transferred first to the central bank would be the respective Government stocks and bonds. After these local assets were exhausted, EACB would then transfer to the central bank the equivalent in Sterling assets it held.

It was further agreed that the advances to commercial banks by the Board would be liquidated by the banks' East African Headquarters in Nairobi by payments to the EACB as and when the advances matured. Ultimately these would form part of the residual assets of EACB to be apportioned to the Goverments/ Central Banks in accordance with the accepted formular.

Finally it was agreed that the central banks would try to plan in order to synchronise the start of their conversions. We recognised that it would cause a great deal of confusion if the Board continued issuing currency for a long time in one country after the other two had started conversion. Such EACB currency would cross into the other two countries for conversion or normal circulation, since it was the authorities' intention to give enough time to the public to exchange their money without undue haste. We anticipated that the EACB currency, bearing in mind the rural communication facilities in East Africa, would be de-monetised after about two years. Residual assets of the Board would then be apportioned on the basis of the proportion of East African currency converted in each country.

The negotiations on the procedures for conversion to the national currencies, and the winding up of the EACB, were concluded about May 1966. My colleagues in Uganda and Kenya, for logistical reasons, were not able to advise their Governments to issue their currencies in June 1966, as we were planning to do in Tanzania. However, they were able to do so in August and September respectively.

Whilst these negotiations were going on, the experts we had agreed to recruit from abroad had arrived, and were carrying out the training of local staff and participating in designing forms for the operations of the Bank. The Manager responsible for Currency and Domestic Banking Operations was from the Bank of England, and his Deputy was from the Danish National Bank. The Foreign Operations Manager was from the Norgesbank, the Chief Accountant from Sweden, and the Internal Auditor from the Reserve Bank of India. A senior economist from the Federal Reserve Board of the United States was able to join us a few months after the Bank started operations, to head the Research and Economic Department. These were the only expatriates, the other staff were all Tanzanian nationals.

I had arranged to recruit middle grade staff locally, mainly from the commercial banks and the universities, and some from the economic ministries and the private sector. These needed and were given intensive reorientation into central banking functions and operations under the expatriate managers, before the commencement of business. They were to prove the backbone of the bank management a few years later, when the expatriate managers started to depart. I was very proud that at the time I left the Bank, eight-and-a-half years later in April 1974, the only expatriate on the management of the Bank of Tanzania was Dr Pendharker, the Economic Advisor, who had held a similar position in the Reserve Bank of India before he retired.

To come back to the preparations for starting full operations, the first shipment of coin arrived in Dar es Salaam harbour in early March 1966. As there was no room for storage of coins in any of the commercial banks' strong-rooms, the Bank arranged for the Tanzania Peoples' Defence Forces Headquarters to accept the huge consignment for storage in the basement of their Magogoni office building. We strengthened the entrance door somewhat, and the Army willingly provided a twenty-four hour armed guard until we were able to move the coin into our own strong-rooms, three-and-a-half years later. Of course, the amount stored at Magogoni got less and less as we put the coins into circulation by supplying them to up-country branches of commercial banks when operations commenced.

The notes started arriving towards the end of April. They were stored on behalf of the Bank of Tanzania by all the commercial banks, the bulk of which was stored at the same commercial bank catering as the currency centre for EACB. This bank had ample space in its stron-rooms It was important that Bank of Tanzania notes and coins should be available in all currency centres and at every branch of the commercial banks up-country before the date of issue. We had agreed with the Government that the date of first issue would be Monday 14 June 1966, a day before the Budget Session of Parliament opened. The Bank of Tanzania would be formally launched by the President being issued with the first note as our guest of honour.

On the appointed day of 14 June, we had only been able to recruit the bare minimum skeleton staff necessary to operate the Bank. Nevertheless, we managed to put up a big show, and invited all the leading bankers operating in Tanzania and the leaders of the business community. The whole Government was there, of course, led by President Nyerere and First Vice-President, Abeid Amani Karume and Second Vice-President Rashid Mfaume Kawawa. All the Members of Parliament, led by the Speaker, the Hon. Chief Adam Sapi Mkwawa, were also present. Acting Chief Justice Biron led the Judges of the High Court of Tanzania.

In my welcoming speech, I thanked the President and the other distinguished guests for agreeing to come so early in the day to grace the occasion. I paid tribute to those organisations which had made it possible for me and the nucleus management staff to build up a team to facilitate the launching of the Bank of Tanzania so soon after the decision had been taken. These included the International Monetary Fund, who provided advisory services and financed most of the experts under their technical assistance programme. I mentioned the central banks, which had agreed to release their staff for assignment with the Bank of Tanzania: the Rigsbank of Sweden, the Bank of England, the Norgesbank, the National Bank of Denmark and the Reserve Bank of India. The Bundesbank of West Germany had been first to arrive, by making

Dr Erwin Blumenthal available. He had studied the situation in East Africa and had written the Report that ultimately led to the decision to establish separate central banks.

Leading First Vice-President Karume and Second Vice-President Kawawa to their seats at the Launching of Bank of Tanzania operations 14 June 1966.

I thanked the commercial banks for their co-operation in releasing staff and in training others, as well as in offering facilities for the storage of our currency. Lastly, I thanked the currency manufacturers for their co-operation in delivering their materials on schedule. Finally, I pledged on behalf of the management and staff of the Bank of Tanzania that we would spare no effort in ensuring that the country and its people would get the appropriate service from their central bank. I then requested the Hon. Minister for Finance to invite the President to give his guidance and to play his part in officially launching the Bank of Tanzania's operations.

In his speech, Hon. Jamal, the Minister for Finance, stressed the role and functions of the central bank as outlined in the recently enacted Bank of Tanzania Act. He asked the Board to act professionally in reaching its decisions on how to run the Bank, and to be bold and truthful in tendering advice on matters relating to policy. He urged honesty and integrity on the part of management and staff, and expressed his hope that the Board would be vigilant in ensuring that the Bank retained a high reputation among the banks and the rest of the financial sector. He ended by thanking the President for agreeing to officiate at the opening of the Bank of Tanzania to the public, and requested him to address the audience before declaring the Bank open.

President Nyerere first stated that he genuinely believed that closer unity among the East African countries was vital for the rapid and sustainable development of their people. He was therefore at pains to explain why his Government had decided to take that apparently retrograde step of launching its own central bank, and winding up the East African Currency Board. First he stressed that a central bank was an essential institution of government of any independent country desirous of effectively managing and controlling its economy. He said that the East African Currency Board was not yet functioning fully as a central bank for East Africa, but it could be developed into such an institution if the partners so wanted. He stated that at the time Tanganyika attained its independence in 1961, the leadership had agreed to retain the Board and the common currency, hoping that the other partners would get their independence soon, and that they would be able to sit together and remodel it as our common central bank.

At that time in 1961, he explained, there were great hopes that on the three countries attaining independence, they would form a Federation of East Africa. Their federal government would then have transformed the EACB into the Federal Central Bank. As it was now obvious, our sanguine hopes for a federation had been dashed, and there were no prospects for a federal government in East Africa for the foreseeable future. He added that the Government had carried out studies to see if the three governments of East Africa could engage in serious negotiations to transform the Board into a central bank to serve us as separate sovereign states. These had reached the conclusion that as the three governments might, and indeed would, pursue conflicting economic and financial policies, a common central bank would find it impossible to render effective service.

The President went on to say that in spite of the three countries launching separate central banks and eventually having no common currency, he still hoped that East Africa could co-operate in the other common services. He was sure that, given goodwill, a formula could be developed to ensure that the common market and common services operate effectively in spite of the use of separate currencies for payments. He asked me as Governor to continue discussions with the new Governors of the central banks of Kenya and Uganda, not only to ensure there was smooth transition to the new currencies but also that there would be collaboration in facilitating operations of the East African common services.

The President ended his statement by warning that although Tanzania was launching her own central bank and national currency, her basic problems of shortage of resources for financing social services and development would remain. Tanzanians should not be misled into thinking that now that we had our own central bank, we could print notes and pay for everything. The only way in which to make our new bank help us develop fast was to redouble our efforts at the workplace: at the farm, factory, mine and office. He said that he was sure the Governor would be reminding us of this all the time.

After the President ended his speech, I led him, the First Vice-President and other leaders to the door opening into the banking hall. He cut the tape and opened the door. I led him further, to the First Teller's booth, where he was served by receiving the first notes in the series. The First Vice-President received the next notes in the series, and the Bank of Tanzania was then opened to public business. Many of the guests were able to exchange their East African currency notes at the Bank. However, as the queue lengthened, they were informed that all commercial banks in the neighbourhood had been authorised to start exchanging East African currency for Bank of Tanzania currency from that morning, and people were able to walk there for service.

There was so much enthusiasm to see what the national currency looked like, that we were informed that many people in the rural areas were walking long distances simply to exchange their old currency for the new. It was essential to issue a statement to clarify that the old notes were still legal, and that if a bank ran out of stock of the new notes, people would be able to exchange when new consignments arrived later. By the end of July the bulk of the old notes had been turned in, and from then onwards, the flow of old notes was only a trickle. Along the border, brisk exchange continued for many months because Kenya and Uganda started converting later and the border trade as brisk as it had always been.

Concurrent with the local preparations for launching the Bank, we had been establishing correspondent banks abroad, so that once we were in operation, we would be receiving and making payments through them. This was the task of the Foreign Operations Department. We decided right from the beginning that we would retain balances in the correspondent banks of our major trading partners, provided that substantial balances with these banks would earn interest. If interest in such banks was not paid, or was non-competitive, we would transfer the funds to London or New York, where our correspondent banks invested them automatically on our behalf, even in interest-earning overnight deposits. In this way, we were active in the market from the start of operations.

As I said before, the Bank of Uganda was scheduled to open in August 1966, and the Central Bank of Kenya about a month later. I am not quite sure about the precise dates of their launching, but by the end of the year 1966, we were all done with the East African Currency Board. The new central banks then decided that the old currency should not be de-monetised for another year in order to give the maximum opportunity, especially to remote rural populations, to exchange their hordes.

On matters of a personal nature, we moved into our new house in Mzinga Way, Oyster Bay, about a month after the launching of the Bank. On 15 July, I collected Johara and our son Mashinda from the Ocean Road Maternity Hospital. Mashinda had been born two days before, and symbolically I wanted him to start living in a house we could call our own. A week later our families in Marangu, including my mother, uncle Aminieli, Ismael and Hassan Melyi Marealle, my father-in-law and his wife, came to Dar and joined in celebrating Mashinda's arrival, the moving into our own house and my highly publicised appointment as Governor of the Bank of Tanzania. This proved the last occasion the older generation members were able to be in Dar es Salaam together at the same time.

The main task before the Management of the Bank at this time was for it to consolidate in order for it to render effective service to the country. We did this by recruiting staff as well qualified as possible and intensifying their training. In addition, the Management of the Bank and I devoted much of our time in ensuring that the new bank building under construction was completed as early as possible so that we could be properly accommodated.

In spite of the lobbying by some senior members of the Government in favour of other architects, Akermalm and I had persuaded the Board of the Bank of Tanzania to agree to the appointment of H.L. Shah as the Architect. We made arrangements for him to visit the Bank of England, the Rigsbank in Stockholm, as well as the Danish NationalBank. After those visits, he produced designs, which the Director General and I discussed and made suggestions for modification. After finalisation, I again insisted that we award the main contract to a local company, and Mwananchi Engineering & Contracting Company (MECCO), the company launched on the initiative of TANU, won the tender.

The company observed the Bank's requirement that local materials would be used to the maximum in the construction, and in the end a very high standard of workmanship was achieved. Elimo Njau, the East African artist, perfected a Mural on the wall of the inside patio, depicting the economic activities of Tanzania. He called it 'Making Money in Tanzania'.

It was possible to invite the President again, on 7 July 1969, just over three years from the date the Bank formally started operations, to officiate at the opening of the Headquarters building. On this occasion I was able to invite a number of central bank governors or their representatives with whom we had cooperated in the establishment of the Bank. Other foreign invitees included our major commercial bank correspondents, with whom we did business.

After a large Reception organised by the Bank that evening and a Dinner Party for the foreign Governors and other distinguished guests, it was possible to put a chartered aircraft at the disposal of the governors and their spouses to visit Lake Manyara, Ngorongoro Crater and Serengeti National Parks. The Governors were spellbound by the experience, and continued to write to me for years extolling the tourist potentials of our country.

The Bank of Tanzania Headquarters Building as it was when opened in July, 1969. Its construction costs amounted to Tanzania Shillings 11 million, at that time equivalent to about US$ 1.6 million.

President Nyerere examines a Commemorative Coin, presented to him at the formal opening of the Bank of Tanzania Building, July 1969.

At my desk in the new BoT Building with a Portrait of President Nyerere in the background, July 1969.

Unfortunately, the Bank of Tanzania Headquarters building was destroyed by the fire of 1984, leaving only the empty brickwork and concrete structure. The meticulous, local hard woodwork inside partitioning, including the exquisite Mninga and Mvule furniture and Elimo Njau's Mural, and all the records and documents were engulfed in that inferno. A Golden Sword hanging in the Governor's Office, presented to me on the occasion of the official opening of the building by Jonathan Frimpong-Ansah, Governor of the Bank of Ghana, and a life-size portrait of President Nyerere I had commissioned the artist Raithatha to prepare, were also reduced to ashes. Nevertheless, it is a credit to MECCO, the main contractors for that building, that the concrete façade of pink terrazzo chippings, which had actually been fabricated on-site, remained intact after the fire. They have continued to distinguish the central bank building as unique in the City of Dar es Salaam, in spite of the fibreglass and other imported materials used during its rehabilitation.

We arranged for my mother to return to Dar es Salaam to stay with the children in October 1970, when I was able to save enough to enable my wife to accompany me on a tour of Europe.

We travelled by air to Rome and from there went by train through Italy, Switzerland, Germany, and the Netherlands to Denmark, where the annual IMF and World Bank meetings were being held. From there we toured Sweden and Norway. From Oslo we flew to London, spent a few days in England before flying back home. As alternate-governor for Tanzania on the IMF Board of Governors, my own fare was, paid by them.

CHAPTER 12

The Arusha Declaration and Birth of the Community

As President Nyerere was making his speech to launch the Bank of Tanzania on 14 June 1966, negotiations with his colleagues in Kenya and Uganda were advancing to devise a formula for continuing with the East African Common Market and other common services in an environment of different currencies circulating in these countries. Very soon after the Bank was launched, a high-powered Commission, composed of Cabinet Ministers from the three countries under the Chairmanship of a prominent Danish economist, Professor Kjeldt Philip, was set up.

The Philip Commission's Terms of Reference were, in a nutshell, to devise means by which the East African Common Market and East African Common Services could be preserved and operated efficiently for the benefit of all the partners. The Commission was to bear in mind the existence of different currencies circulating in the partner states. The Commission was expected to complete its task by the beginning of the following financial year, namely July 1967.

Whilst the Philip Commission was in session and possibly drafting parts of its Report, another event, which was to impact seriously on my career and those of most Tanzanians, took place. The Arusha Declaration was drafted by the National Executive Committee (NEC) of the Tanganyika African National Union (TANU) and promulgated by President Julius K. Nyerere on 5 February 1967.

I had actually been invited as an observer to the NEC meeting in Arusha, in my capacity as Governor of the Bank of Tanzania. Like all observers, I sat at the back of the conference hall, but I was taking copious notes and listening very attentively to all the speakers and following all the resolutions. Towards the end of the NEC meting, as we were giving a standing ovation as the President and his entourage were leaving for the lunch break, the President noticed me, as I was in the gangway in the first seat in my row. He paused, patted me on my shoulder and said quietly "Governor, I am going to ask you to contribute when we come back this afternoon". I replied, "I shall be very grateful, Mwalimu".

I had never had the chance to address such an élite group of the political power-wielders of Tanzania. In the excitement, I could not enjoy my lunch and only managed a piece of sandwich, a samosa and orange juice. However, by the time the President gave me the opportunity to speak that afternoon, I had made up my mind what I to say and had written a few notes.

I decided to be very brief. I stated that it was a privilege and honour for me to contribute, adding that I fully appreciated NEC's concern regarding ownership of the pillars of the economy, its control and guidence. But I said I wanted to use that opportunity to highlight the apparent loss of confidence that the NEC Meeting had engendered, and the flight of capital that was currently taking place. I dramatised this by asserting that as we were sitting there in that hall, East African Airways aeroplanes were flying overhead carrying tonnes of Bank of Tanzania notes for banking abroad. Under international agreement, we had an obligation to redeem them by remitting our meagre foreign exchange.

This was true: that morning I had been informed over the telephone by my staff in Dar es Salaam that the Central Bank of Kenya did not even have to count the notes being airlifted to Nairobi because they were still in the manufacturers' cellophane packages of one million shillings. I explained to the NEC that the immediate task before the Government was to arrest this situation and, if possible, stop it altogether. Otherwise, we would soon be bankrupt as a nation, unable to implement the decisions we were making.

The result of this was that immediately after that session the President asked Hon. Jamal, the Minister for Finance, and me to go to see him at the Arusha State Lodge. We discussed the situation at length and agreed that I should start at once drafting new Exchange Control regulations to guide us in the remittance of funds abroad.

The second point I made in my contribution to the NEC Meeting was to urge caution when implementing the measures translating the resolutions into action. I stressed that proper management was crucial, for without it, production, whether in industry, agriculture, other economic and social services or the mines, would drop and the people would suffer. The mood of the NEC conference was such that I could not dwell too much on the reduction, or complete drying up of capital inflow essential for meaningful sustainable development. But in retrospect, I consider I was bold, even at that session to refer to the necessity of paying fair compensation for nationalised assets, especially if the erstwhile owners were foreigners who had been encouraged by their governments and ours to come to invest in Tanzania. The NEC Meeting ended almost immediately afterwards on either 2 or 3 February. I presume that the President finalised the text of the historic document between then and 5 February 1967, when he promulgated the Arusha Declaration at Mnazi Mmoja in Dar es Salaam.

What followed is a matter of history. The massive nationalisations of the commanding heights of the economy' started on 6 February with all the commercial banks, insurance, trading firms, manufacturing companies, sisal estates being compulsorily acquired with promises of compensation. After nationalising practically all major industries and trading firms, Tanzania was to embark on establishing large new industries by publicly owned parastatal organisations.

It is significant to note that it was not difficult to raise funds abroad or secure suppliers' credit for these new industries, provided the Government was prepared to give the necessary guarantees after 1971, when the world experienced an excess of foreign exchange reserve liquidity (especially Euro dollars) because of the OPEC accumulation of reserves. Even the World Bank easily provided credit to Tanzania under IDA for projects like the cashewnut processing factories.

By the time the Treaty for East African Co-operation, resulting from the Philip Commission recommendations, was signed in June 1967, the Tanzanian economic scene had been dramatically changed. Events in Tanzania were infectious, for very soon President Milton Obote in Uganda was on what he called "the move to the left". He compulsorily acquired majority shares in many privately owned companies, including banks, although unlike the case in Tanzania, previous owners were left with minority shareholdings. Kenya remained basically unaffected, in spite of professing to implement what her illustrious son, Tom Mboya, called "African Socialism".

In spite of the fact that the authorities in Tanzania were pursuing policies diametrically opposed to the capitalist approach in Kenya, the negotiations in the Philip Commission went on uninterrupted. The complaints by Tanzania and Uganda that the Common Market and common services were operating too much in favour of Kenya and to their disadvantage, were to be answered by a number of measures proposed by the Commission: the Corporations, all operated from headquarters in Nairobi, were reorganised so that the Harbours Corporation would be headquartered in Dar es Salaam, and the Posts and Telecommunications in Kampala. The Railways and Airways were to continue to be administered from Nairobi. A new East African Development Bank, to be based in Kampala, was established to finance industrial development in East Africa, with a bias to correcting the imbalance in industrial investments in the three countries, although ensuring that it operated on a commercial basis.

In addition, the Nairobi Headquarters of the East African Community (EAC) were to move to Arusha in Tanzania. A major innovation in this connection was that three resident East African Ministers were appointed to provide political guidance at EAC headquarters, and to chair the Ministerial Councils established to determine policies for the Community. The Finance Council was chaired by the East African Minister for Finance and Administration, who also acted as chair for the E. A. Committee of Ministers. The Common Market Council and the Economic Planning and Consultative Council were chaired by the E.A. Minister for Common Market and Economic Affairs. The Communications Council and the Research and Social Affairs Council were chaired by the E. A. Minister for Communications and Research Services. The East African Committee of Ministers was answerable to the East African Authority for the governance of the East African Community and its Corporations. The Secretary General was the Chief Executive Officer of the EAC, Secretary to the Authority, the Ministerial Councils and the East African Committee of Ministers.

The East African Community was formally launched in December 1967. However, the conflicting policies pursued by the partner states, accentuated by the Arusha Declaration of Tanzania and the "move to the left" in Uganda, were to bedevil the Community throughout its short history of ten years. Coupled with other developments, some of which were outside the control of the East African Governments, the EAC was to collapse in February 1977, when I was its Chief Executive Officer in my capacity as Secretary General.

CHAPTER 13

International Finance and the Payments System

As Governor of the Bank of Tanzania, the Government nominated me as the Alternate Governor for Tanzania on the Board of Governors of the International Monetary Fund. The Board of Governors meets once a year in a joint session with that of the World Bank. The African governors had at this time established an annual get-together (the African Caucus), and it regularly met with the Heads of these two so-called Bretton Woods institutions to raise questions specifically concerning Africa, and to advance proposals for their solution.

In order to present a good, consistent case for the resolution of their problems, the African Caucus required their Alternate Governors to go to the venue of the annual meetings a week or so in advance, in order to prepare the Memoranda for presentation to the IMF Managing Director and the World Bank President. Tanzania was very active at this time in international affairs, including the United Nations where we were championing the case for liberation for Southern Africa. It will be recalled that President Julius Nyerere was at this time Chairman of the Frontline States, and Tanzania hosted the African Liberation Committee. So our contribution, even in the African Caucus of the IMF and the World Bank, was attentively listened to and highly valued by participants.

I regularly attended the African Caucus preparatory meetings in the years 1967 to 1969. During this period, the main problem confronting the international payments system was the functioning of the Par Value system whereby all currencies were valued in terms of gold; international payments were effected in gold and the main reserve currencies: namely the US Dollar and the Pound Sterling. The concern was that payments for international trade and services were dependent on the monetary value of gold and the fiscal and monetary policies of the United States and the United Kingdom. This situation was considered patently unsatisfactory. The reforms of 1968/69 were therefore designed to facilitate the deliberate creation of international reserves to match the needs of international trade and payment for other services. The First Amendment to the Articles of Agreement of the International Monetary Fund therefore introduced the Special Drawing Rights (SDRs) allocated to Members in accordance with their quotas in the Fund.

The African Caucus, in which I actively participated, accepted the proposal for the creation of the SDRs, whilst protesting that they should be issued with a bias in favour of the Less Developing Countries because their adverse terms of trade impacted negatively on their earnings of foreign exchange reserves. The argument by the African Caucus was not accepted by the majority of Fund Members because they felt such action would adversely affect the acceptability of this new reserve asset.

In 1971 I was elected chairman of the African Deputies, who prepared the Memoranda for the Managing Director of the Fund and the President of the World Bank. Our Minister, Hon. Amir Jamal, was the chairman of the African Caucus itself that year. So when the Boards of Governors of these institutions resolved to set up the Committee on International Monetary Reform and Related Issues in 1972 (the Committee of Twenty), I found myself being selected by the African Governors as one of the two Deputies representing English-speaking African members. My leader on the Committee of Twenty itself was Governor Manasse Lemma of the Central Bank of Ethiopia. The Committee of Twenty was composed of one Governor from each of the twenty constituencies or groups of countries entitled to appoint an Executive Director to sit on the Executive Board of the Fund or World Bank; hence its name.

The Committee of Deputies, under the chairmanship of Sir Jeremy Morse, an Executive Director of the Bank of England, in collaboration with the Fund's Executive Board carried out all the necessary negotiations, technical studies and argued and deliberated the various proposals for reform. I found myself travelling to Washington for Committee meetings or to venues in Europe almost every other month. The Committee, under pressure from its Members from the less developed countries (ldcs), examined proposals for the allocation of SDRs for development. It was argued that financing development would enable the developing countries to shop around for the best and cheapest materials and equipment, which bilateral aid did not allow. We also repeatedly advanced strong arguments for the Fund to sell a percentage of its large gold holdings at market price, and the profit so made to be used to finance aid to LDCs.

As a result of the US Government's decision to suspend the automatic conversion of officially held Dollars into gold in August 1971, the price of gold had shot up almost astronomically from its official rate of US $35.00 per troy ounce. The regime of floating exchange rates had set in, and many of us from the ldcs on the Morse Committee felt that it was fair for those who suffered most from the vagaries of international transactions to be thus compensated. Many developed country members who heard us felt we were naïve and our ideas were far-fetched, but we persisted. It is refreshing to note that after so many years, the IMF has now more or less adopted proposals akin to our argument in those days.

Unfortunately, the work of the Committee of Twenty and their Deputies was almost thrown out of gear by the outbreak of the Oil Crisis in 1973. As a result of the Organisation of Petroleum Exporting Countries (OPEC) hiking up the price of oil, many currencies, including the US Dollar, were unhinged from their old rates of exchange. Floating of the currencies suddenly became the norm.

In spite of the turmoil in payments arrangements caused by OPEC's determination to obtain from the world what they considered was the right and fair price for their product, the Committee of Twenty persisted with its work. We, Deputies (popularly referred to as the Morse Committee) started drafting the final report early in 1974. I last attended a meeting of the Morse Committee held in Rome early in April 1974, when the draft of the Amendments to the Articles of Agreement of the International Monetary Fund emanating from our recommendations was substantially advanced. After that meeting, the Morse Committee held only two more sessions before it finalised its work.

As it will be recalled, the Report of the Committee of Twenty and the resulting Second Amendment to the Articles of the International Monetary Fund were ultimately formally approved by the Board of Governors and Member countries of the Fund. The Amendment led to the strengthening of the SDR as a deliberately created international reserve asset. Allocation of SDRs continued to be based on Fund Quotas, but arguments in the Committee resulted in the gradual reduction of the preponderance of votes for the United States and the United Kingdom. As I said above, because of developments back home, I did not attend the last two meetings of the Morse Committee. But Jeremy Morse kindly sent me a year later a commemorative porcelain plate embellished in gold, the centre of which depicts a conference table with all our forty chairs of the Deputies, also marked in gold.

I should mention that a number of people who served on that Committee made it to the top of their careers. The most outstanding example has been Dr Manmohan Singh, the then Chief Economic Advisor to the Indian Government, who subsequently became Minister of Finance and eventually Prime Minister of India. Paul Volcker, who was Under Secretary for Monetary Affairs in the US Treasury, became the Chairman of the Federal Reserve System of the United States. Otmar Emminger of West Germany soon rose to be President of Deutsche Bundesbank. Johannes Witterveen, who was Managing Director of the Fund during this period, was to be succeeded by Jacques de la Rosiere, who, as a Deputy Director of the French Treasury, also served as a Member of the Committee. Members of the Committee who were current Governors of their respective central banks included Victor Bruce (Trinidad and Tobago), Mohamed Ghenima (Tunisia), Pereira Lira (Brazil), Svend Andersen (Denmark) and Erik Brofoss (Norway). In addition, my friend Governor Jonathan Frimpong-Ansah took leave from the Bank of Ghana to serve as Vice-Chairman of the Committee. So, in my membership of this Committee, I brushed shoulders with luminaries in the world of finance and central banking.

CHAPTER 14

Growing in the Bank

At the Bank of Tanzania, right from its inception, training and promotion of local staff had proceeded apace. The Headquarters building had been designed and constructed so that at least in Dar es Salaam we were able to move from rented accommodation into our own in July 1969. Akermalm, the first Director General, left in 1970 and was replaced by a Danish senior central banker, Borge Andersen. I had been offered a second term of five years as Governor at the beginning of 1971. When Andersen left in 1972, a New Zealander by the name of Paul Martin came briefly for a year, after which it was decided that my Deputy should be a Tanzanian. Charles Nyirabu, a senior economist who had been working with the Ministry of Development Planning, was then appointed Director General. It was decided soon afterwards to change the title to "Deputy" Governor, as well as introduce a few other amendments to the Bank of Tanzania Act, which we felt were necessary because of our experience. By this time, all the expatriate management staff had left the Bank, except Dr Pendharker, the Chief Economic Advisor.

In terms of the physical facilities, all the currency centres previously used by the Currency Board, became our centres. In Moshi and Zanzibar the Bank, soon after the start of operations, moved into its own rented accommodations rather than use the commercial banks' strong-rooms. This was possible, following the establishment of the National Bank of Commerce (NBC) by the February 1967 nationalisation measures. The NBC did not require all the old branch buildings in these two towns (Moshi and Zanzibar), and so we rented them as they had strong-room facilities.

We also decided to start to design and build our own branches in the main commercial centres up-country, namely Arusha, Mwanza and Mbeya. At Arusha, the facilities were deliberately designed so that they could in the future be converted into nuclear office for an East African federal central bank. During this time, I had envisaged that I would be able to lobby for the newly established African Centre for Monetary Studies to make

Arusha its headquarters. The Government of Senegal was, however, more aggressive in 1975 in its lobbying at the meeting of the Association of African Central Banks, which deliberated on the site, and Dakar was chosen as the headquarters. By this time I had already left the Bank of Tanzania.

During my tenure as Governor of the Bank of Tanzania, I was invited almost every other month to address Chambers of Commerce and Industry in Tanzania, conferences of heads of parastatals, university students and other academia. Sometimes it was to explain policy decisions of the Bank; sometimes it was just to educate the audience so that the role of the Bank would be better understood. Our membership of the International Monetary Fund and the role of that institution also figured as subjects of various other addresses I gave. At seminars of Parliamentarians or senior government officials, either as guest speaker or as a participant, I was also invited to speak. I therefore visited almost every regional headquarters, and got to know my country well.

During this period, the political leadership of Tanzania required that all public servants should become members of the sole political party in the country (TANU/ASP, later CCM). As I had already joined TANU in 1957, but kept a low profile as a civil servant, I had no hesitation at this time to participate publicly. Furthermore, as part of the mobilisation of the people to participate in self-help projects, political leaders physically worked with the people, sometimes for prolonged periods. Especially at the height of the wholesale establishment of the Ujamaa Villages, politicians lived and worked with the people being resettled: building shelters, houses or community centres, schools or health centres. Irrigation dams and trenches for the laying of water pipes for the new villages were being established all over the country, and leaders physically participated to inspire the public.

At my own birthplace in Marangu, I sponsored the development of a Piggery Unit, to which the Bank donated an amount of One Hundred thousand Shillings, which it had earned as a result of participating in the UN Food and Agriculture Organisation (FAO) Scheme to encourage the growing of food. A commemorative coin, designed to encourage the growing of more food, was issued and sold to collectors and numismatists for a higher price than its face value, and the profit thus realised was donated for development of the piggery. Later, I also managed, with my uncle Aminiel's assistance, to persuade the villagers in central Marangu to excavate a seven kilometre trench in which we laid government supplied galvanised pipes to bring water into the villages of Arisi, Lyamrakana and Sembeti in 1972. The water engineer, a Biafran expert, agreed a design with me which ensured that after every five homesteads there was a standpipe at which the people could draw water. It was at this time also that I was able to have piped water in the house I had built between 1957 and 1960.

After this exercise, I was able to prevail on the Tanzania Electric Supply Company (TANESCO) in 1973, to construct a powerline from *Nyumba-ya-Mungu* hydro-electric power station to Marangu, so that electricity on the national grid was available at Kibo Hotel, Marangu Teachers' College, Ashira Girls' School and for other residents able to pay for it, including the Chief and my own house. At first a number of local leaders at Marangu were reluctant to cut trees in their homesteads that were obstructing the power line, and opposed the project. But in the end they gave in, and the line was built to their lasting benefit.

In the end, senior officers in the civil service and the parastatal sector were more or less compelled to participate in community work, in order to show a good example and enthuse the public to "build the nation"!. In spite of my voluntary work at Marangu, I considered that running the central bank and attending to all tasks relating to it, in Tanzania and outside the country, was more than enough of the contribution I could make. Nevertheless, I went to Chamwino in Dodoma, on one occasion, when the President was working with the people there. As a token, I assisted in carrying some bricks to the masons on-site, but my main reason for going there was to consult with the President. I also visited Geza Ulole, in the Dar es Salaam region, for curiosity's sake.

However, the one occasion when all the heads of ministries, departments and parastatals were required to go and participate in "building the nation", was when constructing the Ntomoko water supply, in Kondoa District. An enthusiastic socialist Area Commissioner, Nsa Kaisi, had realised that his recently established Ujamaa Village of Ntomoko did not have water, even though it was the rainy season. In surveying the surrounding area, a stream was located with the water spring from which it started. Nsa Kaisi decided that a pipe must be laid from the spring to Ntomoko Village, and on to Kondoa town, his district headquarters. The distance was about 30 kilometres. The whole district population was mobilised to excavate the trench for the pipe.

Dar es Salaam was informed of this effort, for in any case, pipes of that length and size had to be procured, and Nsa Kaisi could not have budgeted for this in the District finances. President Nyerere visited this cadre of CCM, was impressed, and participated in the excavation of the trench with the people for some time. On leaving Kondoa he directed that this was a project to be physically supported by the whole senior cadre of the Government, including the parastatal sector. I received instructions from State House on this, and a few days later, it was our turn to go to Ntomoko.

Early in the morning, we boarded a Military aircraft, the Canadian-made Carribou, which flew us in the roughest of clouds I had ever experienced. We strapped ourselves to the canvass seats, but the swings, the bumps and the sudden drops as air pressure outside the aircraft abruptly changed, made many of us think of the worst. A colleague head of a parastatal strapped in the seat next to me regretted loudly that he had not finished writing his will. We knew the geography of the route we were taking to Kondoa, and I imagined any time we could hit one of those mountain peaks and perish in a bonfire. I continuously prayed for the forgiveness of my sins during that frightful flight, which seemed to last for hours and hours without end. The army pilot was aware of the fact that his VIP passengers were frightened out of their wits, and said nothing except the initial instructions for us to fasten our seat belts. We would not have heard anything even if he had decided to speak to us because of the loud noise of the engines. It was absolutely deafening.

Our prayers were ultimately apparently heard, and at 10.30 a.m. we landed at the Kondoa airstrip. It was just a flat area, whose bushes had recently been cleared. When we touched down and were taxi-ing towards the group of people waiting for us, there was a fantastic sigh of relief. We all looked at one another wondering in disbelief if it was true that we were on hard ground at last. As soon as the aircraft came to a halt, we scrambled to get out and the people waiting for us, including Nsa Kaisi, walked towards us to shake hands. Most of them were very senior officers in institutions based in Dodoma Region.

One of them was Dr Widmel Pendaeli, a former schoolmate and collegemate. He was the psychiatrist in charge of the Mirembe Mental Hospital. We had not met for years, and after hugging and greeting, he invited me to ride in his car with him. When we had exchanged information about our respective families and were seated, I asked him if he was also in the trench-digging exercise. He confirmed that he was and I asked, "What about your patients at Mirembe? Who is looking after them?". He replied, "Well, my assistants will take care of them. After all, Edwin, most of my patients do not know that they are sick until I tell them. I can be a consultant here too". I got the message, and began to describe to him the last two-and-a-half hours ordeal on the part of the twenty or so Heads of the top parastatals in Tanzania in that godforsaken military aircraft.

We soon reached the tented camp in which we were to live for the next four days of hard labour. I was shown my tent, took working clothes from my bag and dressed ready for trench digging. When we were having tea and sandwiches, the District Engineer supervising the digging gave explanations regarding the programme of activities during our stay at the camp: We would start the digging immediately after tea and end the morning work about 1.00 o'clock. After washing up, lunch would be served. At 3.00 p.m. we would resume digging and close the day's work about 5.30. Dinner would be served between 7.00 and 8.30. At 8.45 we would assemble for discussion on any topic of our choice, but it was hoped that the policies of Tanzania would be our major interest. We would retire to bed about 11.00. Breakfast would be served from 7.00 so that we would be ready for work at 8.30, prompt. After these explanations, each one of us was given a hoe, shovel and pickaxe, and trooped behind the Engineer to be allocated his portion to dig. Those who feared that their hands would develop blisters were each given a small bottle of Vaseline petroleum jelly.

Each of us was allocated two metres of ground marked with pegs and rope, so that the trench would be straight and there would be no-one accidentally hitting his neighbour with his hoe or pickaxe. The trench would be half a metre wide and an average three-quarter of a metre deep. It was a tough exercise and many of us soon started panting for breath and resting to regain strength.

Very few of us were used to this type of job, and those who had experienced it in the past, had long since got used to sedentary office work, and so did not fit in easily to this sudden change. Many had blisters on their hands almost immediately, and the petroleum jelly proved useful. At least we only had to dig for one-and-a-half hours before the lunch break. When we resumed at 3.00 o'clock, many were complaining of pulled muscles, and others had backaches, but no-one was so bad as to be unable to return to his shallow trench. In order that I would be able to finish, I decided to work at my own pace, without too much exertion. By 5.30, when we closed for the day, I had gone 0.4 metres down. Some of our colleagues had finished, but the Governor's performance surprised those who remained. Luckily, I had encountered no stones and the petroleum jelly, which I applied before starting to dig, protected my hands from blisters.

After dinner the large dining tent was turned into a meeting room. As the most senior of the parastatal heads, the Governor was elected chairman of this first discussion group. I asked for suggestions regarding topics for discussion. One member suggested that I should explain the benefits of the recent decision not to devalue the Shilling along with the Pound Sterling. As chairman, I explained that I would prefer to talk about that on the following day, when I would not be presiding over the discussions. The group agreed, but no one was forthcoming with another proposal for discussion.

Then I noticed Dr Widmel Pendaeli sitting near the front row of chairs. and recalled his remarks when I was in his car that morning. I asked him if he would like to elaborate on his remarks that he could be useful here among us as a psychiatric consultant, since none of his patients knew that he was sick until he himself told him. Widmel was a little reluctant, but he explained that after hearing from the Governor what an ordeal the high-ranking passengers in that military aircraft had passed through that morning, he thought that those who decided on trips like this might need to consult him. He added that he appreciated the need for mobilising the population for self-reliance and he himself was ready to participate. But it was vital to consider the true costs of such mobilisation. There could also be high risks and losses which might adversely affect our capacity to fulfil the objectives of the very projects we were mobilising the people for in the first place.

The doctor's remarks provoked a very lively debate. Many of the heads of parastatals asked whether TANU leaders were aware that our salaries were so high that, if we contributed only a day's pay, we could hire a bulldozer to finish the whole job we were trying to do in a matter of days. Others lamented that their absence from their normal professional assignments at that particular time could be critical for the operations of their institutions, and adversely affect the profitability of their corporations, and even the economy. The fellow who had regretted in the morning not having finished writing his will, was vociferous in blaming the authorities for putting almost the entire élite of Tanzania's parastatal management in one single plane, hazardously flying over mountainous country in very inclement weather. He asserted that it was foolhardy. We are all crazy, he asserted.

Another fellow stated that in his home area, it was a tradition for residents of a village to devote one day in the week for communal projects. On such days they dug trenches for water pipes, or dug furrows or dams for irrigation. On other days they maintained or repaired the roads or furrows of the past. He suggested that the people of Ntomoko should be encouraged to adopt such an arrangement because "spoon-feeding" them by visiting VIPs from Dar es Salaam and Dodoma was a totally unsustainable way of doing things. In the end, as chairman, I thanked Dr Pendaeli for his bold and provocative remarks, which had stimulated such lively discussion. I said that at some stage of development, it was essential for leaders to show the people they lead that they themselves could actively engage in certain projects, in order to inspire the people. However, it was necessary to weigh the cost of political mobilisation. I said that I noted that Nsa Kaisi was taking notes and that it was to be hoped that the message would reach the powers that be.

The following days we had very interesting debates on various subjects of political and economic interest. When we left Ntomoko, at the end of those four days, at least we had had the opportunity to get to know one another much more than it would ever have been possible in any of the seminars held in lavish hotels. The Ntomoko project, however, proved a disaster: the expensive pipes laid in that trench were never filled by water from the intake spring as planned. The spring dried up after the rainy season. Apparently there had not been any in-depth hydrological survey of the area to establish where to tap a permanent water spring. In fact, Ntomoko was only one of many abortive projects, hurriedly conceived and extravagantly implemented prior to proper feasibility studies. It was such projects which partly contributed to the eventual near collapse of the economy, and the unmanageable foreign debt.

Before I left Dar es Salaam for Ntomoko, I had given instructions that my official car should follow me to Kondoa on the day the Ntomoko exercise was expected to end. I had planned to return via Arusha, as at that time, August 1973, as the Bank of Tanzania branch was under construction, and I wanted to see how it was progressing. This plan proved very convenient, since I would not have wanted to fly back in that military aircraft. Indeed, I gave a lift to a fellow who swore that he would never take such means of transport again. As I was planning to spend a few days in the North, he took a bus from Arusha the following morning to return to Dar es Salaam.

CHAPTER 15

Back to an EAC on the Brink of Collapse

As I said above, the Morse Committee was planning to have another session in Washington in May 1974 when I returned home in the third week of April. However, on 22 April 1974 President Nyerere summoned me to his office. He informed me that he had consulted with his East African colleagues, Mzee Jomo Kenyatta, President of Kenya, and President Idi Amin of Uganda and that they had agreed to appoint me Secretary General of the East African Community. This was a most unexpected revelation. The President proceeded to tell me that as Governor, I was to hand over to my Deputy, Mr Charles Nyirabu, immediately and proceed to Arusha since the retiring Secretary General, Mr Charles Maina of Kenya, had been summoned by his Government for an urgent assignment and had actually already left Arusha.

I was momentarily stunned, but when I regained composure, I thanked the President for this new consideration and left to prepare for my new job. Two days later, on 24 April 1974, I reported at my new office in Arusha. However, that very evening I had to board an EAA plane for Kampala, Uganda, where the East African Legislative Assembly (EALA) was holding its Budget Session. As Secretary General, I was ex-officio Member of EALA and had to attend.

On arrival in Kampala, I was sworn in the following morning as a Member of EALA by the Speaker of the Assembly, who happened to be my old roommate and classmate at Old Moshi, Hermangild Elias Sarwatt. I remember being asked to wait in the lobby outside the Assembly Hall until the Prayers were said. The Minister for Common Market and Economic Affairs, the Hon. Robert Ouko, then came out and ceremoniously escorted me into the hall with the Members standing and applauding. I swore my oath of allegiance to the East African Community and their leader, signed it, and was then led by the sergeant-at-arms to the official front bench to sit with the East African Ministers.

Being welcomed by Robert Ouko (left) to the EALA Chambers, for swearing in as a Member, 25 April 1974.

My appointment as Secretary General had come so unexpectedly, and I had to report so quickly, that I left the packing up for the move to Arusha entirely in Johara's hands. The EALA session in Kampala was going to last until the second half of May, and I had to be there in person to follow up questions related to the Secretary General's Office. Whenever I was free from EAC matters, I would scribble notes concerning the "Handing over of the Bank of Tanzania" to my successor.

At weekends, I took the Friday evening EAA plane from Entebbe to Nairobi, and then the Saturday morning plane from Nairobi to Dar es Salaam, in order to sort out problems relating to the arrangements for the transfer to Arusha. I had to organise the renting out of our house, and the transfer and admittance of the children to appropriate schools in or near Arusha. The Headmasters and Headmistresses of their schools as well as the Ministry of Education had to be approached to give formal approval for transfers in mid-term. I should mention that by

April 1974 we had five children, Melyi having been born in 1968 and Kineneko in 1972. Except for the youngest, who was going to the kindergarten, and Nora, who would transfer to a boarding Girls' Secondary School in the North, the others were enrolled at a Primary School in Arusha.

I spent one weekend in Arusha, where I saw the house allocated as my residence, and gave instructions regarding its remodelling and refurbishment. I also saw the schools to which our children would transfer. I was also able to deal with some papers at the Secretary General's office, which could not be brought to me in Kampala. When the EALA Session ended, I flew to Dar es Salaam where I was able to discuss with my successor at the Bank regarding the handover notes I had written while in Kampala, and made arrangements to join my family for travelling to Arusha. Before we left Dar es Salaam, the Bank of Tanzania organised a big Farewell Party in my honour, and gave me beautiful presents that I have always treasured.

Working for the East African Community in what proved to be the last three years of its existence, was very hectic and strenuous for me. Since the overthrow of Milton Obote in 1971 by Idi Amin, the East African Authority had not been able to meet, as Nyerere refused to sit at the same table with Amin. Many problems requiring the Authority's decision had remained unresolved. The Secretary General, in collaboration with the Committee of East African Ministers, resorted to writing letters to Members of the authority in an attempt to get each Member to agree to proposed solutions. As every decision required unanimous approval, it took a very long time to proceed. The fact that the Treaty for East African Co-operation had reserved for the Authority rather too many functions and powers, made matters worse. If a decision was not reached quickly enough, I, as Secretary General, would make trips to the three capitals and plead with the Presidents, or their Permanent Secretaries, to bring my correspondence to their Excellencies' attention, in order to elicit a favourable reply.

The World Oil Crisis, which began in 1973, precipitated serious balance-of-payments problems in all the partner states and made it very difficult to manage the corporations. Funds earned by their operations were not freely remitted to the corporations' headquarters because of the shortage of foreign exchange.

At my desk as newly appointed EAC Secretary General, May 1974.

The three Governors of the central banks, who under the Treaty formed an East African Monetary Committee to resolve problems of this nature, were unable to intervene to ensure that headquarters regularly received surpluses from all the corporation branches. The EA Ministerial Communications Council asked the Governors and the Chief Executive Officers of the four Corporations to constitute a special study committee, under my chairmanship, to devise a formula to facilitate easy and prompt remittances. We held several meetings in Nairobi, Arusha and Mombasa, and produced some recommendations. The recommendations were implemented for a few months, but as the strain on foreign exchange got worse, the banks defaulted, and non-remitted balances accumulated.

I should mention that whilst the East African Corporations were limping on, I received an invitation in 1976 from Kurt Waldheim, the United Nations Secretary General, to serve on a Committee of Eminent Persons to deliberate and recommend a Code of Conduct for Multinational Corporations. The Committee, under the chairmanship Mr Jha, the Governor Emeritus of the Reserve Bank of India, included prominent commercial bankers and industrialists from Europe, the Americas and Japan.

We were expected to produce a Report for the Secretary General to submit to the United Nations Economic and Social Council (ECOSOC) on how to regulate and guide multinational corporations in their operations. All three of the Committee's meetings that I was able to attend were held in Geneva. I was unable to attend its last two sessions, as these were held after February 1977 when I had been summoned to Dar es Salaam and appointed Minister. I was, however, able to nominate as my representative on the Committee, Professor Justinian Rweyemamu, who was then serving as Economic Advisor to President Nyerere. The Committee's final Report was submitted by the Secretary General to ECOSOC and resulted in the setting up of the UN Centre for Transnational Corporations. I am, however, not sure how that Centre fits in (if it still functions) with the globalisation and free trade of today's world.

The collapse of the East African Community came as my tenure of three years as Secretary General was about to end. However, this collapse had been threatening ever since Idi Amin took over from President Milton Obote in the military coup of 1971. Obote had been attending a Commonwealth Heads of Government Meeting in Singapore when Amin staged the *coup d'etat*. As he could not return to Uganda, Obote sought political asylum in Dar es Salaam, and his friend Nyerere readily granted it. Many governments abroad, however, soon recognised the new Uganda regime, including the United Kingdom and even Kenya. Of course, Tanzania would not do so, partly because of Obote's influence. A brief account of incidents, each of which almost precipitated a collapse of the EAC and ultimately eroded its foundation, might be appropriate here.

Very soon after Amin's coup, a Session of the East African Legislative Assembly was due to take place in Nairobi. Amin had disbanded the Uganda Parliament, and since Members of EALA, under the provisions of the Treaty, were elected by their respective National Parliaments acting as electoral colleges, Amin decided to nominate new Uganda Members. A crisis was precipitated when these new Uganda Members of EALA entered the Assembly Hall: One of the Members from one of the other two partner states raised a point of order, asserting that the new Uganda Members could not be sworn in, since there was no Parliament in Uganda to "elect"them.

Without the Uganda Members, the EALA could not proceed, and so the Estimates of Expenditure for the East African Community could not be approved. A crisis of imminent collapse was at hand! The Speaker, Hon. Herman Sarwatt, promptly adjourned the Assembly in order to consult, seek legal advice and deliberate on the matter. After a day of suspense throughout East Africa, the Speaker gave instructions for the Members to reassemble; and when they were all seated, he read his statement. In it, he said that Idi Amin had assumed the role and powers of Parliament in Uganda since the coup. He had indeed passed and enacted some national laws currently operating in Uganda. Many Governments as well as international organisations had recognised his Government and were transacting business with Uganda. The Members selected by President Amin, in his capacity as the President and "Parliament" of Uganda, were therefore properly elected and he, Sarwatt, as Speaker of the EALA, was prepared to swear them in as properly elected Members of the East African Legislative Assembly. With this bold and pragmatic interpretation of the situation in Uganda, the first crisis ended.

Another crisis followed some months later when Uganda exiles, who had followed Obote to Tanzania, planned to oust Amin by seizing Entebbe International Airport. With co-operation from some Ugandan pilots of the East African Airways, they took off at night from Dar es Salaam and were planning to load arms into those EAA civilian aircraft at Kilimanjaro International Airport (KIA). However, at KIA one of the aircraft developed engine troubles. The pilots were unable to repair it until dawn. They had to abandon their mission, embarrassed as to how to explain the presence of several aircraft at KIA. When Idi Amin got news of this fiasco, he was furious and started eliminating any of his subjects he suspected of being loyal to Obote. He also reacted by expelling Tanzanians living in Uganda, including those working in East African Community institutions. However, as Uganda needed the Community, especially the access to the sea, Amin would not take further steps to damage the EAC.

With Amin's intensified and systematic elimination of victims suspected of being Obote supporters, the number of Ugandan exiles in Tanzania swelled, and their determination to rid their country of the dictator increased. In spite of the botched-up invasion at Entebbe International Airport, they soon staged another attempt, this time through Mutukula, in the Kagera Region. Because of its good intelligence network, Idi Amin's army was ready to meet them and Hans Poppe, the Police Commander for Tanzania's Kagera Region, who was on duty in the area, was actually arrested by the Ugandan Army, taken prisoner and killed. Poppe happened to be of mixed blood (Tanzanian and German ancestry). Amin took his body to display in the centre of Kampala, claiming that Poppe was Chinese and that the Tanzanian army led by Chinese mercenary officers had assisted the Ugandan exiles in the invasion. We all thought that this must mean that the end of the Community was near. However, tempers soon cooled down, and Ugandan officials re-joined their East African colleagues in keeping the EAC staggering on.

When Amin turned to Kenya and claimed that a large part of Western Kenya ought to be Ugandan territory, we again felt that the end was near. Fortunately, the authorities in Kenya took those statements lightly, and in the end Amin was ignored. But this also meant that, whereas previously Kenya could play the role of conciliator between Tanzania and Uganda, that role vanished.

In spite of these frustrations and the gathering storm of an impending collapse, most of the technical operations of the Departments and the Corporations staggered on. The Civil Aviation and Meteorological services, as well as the East African scientific research organisations in agriculture, forestry, fisheries and industry were maintained; and also medical research into viral diseases, trypanasomiasis, leprosy, malaria and vector-borne diseases continued functioning, through the provision of funds from the EAC General Fund. The East African Customs and Excise Department, of course, collected revenue for the three East African Governments and, as stipulated in the Treaty for EA Co-operation, passed on the appropriate share to EAC Headquarters, which administered these "General Fund" Services.

As Secretary General, I was even able, during this crisis-laden period, in close collaboration with Al Noor Kassum, the East African Minister of Finance and Administration, to organise the building and completion of the East African Headquarters building complex, after EAC secured a loan from a consortium of Italian banks guaranteed by the three East African Governments. With this loan, it was also possible to add substantially to the housing facilities of the Municipality of Arusha. Subsequently, the EAC headquarters complex became part of the assets accruing to Tanzania on the collapse of the Community and was turned into the Arusha International Conference Centre.

In the end, the corporations, especially the Railways and the Airways, started to experience serious difficulties in continuing to have funds earned in Tanzania and Uganda remitted to their Nairobi headquarters. I have already referred to the working group which was chaired by the Secretary General, which produced a formula for remittance. This arrangement lasted for only a few months. The performance of these corporations therefore left much to be desired.

The disenchantment of Kenyan leaders with the malfunctioning of the corporations and also with the socialist policies of Tanzania and the idiosyncracies of Idi Amin in Uganda, led to their increasing lack of enthusiasm for the EAC. When Tanzania banned Kenyan-owned heavy trucks from using the road to Zambia, there were very angry reactions from Kenya. It was probably at this time that the Kenyan authorities initiated deliberate steps to sever relations. The trains from Mombasa were not allowed to cross into Tanzania. One of the boats of the East African Marine Services on Lake Victoria was detained at Kisumu and actually used as a night club. Tanzanian and Ugandan nationals working at the Railways headquarters were sent back home.

There was even new construction at the Taveta Railway Station by the Kenyan authorities, to make it possible for locomotive engines to turn around and return to Mombassa or Nairobi once they had off-loaded their cargo or passengers at this border station. Accompanied by Hon. Captain Hussein Marijan, the EA Minister for Communications, who was Ugandan, I made a special inspection by motor trolley from Moshi along the Rail link to Taveta to ascertain what was happening. On reaching Taveta we were actually detained and arrested by the Kenya Police authorities for 'entering' Kenya illegally! It was, of course, a farce: as EAC staff, we were free to enter and leave Kenya at any time. The East African Community flag was even flying on the cars, which had proceeded to Taveta by road in order to drive us back to Arusha through Himo and Moshi.

However, after protracted arguments with the Kenyan Police, I was able to talk over the telephone with Geoffrey Kariithi, the Permanent Secretary to the President in Nairobi. After some heated exchanges, since everyone was rather irritated, Kariithi gave instructions that we be released. The harm had, however, already been done, because before we reached Arusha, all the radio stations in East Africa and even the British Broadcasting Corporation in London had announced our arrest as evidence of the impending breakup of the East African Community.

In the end, the frustrations engendered by lack of political goodwill and co-operation in the working of the Community were highlighted, and in my view exaggerated, by the media in Tanzania and Kenya. Editors, especially of the ruling Party or Government-owned newspapers, and the national radios engaged in very hostile comments. Name-calling and abusive language were used to castigate the leaders of each other's countries. I personally had to go down to Dar es Salaam to plead with the Government to tone down the language, especially on Radio Tanzania, as I was finding it very difficult to engage in meaningful dialogue with officials in Kenya, who felt that they were being personally targeted. My plea in Dar es Salaam was of no avail as the Kenyans responded with gusto before I even left Dar for Arusha.

This was at the beginning of 1977, when the Tanzanian authorities were preparing to celebrate the Tenth Anniversary of the Arusha Declaration. They also decided that the merger of the ruling parties (TANU and the Afro-Shirazi Party) should be formally proclaimed on 5 February 1977 to create Chama cha Mapinduzi (CCM). These twin events were planned to take place in Arusha and Zanzibar.

At about this time, I also decided to write a letter to Members of the East African Authority informing them that my three-year contract of appointment as Secretary General of the Community would expire in April. I advised that they would need to set the necessary machinery in motion to appoint a new Secretary General. It was Uganda's turn to provide a candidate. Because of the inability of the Authority physically to meet, I had readied myself to go to Uganda, around February or March 1977, to hold discussions with President Amin so that his Government could nominate someone whose name and curriculum vitae I would then take to the other Presidents for approval. This procedure had become routine as a way for us to get the Authority to agree to non-controversial decisions, and I wanted to be able to hand over to my successor in person, to prevent the recurrence of the difficulties I had suffered in 1974. Indeed at this time I had reckoned that I would not be able to fit into the Tanzania Government system, and so I had already started looking for an affordable coffee farm around Arusha to buy and then work as a businessman /farmer.

As the preparations for the Tanzania celebrations went on, we at the EAC were aware that the East African corporations were in great difficulties. In particular the Airways were no longer able to buy essential spare parts to service their aircraft properly, and their debts in respect of supply of emergency spare parts, refuelling and landing fees in Europe were mounting. The Railways were unable to service their debts, and even Tanzanians and Ugandans working at headquarters or in other areas of Kenya, as I noted above, had been sent back to their own countries.

The EA Communications Council was impotent to intervene, and funds earned by the branches were not remitted to headquarters to relieve the financial crises. The other corporations, namely the Harbours, and the Posts and Telecommunications suffered similar problems of non-remittance to headquarters, but their strain was less severe since earnings in the countries of their location more or less matched their urgent requirement for funds. It was only when it came to the servicing of foreign long-term debts that it proved critical to have funds from all branches. And some of these debts were kept unpaid pending the resolution of the problems.

Early in February 1977, President Nyerere arrived in Arusha, ready to receive the state guests invited for the celebrations. Most were expected to come to Arusha first, for the Arusha Declaration's tenth anniversary celebrations in the morning; and afterwards, they would fly to Zanzibar for the afternoon launching of Chama cha Mapinduzi. On about 3 February, a creditor of East African Airways in Europe decided to get a court order to detain one of the aircraft of the Corporation at an airport in Europe, in order to force EAA to pay its outstanding debts. When the Kenya Government was informed of this, it reacted by grounding all EAA aircraft at Nairobi International Airport without consulting the other partner states, ostensibly to prevent their being seized by other creditors. Guests bound for Arusha and Dar es Salaam who had flown in by EAA or were to board EAA planes from Nairobi for KIA found themselves stranded.

Nyerere was infuriated on being informed of the Kenya Government's decision. He reacted by closing the Kenya-Tanzania border immediately. In this way the East African Common Market, which had lasted since the British took over the administration of Tanganyika in 1919, came to an abrupt and unceremonious end. The EA common services staggered on until the end of their financial year, on 30 June 1977, when they formally ceased to function.

As I have intimated above, the collapse of the East African Community had been expected at any time after 1971, when relations between the partner states became continuously strained. Amin was not the only stumbling block: the purposes for which the reorganisation of 1967 had been made were not being fulfilled. As a result of the irreconcilable economic policies of the three countries, and the delaying tactics on the part of the most advanced partner, namely Kenya, to avoid implementing corrective measures in industrial allocation, the complaints of the past persisted. So even in official circles in Tanzania, the EAC had not served much purpose. As I have indicated above, even Kenya officials were hostile to the Community, many of them because of selfish personal interests.

Nevertheless, the abrupt closure of the Tanzania-Kenya border, literally ending the fifty year old Common Market, came as a shock. Some officials in Kenya thought that the border would re-open quickly, as they believed Tanzania badly needed goods and services originating from Kenya. Those with personal interests in the collapse of the EAC corporations actually celebrated. In

Tanzania a number of officials, including myself, thought and hoped wrongly that Mwalimu would re-consider his decision, once tempers cooled down.

Indeed, discussions between Tanzania and Uganda did take place in March/April, 1977, the Tanzanian delegation being led by VicePresident Aboud Jumbe, whom I accompanied in my new capacity as Minister of Finance and Planning. But Amin's insistence that he must discuss matters face to face with Nyerere, aborted the effort. So the East African Community, its corporations and the Common Market died unceremoniously.

Even though the Kenya-Tanzania border had been closed on 4 February 1977, I had remained for a few days, mistakenly optimistic that tempers would cool, and that some means would be found to continue to operate the EAC and the Common Market. At that time, my main concern was to get permission for EAC staff stationed in Tanzania, who happened to be in Kenya prior to the closure, to cross the border back into Tanzania. Similarly, I wanted to get permits for my Kenya-based staff who were on duty in Tanzania to go back to their stations in Kenya.

Officers of the Tanzania Immigration Department were very tough and excessively bureaucratic in processing the permits, and many of the EAC staff affected became hardship cases. I myself had to make a number of trips to Nairobi and had to go through all the red tape of permits and rigorous inspections at Namanga. The flying of the Community flag on my car now meant nothing to those bureaucrats. It was a genuinely sad sudden turn of events. In Nairobi I managed to meet Geoffrey Kariithi, the Permanent Secretary to the President, who was in no mood for dialogue on the Community. But at least I was able to get some background to recent decisions taken by Kenya. I was also able to leave him with a copy of my letter to the Authority relating to the need for them to appoint a successor to me in April.

CHAPTER 16

Back to Finance

When I returned to Arusha and decided to go to Dar es Salaam, I had to fly in an aeroplane on loan to Tanzania from the national airline of Mozambique! Only two aeroplanes of the EAA fleet were in Tanzania at the time the Kenya Government grounded the airline, and they were either operating elsewhere or not serviceable on that day. It was 11 February when I went to see Timothy Apiyo, the Principal Secretary to President Nyerere. After discussing matters relating to the EAC and my letter on the appointment of my successor, he intimated to me that the President wanted me to head one of the major parastatal organisations in the country. I assumed that such appointment would begin after April, when my assignment with the Community would formally end. I therefore told Mr Apiyo that I would discuss this matter with my wife and would contact him later. Actually, I was not enthusiastic to work in a parastatal again, having headed the Bank of Tanzania, the most prestigious of them for nine years, and the EAC for the last three. From the State House, I drove to the airport to catch the afternoon plane for Arusha.

In the evening Mr Apiyo telephoned me from Dar es Salaam. He said he had thought that I had gone back to my hotel, and that he had been in contact with some of my friends in Dar es Salaam, attempting to trace my whereabouts. He added that the President wanted to see me urgently and that I should get into the earliest plane the next day and return to Dar es Salaam. So on 12 June, I managed to catch the afternoon flight back to Dar. I was met by a State House driver at the Airport. I checked into the Hotel Kilimanjaro and at about 4.00 o'clock was driven to the President's Msasani residence. At Msasani, I met Hon. Edward Sokoine, then Minister for Defence, and greeted him as he was getting into his car to leave. A Presidential aide gave me some tea as I waited to see the President. Mr Pius Msekwa, who was to be the Vice-Chancellor of the University of Dar es Salaam, walked out of the President's office, and we exchanged salutations. I was then ushered in.

The President referred to my discussion with Apiyo the previous day, and the fact that I had said I wanted to discuss the proposed appointment with my wife. When I tried to explain that I had thought the appointment would not start until after my contract with EAC expired in April, allowing me ample time to think about it, he interrupted saying: "Edwin, I am going to nominate you to be a Member of Parliament. Then I will make you my chief economic advisor by appointing you as Minister for Finance and Planning". I was stunned. With my mind fixed on the EAC assignment, I could only ask: "With effect from what date, Mwalimu?". He replied, "With effect from today". I was momentarily confused, but after regaining my composure, I thanked him for the confidence and consideration he was giving me. I added that I would try my best to render service to my country and that I would depend on his guidance and direction in the execution of my duties. After a few more pleasantries, he stood up, we shook hands, and I left.

On leaving Msasani, I went straight to my room in the Hotel Kilimanjaro. I telephoned Johara so that she would get the news from me rather than from the seven o'clock news broadcast by Radio Tanzania, Dar es Salaam. She was thrilled; but I stressed that she again had a tough job ahead, packing without much assistance from me to return to Dar es Salaam. She replied that she was getting used to such packing, and that she would not mind doing so this time. I thanked her, rang off, had a bath and then ordered dinner in my room. As I ate, I listened to the Radio and telephoned other close relatives and friends in Dar es Salaam to tell them of my new appointment.

The swearing-in ceremony for Ministers took place the next day. Besides the new Prime Minister, Mr Edward Moringe Sokoine, and myself, newly appointed Ministers sworn in at that ceremony included Mr Benjamin Mkapa, previously our High Commissioner in Nigeria, who became Minister for Foreign Affairs. He was later to be the third President of Tanzania. My colleague at the EAC, the EA Minister for Finance and Administration, Al Noor (Nick) Kassum, was sworn in as Minister for Water and Mineral Resources. Dr Nicholas Kuhanga, who previously was Vice-Chancellor of the University of Dar es Salaam, became Minister of Education. Mr Jackson Makwetta became Minister of State in the Prime Minister's Office. My immediate predecessor in the Ministry, Mr Amir Jamal, was transferred to Communications and Works. Mrs Tabitha Siwale, previously Minister of Education was transferred to Lands and Housing. The preceding Prime Minister, Mr Rashid Mfaume Kawawa, became Minister for Defence and National Service. Others were reshuffled, and were also sworn in as ministers in their new portfolios. It was a real shake-up.

After the ceremony I went to my new office at the Treasury where I met the newly appointed Principal Secretary to the Treasury, Ernest Mulokozi. Ernest had been General Manager of the National Development Corporation and had just handed over to Arnold Kilewo, ex-Chairman of the collapsing East African Airways Corporation. Arnold, Nick Kassum and I were leaving EAC as it crumbled to pieces, and were taking further steps up the ladder. "Every cloud has its silver lining"; we seemed to be telling ourselves.

The immediate task before the Government was to integrate the various EAC Departments and Corporations into its administrative structure. The Tanzania region of the East African Customs and Excise Department became an integral part of the Ministry of Finance; and its head now looked to the Principal Secretary for leadership and guidance, rather than to the East African Commissioner General for Customs and Excise, who until then had been based in Mombasa. Similarly, Departments such as Civil Aviation, Meteorological Services, Agricultural, Medical and Industrial Research institutes were integrated into their respective ministries. The ministry responsible for Communications had a tough job in embarking on the creation of national corporations from the regional branches of the East African Corporations, and Amir Jamal had this arduous task.

There were problems in connection with the absorption of Tanzanians who were employed in general administration at the Central Secretariat of the Community. They were instructed to apply for jobs in Government in accordance with their specific qualifications, and whenever they were fitted into government, they were to be treated as transferred from their pensionable employment. Those who could not be so absorbed were either retired on 'abolition of office' terms, or they remained in the

Caretaker's Service until the disposal of the Arusha Community Building complex.

An additional task fell on my shoulders in my new capacity as Minister responsible for finance. This was to negotiate with the other East African governments on how to apportion the assets and liabilities of the Community and its corporations. Fortunately, the Ministers assigned for this task were Robert Ouko in Kenya and Jack Ssentongo in Uganda, whom I knew well and who were personal friends. We met after the Budget Sessions in June and agreed that we would request the World Bank, as the major creditor to the EAC Corporations, to provide technical assistance for this purpose. In October the three of us met in Washington during the World Bank/IMF annual meetings, and jointly interviewed the candidate proposed by the World Bank. We agreed that he should start his assignment as soon as possible. Thus was Dr Victor Umbricht appointed Conciliator in the apportionment of assets and liabilities of the defunct East African Community.

The Umbricht Conciliation exercise involved a long drawn-out study, delving into the history, analysis and valuation of all assets of the East African Community and its Corporations, identifying their location and all liabilities attached to them. The Conciliator was then expected to recommend the apportionment of the assets to the partner states in a practical and fair manner, having regard to attendant liabilities and their ultimate settlements. Dr Umbricht had to present interim reports in order to reinforce the operations of the successor national institutions or departments, whilst he was perfecting his final report and recommendations. It was a laborious job, delving into the background of assets and institutions dating as far back as the nineteenth century, with a number of them inherited by governments; whose officials did not care much about the preservation of documents, or whose records had got lost or destroyed.

By the time he presented his final conciliation report in 1985, tempers had cooled down in East Africa, and many of the leaders had thought again about their 1970's attitude to co-operation, or had left the scene altogether. It was therefore possible to include in his recommendations some seeds of a revived community. At that time, I had myself moved to Washington to represent East Africa and other English Speaking African countries on the Executive Board of the International Monetary Fund.

Victor Umbricht, who had become a frequent visitor and a personal friend, brought me in 1985 a copy of his final Draft Report, which he was expected to present to his sponsors, the World Bank. We discussed at length some of his proposals for the resolution of EAC problems, and he thanked me for the advice and information I had readily given him since 1978, while he was developing his recommendations. He had visited my home whilst I was in Dar as well as when I moved to Arusha. During our discussions, I was able to take him to lunch with me at the IMF Executive Directors' Dining Room before he left for Dulles International Airport for his native Switzerland. Victor Umbricht was an accomplished diplomat and a dedicated, fair and balanced international arbitrator. East Africa was lucky to have him.

His specific recommendations on how the moneys in the EAC Pension Fund were to be apportioned to the respective states were subsequently botched up due to the Tanzania Government 'borrowing' this foreign exchange and spending it during the crisis of 1987. The result has been that the Tanzanian EAC pensioners have not been paid, or have been paid the TShilling equivalent as it was in 1987, causing untold hardships to these now elderly people. A fair solution lay in the Government either paying them in pound sterling or reimbursing their Pension Fund with the foreign exchange borrowed in 1987 plus accrued interest.

Reverting to the subject of my Ministry, I should stress that the most absorbing task for the Minister and his senior advisors in the first half of the calendar year is the preparation of the Government Budget for the fiscal year beginning on 1 July. At the time I took over, the estimates of expenditure for the year 1977/78 were being received from ministries and independent departments. These had been prepared on the basis of guidelines agreed by my predecessor, and issued in the previous November. They were being scrutinised by desk officers in collaboration with senior officers from the line Ministries, prior to being passed on to the Principal Secretary. The Principal Secretary was expected to discuss any problem in this connection with his counterpart, or even with the relevant Minister concerned, before bringing them to me. I had gone through this entire procedure during my brief tenure as Permanent Secretary to the Treasury in 1964/65.

However, this time, as a result of the collapse of the Community, the Treasury had to include in its own estimates a new Department of Customs and Excise. Similarly, all the Ministries affected were instructed to submit additional estimates for departments and research institutes that were being absorbed from the EAC. The self-financing corporations' budgets were not part of this exercise, although government intervention and financial assistance was required in order to launch their formerly Tanzania-based regional components as new national corporations.

Whilst the estimates were being scrutinised, the Minister and the Principal Secretary, in collaboration with the Chief Economist and Heads of the Revenue Departments critically examined the performance of each item of revenue (such as taxes, duties, levies, licenses, royalties, cesses) during the then current year. We tried to forecast whether by the end of June 1977 the overall revenue performance would enable us to balance the Budget. We examined why each item had performed as it did and forecast performance for the new financial year if rates were to remain unchanged.

Together with the Principal Secretary and the Chief Economist, I discussed various options of taxation, and the economic and financial policies we wanted to follow in the new financial year. First, having regard to the closure of the Kenya border, we wanted to encourage and support the manufacturing of consumer items that had been erstwhile imported from Kenya. Secondly, it was vital to encourage exports and their production, if the deteriorating balance of payments was to be arrested. On this basis we wrote a Paper for the Economic Committee of the Cabinet. As usual, inputs from the Governor of the Bank of Tanzania were sought regarding foreign exchange policy and borrowing for purposes of financing part of the budget expenditures. By the end of April, the general framework of economic and financial policies for the next financial year had been approved by the Cabinet. What remained was for the Treasury to make adjustments in the estimates of expenditures to fit in with the anticipated revenue. I should mention that, because of the need to maintain confidentiality, having decided on policy, the Cabinet as usual, left specific rates, and even the types of taxes to be imposed, for the Minister to agree with the President before presenting the Budget to the National Assembly.

There was a great deal of public sympathy with the Government in its efforts, as demonstrated in the 1977/78 Budget, to set matters right after the collapse of the East African Corporations and the closure of the Kenya border. However, because the international coffee prices were high, the Government persisted in retaining the export taxes imposed the previous year. My arguments that in most other countries exports were actually subsidised rather than taxed, fell on deaf ears. A majority of my colleagues in the Cabinet argued that the export tax would make every peasant producer contribute to public revenue in the spirit of self-reliance. For those who did not produce for export, they argued that they should pay the Development Levy in order to play their part in self-reliance. My rejoinder was that maximising peasant incomes by abolishing export taxes would boost production, increase foreign exchange earnings and reduce poverty across the board. This would enable them to purchase more goods bearing customs duty and sales tax, which would more than compensate for the loss in export tax. But this argument was of no avail.

I have deliberately given my stance on taxes, including those imposed on exports, because I have the impression that, even today, Tanzania has not fully accepted this rationale. As a result, our agricultural exports have continued to stagnate, reducing most of Tanzania's rural pesantry to indigent paupers.

The statement by the Minister for Finance when presenting the Government Budget to Parliament is an overall statement of Government policy, and could not contain views that had not been accepted by the President in Cabinet. However, my insistence that exports must be boosted, especially traditional exports, if the economy were to grow, remained a major theme in all of the three Budgets I was able to present. In my last Budget, 1979/80, I even quoted the famous Finance Minister who told his country to "export or die". Looking back on those years, I am happy to note that the Government in Tanzania has come a long way in embracing a policy of no taxes on exports, although it is still ambivalent on subsidising agricultural exportss. The practice is in Europe, United States and Canada.

Presenting my budget in parliament as Minister of Finance in 1978 (Courtesy: *Daily News*).

I have decided to include in this story of my life, major policies and procedures for the institutions I was entrusted to run or manage, so that readers can understand, in a layman's language, what went on then and /or even some of what goes on today. It is my hope that this will explain the impression of secrecy surrounding the budgets, and also remove the wholesale blame piled on the Finance Minister when aspects of policy begin to cause pain to some sections of the people. Finance Ministers do not and cannot act alone.

During my tenure as Minister I made many trips to regions up country, but in most cases I was "the duty Minister", accompanying the President or the Prime Minister. The only region I was able to tour alone in my capacity as Minister was Morogoro. I saw this rich fertile region with more than adequate rains in all its districts. I toured the budding industries, mainly initiated by the famous Member of Parliament for Morogoro, Amir Jamal, when he was Minister for Commerce and Industry. I spent a day in the Mikumi National Park seeing the wildlife, for a change, and stayed overnight at the Wildlife Lodge. The potential for a flourishing local tourist industry, in view of its proximity and easy access to the City of Dar es Salaam, was obvious.

We next went to see the Sugarcane Plantations in the Kilombero District. The management arranged for us to tour the twin plantations. With such abundant water and land, this country should be self-sufficient in sugar, particularly since there is more than ample land which can be made available to out-growers. As you approach Ifakara, you realise that nature made that land ideal for paddy. The vast Kilombero Valley could become the granary of Tanzania and even East Africa, if only our people could be given the incentives, expertise and the necessary tools.

Precarious crossing of the Kilombero River took us to the Ulanga-Mahenge District. This vast district, so close to the coast and Dar es Salaam, yet so remote because of the absence of a reliable bridge across the Kilombero, has a very pleasant climate and great agricultural potential. I enjoyed the hospitality of the Catholic Fathers at their monastery in Mahenge in lieu of a hotel. The small Mahenge government guesthouse, in which I could have stayed, accommodated Ms Anna Abdallah, the then Morogoro Regional Commissioner, who was accompanying me during my tour of her region. I returned from Ulanga-Mahenge after visiting most of the wards where self-help projects were being implemented by the residents. There were primary schools, medical dispensaries and earth roads being built under the supervision of the District Engineer, whose parents I knew well as they were my neighbours back in Marangu. The urgent need to have all-weather roads in that potentially rich agricultural district, and the necessity to build a permanent reliable bridge across the river could not be over-emphasised.

On our return journey, I persuaded Ms Anna Abdallah that we should visit the Kilombero Agricultural Training and Research Institute at Ifakara. A cousin of mine, Geoffrey Nderingo Mtei, was the resident agricultural engineer at the Institute, and I had not seen him for years. Geoffrey and Crecentia, his newly wed wife, were excited to see me, and considered it an honour to provide lunch for the Regional commissioner and the Minister for Finance. After lunch we drove on to the Wildlife Lodge at Mikumi where we spent the night before going on a tour of Kilosa District.

Morogoro North, which has now been renamed Mvomero District, was our next destination. The road through Dakawa, Turiani and on to Mtibwa Sugar Plantation and Mziha was familiar to me. It was the same gravel road we drove in those Tanganyika Railway Buses back in 1951/52, on our way to and from Tabora High School. I also drove myself on this road on that day in July 1960 when Johara and I had the accident in my Fiat 1100. Now in 1978, more than 18 years later, the road had even worse potholes as it was rarely used for trunk traffic to the North. The Chalinze Segera tarmac road had been built and was now the trunk road to the Tanga and Kilimanjaro Regions. It was a pity to see a road that provided access to such currently productive areas as Turiani Madizini and the Mtibwa Sugar Works being neglected, rather than macadamised; at the same time, preference was given to the eastern route, which passed through almost virgin land. Our priorities appeared to be wrong, and I said so to Ms Abdallah as we were about to reach the Mtibwa Sugar Factory, where we were to be accommodated by its management. She had been thoroughly softened by the humps and bumps in those potholes, weakening any inclination to disagree.

At Mtibwa about one thousand workers and other residents lined up along the driveway to cheer us as we walked from the factory to the VIP guest house. My own half-brother, Hermas Eliapenda Mtei, (son of my father and his second wife), a teacher at Turiani Primary School, was among those waiting to welcome us. When I was near enough to recognise him, I shouted Hermas!, and he came out of the crowd and we hugged one another. My police bodyguard, who was walking behind me, reacted immediately and tried to separate us, as he thought I was being molested. It was only my saying *Mdogo wangu mpendwa! Mdogo wangu mpendwa!* ('My dear young brother! My dear young brother') that prevented the policeman from the instant use of his baton!

On reaching the guest house, and after a bath, I asked the Regional Commissioner to excuse me so that I could spend the evening with Hermas. I found that at his residence he had assembled all his friends for a proper *ndafu* (he-goat) roast party, Chagga-style. We had a superb time with his friends and particularly his young children, who marvelled at their uncle having only heard of or seen him before in newspaper photographs. The next day Ms Anna Abdallah and I drove back to Morogoro passing through Dakawa and observing this other potential granary of Tanzania.

The salient points observed during my tour of Morogoro Region were reported verbally and in writing to my bosses, the President and the Prime Minister. They both thanked me for my analysis, both of the potential of the region, and its problems. They noted that I was one of the rare Ministers whom put their reports on paper. They remarked, however, that since I was the Minister for Finance and Planning, they would be glad to see me co-ordinate with other relevant Ministers to hasten the solutions to the problems I had raised. I entirely agreed with them and I braced myself for action.

However, this was 1978, and very soon afterwards Idi Amin invaded Tanzania and pushed his troops to the northern bank of the Kagera River, destroying and devastating the countryside. An all-out national effort was required to drive the invader out, and to ensure that this danger would not recur. My role as Minister for Finance and a Member of the Defence Committee of the Cabinet was to ensure that funds were diverted and others mobilised for the war effort to ensure a swift victory, whilst minimising the disruption of essential services and ongoing projects.

A Supplementary Budget had to be prepared and passed by Parliament, which at first involved the virement of funds from votes/allocations which catered for services and projects which could be postponed partly or wholly. When the new financial year started later, we fully budgeted for war. As part of the mobilisation effort, I visited some of the countries which had offered us financial or other material assistance. Most of those ready to assist were desirous of appearing neutral, and were unwilling to be seen as publicly taking sides in this East African confrontation. So they preferred the Finance Minister to make the visit, rather than the Defence or Foreign Minister. I found myself making trips abroad accompanied not only by officials from my own ministry, but also with colonels or majors from the Ministry of Defence. I mention this role because the impression has been gained only the leaders who went to the front contributed to the war effort. I participated in the negotiations for loans and supplies given on credit, and signed some of the agreements with those governments.

In the second half of 1979 victory over Amin's army was attained, and the entire Cabinet and other senior Government officials went to Kagera to celebrate; and to receive a large contingent of the Tanzania Army not required in Uganda for the initial maintenance of peace, law and order. I was among this group, and had opportunity to inspect some of the devastation and destruction caused by Amin's army. We crossed the Kagera at Kyaka and went all the way to Mutukula to see with our own eyes how the countryside had been ravaged. It was obvious that this area would require special assistance to enable the inhabitants re-establish themselves in homesteads ransacked by the marauding troops. Indeed, the whole of the Kagera Region and the country at large would, in my view, within the next year or two, have to revive the projects abandoned or shelved because of our pre-occupation with the war.

Our major task in the folowing few months would be to assist in the de-mobilisation and return of the many volunteers who had gone to the front, in order that they could get back to their old jobs. My ministry had to gauge as accurately as possible what costs had to be incurred in the immediate future to be able to restore to orderly service, facilities and infrastructures that had been destroyed, abandoned or postponed as a result of the war. Fortunately, many bilateral donors and even multilateral institutions, such as the World Bank and the International Monetary Fund, as well as the United Nations Development Programme were ready to assist. Many donors were only waiting for the Government to put forward a consistent and viable rehabilitation programme before granting us assistance or giving us favourable credits. I cannot recall the precise figure, but we reckoned that over the next two years, Tanzania would require from abroad something in the order of US$ 375 million for rehabilitation. In addition, balance-of-payments support of some magnitude would be required from the IM F.

Early in September 1979 the IMF and the World Bank sent teams to Tanzania at my request. They studied the situation and left us with some proposals to consider. The Annual Meetings of the Board of Governors of IMF and World Bank were due to be held in Belgrade, Yugoslavia, at about the end of September or beginning of October, and I arranged to continue the discussions whilst in Belgrade. In the meantime, I consulted with the President about the major proposals of the IMF and the World Bank before I left for Yugoslavia and he agreed that the approach I was taking was right and in the interests of Tanzania.

I should mention that when I returned to the Treasury in 1977 as Minister, I resumed the very friendly contacts I had established with other African Ministers of Finance and Governors of central banks. I have already referred, in this narrative, to their selecting me in 1972 to serve as a Member of the Deputies of the Committee of Twenty (the Morse Committee). At the Belgrade Annual Meetings, African Governors were expected to nominate an African Minister for election by the Conference as Chairman of the Boards of Governors for the ensuing year. Prior to the Meeting, the Executive Directors serving our constituency on the Executive Boards of the IMF and World Bank had visited me in Dar es Salaam to suggest that I should offer my name to the African Caucus for this purpose.

At the African Caucus meeting in Belgrade, it was resolved that only my name would be submitted for the vote during the last plenary session of the Boards of Governors. As Governor for Tanzania for the IMF and World Bank, I was therefore elected Chairman of the Boards of governors of the two institutions for the 1979/80 fiscal year. It was an honour for Tanzania and recognition of the active part we had played in advancing African interests in the Bretton Woods Institutions. I felt very proud to have played a part in that achievement.

As Minister responsible for planning, I found myself serving as Member or co-Chairman of Joint Commissions of Co-operation between Tanzania and a number of countries friendly to us. In that capacity, I led a ministerial team which toured Mozambique. Later, I led another high-powered delegation to India after hosting my Indian counterpart, who happened to be Hon. Behal Vajpayee, the then Foreign Minister of India, who subsequently assumed office as Prime Minister of India. During my visit the Indians put on an extensive tour for us in the sub-continent, taking us to see the breath-taking beauty of the Taj Mahal and the industrial complex of Bangalore in South India. When I was in New Delhi, I was able to pay a courtesy call on President Sanjiva Reddy.

On official visit to India, I paid a courtesy call on President Sanjiva Reddy, 1978 (Courtesy *Daily News*).

During this period, I also organised the first meeting of Planning Ministers of Southern African countries, which broached the need for joint action to lessen our dependence on apartheid South Africa. President Nyerere, as Chairman of the 'Frontline States-', had been reluctant to open the Conference, but he extended an invitation to Sir Seretse Khama, President of Botswana, who came to Arusha specifically to open the procedings. Follow-up of that Conference culminated in the launching of the Southern Africa Development Co-ordination Community (SADC) in 1980.

With President Sir Seretse Khama, after he formally opened the Southern African Conference of Ministers of Planning on Lessening Dependence on apartheid South Africa, 1979.

CHAPTER 17

Events Leading to My Resignation

As I said earlier, we were expected to pursue in Belgrade the negotiations which had started with the IMF and World Bank in Dar es Salaam. After several meetings with these officials in Belgrade, I invited the IMF mission to return to Dar es Salaam in November, hoping to conclude the negotiations then. The World Bank agreement to provide the long-term credits to Tanzania was, in any case, contingent upon the IMF reaching agreement with us on the adjustment measures and the provision of their balance-of-payments support. So when we returned to Dar es Salaam, I concentrated on working with my staff on a programme which would be acceptable to both the President and the IMF.

Bo Karlstrom, a senior member of staff of the African Department of the IMF, led the mission to Tanzania in November 1979. They arrived in the third week and were booked into the Hotel Kilimanjaro. They worked with us for about a week before finalising a package of proposals I could put in front of my colleagues in the Government. The proposals included a programme of adjustment measures, accompanied by credit facilities and possibly bilateral grants for the rehabilitation of the economy. I kept the President briefed continuously on the salient points of the negotiations as we progressed.

However, although he was prepared to accept most of the proposed financial assistance measures, he was adamantly opposed to any proposals to strengthen the management of the parastatals by involving outside participants as shareholders. He was also adamantly opposed to the devaluation of the Tanzania Shilling. It was apparent to me that he was being advised by other persons against doing anything affecting the exchange rate or touching on publicly-owned corporations that were either bankrupt or loss-making.

The President was aware of the huge Treasury subsidies being given to many of these corporations. Their indebtedness to the National Bank of Commerce had grown, in my view, to an alarming proportion and was threatening the very solvency and viability of that bank itself, since repayment of bank loans was proving impossible in many cases.

I had myself commissioned a Danish expert, who studied the National Milling Corporation's operations. The study had revealed rampant misuse of their trucks by uncontrolled and dishonest officers and drivers which, in my judgement, could only be rectified by managers or supervisors having a stake in the NMC trading operations. This suggestion smacked of capitalism, and was, of course, taboo in those days. But it was necessary to be frank with the President, since I could not think of any alternative solution. At this time, I had in mind the possibility of inviting people such as those who had previously owned Chande Industries to repossess part of their old shares in National Milling in order to re-instil a sense of stake-holding to facilitate better management and control of the assets. After all, it was Andy Chande himself who was the first Managing Director of the giant state-owned National Milling Corporation, and he had initially been quite successful in reorganising and running it.

Regarding the exchange rate, I should mention that in the eyes of many observers at that time, the Tsh was highly overvalued. The official rate of exchange was fixed at US$1.00 = 9.60Tshs. This was the rate the Bank of Tanzania was using to buy Shillings smuggled into foreign centres, including Zurich, London and even Nairobi. Because of the lack of confidence in the future of the Tanzanian economy, these smugglers were prepared to surrender their Shillings at rates between US$ 1.00 = 20.00 and 30.00 TShs. The Kenya Shilling had recently been devalued to US$ 1.00 = 12.00 KShs. But even at the devalued rate, the Kenya Shilling was being exchanged in the black market and along our 'closed' shared border at the rate TShs 3.00 = KShs 1.00. I therefore failed to understand the advisors who were briefing the President on this matter.

The IMF Mission considered that if we took the other measures, such as reducing defence spending and improving the management of the parastatals in order to avoid the huge subsidies currently going to them, we could devalue to US$ 1.00 = 12.50 TShs and thereafter run things smoothly. I recall that I was able to persuade them to agree to a two-step adjustment:first to US$ 1.00 = Tsh10.80, and after about six to nine months, to move to US$ 1.00 = 12.50 TShs. I argued that the interim period would give us time to see whether the balance-of-payments relief and the other rehabilitation measures were bearing fruit. I was banking on injecting enough foreign exchange into the economy to ensure that the shops would be properly stocked with consumer goods, to dampen the inflation and ensure repairs of the infrastructure and industrial equipment, thus substantially restoring confidence and the efficiency of economic activities. I explained our counter proposals to the President and how I envisaged the economy would be put on an even keel. But to him, the idea of devaluing the currency or reforming the parastatals in the manner I was proposing was out of the question. This uncompromising attitude on the part of my boss was not only disappointing but started to worry me.

I discussed the President's reactions to the proposals with Mr Karlstrom. He suggested that if he had an audience with the President, he might be able to soften his attitude. I therefore requested an appointment for a courtesy call by the Leader of the Mission on the President on 29 November, and this was granted for 4.00 p.m. at his Msasani Residence. I went to Msasani, accompanied by Karlstrom and one of his assistants. The Principal Secretary to the Treasury, Ernest Mulokozi, was also with me. After the introductions and the normal salutations, Mr Karlstrom gave some details regarding the proposals and set out how he envisaged the performance of the economy would turn round and improve, on the measures being implemented. I could see that the President was not happy with these explanations, and was becoming agitated. In the end, he thanked the Leader of the Mission and said that he was unable to accept the advice to devalue our currency, but would certainly like to strengthen the management of the public corporations in a manner he considered acceptable and workable and at an appropriate time. He then abruptly stood up, and left us standing at the meeting place on the veranda. He then walked to the beach front of his residence.

We were all perplexed and I decided to follow him to the beach, at least to bid him farewell. When I was able to talk with him, he indicated that he considered the visitors were insolent and added that he would never allow his country to be run from Washington. He told me to tell them to go back to Washington. He added that, whatever arguments were advanced, 'I will devalue the Shilling over my dead body'. After hearing this categorical statement, I did not want to prolong the discussion. I thanked him, and left to rejoin the Mission leader and his colleague who were waiting to hear what he had said. I asked the others to follow me whilst I rode with Karlstrom in my car to my residence where we could have tea and talk.

At my house, whilst tea was being prepared, I explained that the negotiations had broken down, but the Government would be in correspondence with the IMF in the future on this subject. After noting my explanations, they reacted by stating that they would have been glad to leave for Washington the next day, but their bookings were for Saturday and it was difficult to get connections in Europe with such short notice. It was Wednesday and I suggested that they transfer from the Hotel Kilimanjaro to the Bahari Beach Hotel where they could go swimming, surfing, or scuba-diving until the time of their departure. They were pleased with the suggestion, and I booked them into the Bahari Beach Hotel by telephone from my house. They checked out of the Hotel Kilimanjaro and transferred to the beach hotel that evening.

The IMF mission left on Saturday morning, and I did not meet Bo Karlstrom again until about four years later, when fortunes for both of us had almost diametrically changed. I gathered in 1983, when I moved to start work at the Fund, that after President Nyerere had strongly attacked the IMF, his superiors thought Karlstrom might have made his presentation in an improper, non-diplomatic manner. As he considered that he acted correctly, he decided to leave the Fund in order to take another job in his native Sweden. I can state categorically that in my view Bo Karlstrom acted absolutely correctly during that audience with the President and that no presentation- however cogent or diplomatic, would have persuaded Nyerere to change his mind at that time.

That night I was unable to sleep. The next day was a public holiday, but early that morning I went to my office and drafted a letter to request the President to relieve me of my job as Minister for Finance and Planning. I explained that over the past few months I had become aware that my advice to him, even on matters related to strengthening my Ministry administratively and the financial sector generally, had not been acceptable to him. I then touched on the negotiations with the IMF and the fact that I had spent many days and nights trying to come up with proposals, which in my conviction would have gone a long way in resolving many of Tanzania's economic and financial problems.

I acknowledged in that letter that the Fund appeared rigid in their insistence on solutions which might not work in certain circumstances; but that was why we, as a Government, had to have local staff capable of arguing with them and offering alternative workable proposals. I asserted that I had done my best with the local experts at my disposal and that I had substantially modified the IMF's stand as originally presented; but he, as President, had rejected the proposals *in toto*. I further stated that I frankly believed that the proposals as modified, if implemented, would in the long run be beneficial to the country. I therefore requested him to look for another Tanzanian whom he could trust more, and whose advice he would more readily accept. I finally suggested that since my resignation as Minister for Finance might adversely affect the financial situation somewhat, we could explain that I had resigned for health reasons. I had not properly slept for some nights previously, and after finishing that letter I already felt relieved enough ready to go for an afternoon siesta.

As I finished writing the letter, I had a telephone call from the Minister for Agriculture, Hon. John Malecela. He said that the President wanted to see both of us. I left the letter on my desk, expecting that I would have it typed the next day when my personal secretary would be on duty. I left for Msasani, driving myself as my official driver was, like everybody else, not on duty. I found Malecela already at Msasani, and we went into the President's office together.

The President wanted to discuss the acquisition by the Government, of the Danish-owned Tanganyika Planting Company (TPC) at Arusha Chini, in Kilimanjaro Region. I knew about the proposal by Mr Moeller, the Danish shipowner magnate, who owned this sugar cane plantation and wanted to get rid of it. His reasons for selling were twofold. First, the Bank of Tanzania had been unable to allow the remittance of dividends to him for four years as the foreign exchange position was highly strained. Secondly, those dividend moneys, plus other funds locally generated by TPC, could not even be remitted to purchase irrigation equipment and other machinery urgently required for rehabilitating the plantation. Mr Moeller therefore offered to sell the plantation to the Government for what the President and the Minister for Agriculture considered was a very low and reasonable price. The one condition that the Bank of Tanzania and I had not accepted in the discussions we had held with Mr Moeller was that the price money should be remitted immediately in a lump sum.

I explained to the President that although it would be good for the Government to acquire TPC for the price agreed, Tanzania literally did not have the foreign exchange to allow immediate remittance. I mentioned that the Governor of the Bank of Tanzania had himself already intimated to me that even for national foreign debts that were due for repayment, we might in the very near future, be unable to make the necessary foreign exchange available. In my view, such a situation was very serious, because the country's creditworthiness was at stake. At that time (1979), it was unheard of, for a sovereign country to default on the repayment of a long-term debt.

Both the President and Mr Malecela looked at me incredulously. Then the President stated that the Government must buy the Plantation, and the money must be found. I said that that decision was his, and hoped that funds would be found somewhere, somehow to meet his directive. I left the office and drove behind Mr Malecela's car so that I could discuss this further with him in his office. After I had explained to Mr Malecela how precarious the financial situation was, he seemed to appreciate my difficult position, but added that he hoped that Treasury would be able to implement the President's directive. I replied that I hoped so too, but intimated to him that because of this and many other problems, I was finding it impossible to carry on as Minister, and would resign. When I left Malecela's office, I was determined to go to send the hand-written letter to the President. I was so tense when going to my office that I hit a car in front of me when its driver slowed down in order to turn right. The driver happened to be Andy Chande, and as the damage was very minor, he excused me and I went on to my office. I finalised the letter in my own hand by rewriting a page I had corrected, signed it and put it in an envelope to go to deliver it personally to the President.

As I was coming out of the Treasury building I met Batao, one of the junior Personal Assistants to the President. He gave me a letter which apparently was supposed to be delivered to me personally, and I signed for it in his Delivery Book. I put it on my car seat as I drove back to Msasani to take my letter to the President. When I reached Msasani I enquired if the President was still in his office. He was and I was ushered in. He was not expecting me to return so soon. I explained that after our discussions the previous day, I had written a letter to him that I intended to have typed before delivery. However, following the morning's meeting, in which Mr Malecela also participated, I had decided not to wait for my personal secretary to type it after the public holiday. I therefore requested him to accept that letter as it was. I was shaking with emotion as I handed the letter to the President.

After reading the letter, the President asked me whether a messenger had delivered a letter that he had written to me that morning. I replied that Batao had given me a letter outside the Treasury Building as I was getting into my car to bring mine to him, but it was on my car seat and I had not yet read it as I had felt so tense. He then thought for a while and said: "Well Edwin, I thank you for your letter". He then pressed his bell for an assistant and asked for Paul Sozigwa, his Press Secretary. When Paul came in, he informed him: "Edwin has tendered his resignation as Minister of Finance and Planning. I have accepted his resignation with immediate effect. I shall give an explanatory statement later. Go and make a statement to the press to that effect". So I parted with President Nyerere. He and I shook hands as I stood up to leave. I went back to the office to collect my personal documents and papers.

I read the letter delivered by Batao on getting into my car. It was very brief and was signed by the President himself. It said that he had decided to revoke my appointment as Minister of Finance and Planning. He added that he could not allow his Government to be run from Washington. Another sentence said that he had directed me to expel the IMF team, but I had not followed his instructions. Apparently, my hosting of the members of the Mission for tea and discussions at my house, and their move to the beach hotel, were being trailed by the National Security Service. The Security personnel mistakenly regarded them as saboteurs!

I could not, of course, reply or even write to the President to explain because I regarded his verbal reaction to my own letter as withdrawal of his. But to imply that the IMF package of proposals was wholly dictated from Washington without our input was most unfair to those of us who had worked so hard on the final version. Secondly, I could not have interpreted the President's instruction to "tell the Mission to return their home in Washington" as meaning they were to be expelled or declared prohibited immigrants. In any case, I was not the Minister responsible for "expelling" undesirable immigrants or visitors. I considered that whether or not Tanzania accepted the IMF conditions, we were still members of that institution, and it would have been disastrous to part with the delegation in an undiplomatic manner. I therefore considered my interpretation to be in the national interest in the long run.

That evening, Radio Tanzania Dar es Salaam announced my resignation exactly as the President had directed. However, it was the foreign press which explained that the cause of my resignation was occasioned by differences on economic and financial policies. Kenya Radio and the British Broadcasting Corporation were particularly strong in their criticism of President Nyerere at this time, and were to some extent sympathetic to me. The local newspapers on 1 December carried the brief statement on their front pages, with a sad picture of Edwin Mtei, and no editorial comment was made, either then or later. Many relatives and friends, including Ministers, came to see me at my residence the next day, sympathetic and surprised. Even John Malecela came.

I wanted to avoid any confrontation with the Government and refused to be interviewed by any member of the press. I should also mention that I immediately embarked on the plan I had initiated prior to leaving Arusha in 1977, namely to acquire a coffee farm. Within a week, Hermanus Steyn, the owner of Ogaden Estate came to Dar es Salaam at my request, and we reached an agreement to swap my house in Mzinga Way for Ogaden Estate, subject to an independent valuation certifying the market price of each property, with any difference being settled between the parties. Herman was anxious to acquire a house in Dar so that his family could live there to enable his children to attend the International School. I flew with Herman in his personal aircraft to inspect the farm, and I was satisfied that we could live there and operate as farmers, and if possible or necessary do other business. Fortunately, my house in Dar es Salaam was valued a little higher than Ogaden Estate, and Herman agreed to give me an extra tractor and a Peugeot pick-up vehicle from his Manyara Estate as compensation.

However, before detailing my life as a farmer and subsequent events, let me give my own brief assessment of the Nyerere regime's economy and policies, before and after my departure.

Chapter 18

Economic and Other Policies of the Nyerere Regime

The Nyerere Regime lasted for twenty-four years, 1961-85. The brief period when Rashidi Mfaume Kawawa was Prime Minister following Nyerere's resignation early in 1962 was, for all intents and purposes, under Nyerere's control. His main task at that time was reorganising TANU which, in any case, prescribed all the policies. I can identify several phases in the evolution of the country's economy during this quarter-century.

The period ending with the promulgation of the Arusha Declaration in February 1967 can be regarded as the first phase. TANU had promised during the independence struggle to rid Tanganyika of poverty, ignorance and disease. The people's hopes were high. Most people were also ready to apply themselves to hard work in the offices, farms, factories and mines, although as far as Government was concerned, the Adu Commission had prescribed lower salaries in Tanganyika than those commonly obtained in Kenya and Uganda.

At the time the British left, there were only a handful of factories as most manufacturing had been based in Kenya. Nevertheless, the motto of that period for the people of Tanganyika was *uhuru ni kazi* (freedom is work) and, in my view, Tanganyikans at this time did work hard. There was a feeling that the leadership was committed and honest, and we accepted there was no cure for our problems except determined application.

Regarding development finance, during the independence negotiations, the British had agreed to only modest financial assistance to Tanganyika. Indeed, the bulk of that assistance, as I have remarked elsewhere, was earmarked for compensation to the departing, prematurely retired British civil servants under the so-called "golden handshake".

Most of Tanganyika's foreign exchange was earned by the exports of sisal, grown mainly on expatriate-owned estates; coffee, mainly from peasants and some estates in Northern and Southern Highlands Provinces; as well as peasant grown cotton. In addition, tea, mainly grown on estates, and tobacco, partly grown on estates supplemented by peasant grown, all made contribution to foreign exchange earnings. The Williamson Diamond Mine at Mwadui in Shinyanga Region, which was already partly Government-owned, was a major source of mineral exports. It was within this context of modest resources that Tanganyika's First Development Plan of three years was designed. Complaints by Members of Parliament and the public generally that we ought to be more ambitious in state planning for the future prompted the President to coin that famous phrase *"kupanga ni kuchagua"* (to plan is to choose). We had to be selective in deciding on our projects, and had to choose in accordance with our priorities and the available resources.

Under the Plan, Tanganyika embarked on a number of pilot projects to develop villages by integrating communal work with individual private enterprise. As Permanent Secretary to the Treasury, I recall having taken overseas visiting dignitaries, including Mrs Barbara Castle, the then British Minister for Overseas Development in the Labour Government, to Upper Kitete near Lake Manyara. This was our showpiece for what could be done under the "integrated development villages" approach. The modest funds that could be allocated for capital development were used to build schools, training institutes and hospitals. The intensive training for local staff under the Africanisation programme also attracted a relatively large share of available resources, including donor funds.

On the industrial side, some consumer goods manufacturing had started to relocate in Tanganyika at this time: these included British American Tobacco, Unga Limited and Aluminium Africa. It was the frustratingly slow pace of economic development caused by the scarcity of long-term financial resources, among other reasons, I guess, that led President Nyerere to take the route via the Arusha Declaration. He expected that this would facilitate a faster and fairer way to development. Steady and uninterrupted external inflow of capital as sine qua non for take-off in small economies did not occur to him.

On promulgation of the Arusha Declaration in 1967, the second phase of the economy under the leadership of Nyerere began. The nationalisation of all the banks, insurance companies, major manufacturing and trading firms, and sisal estates immediately followed. Uncertainties on the part of owners of substantial assets in the country caused a massive flight of capital, in spite of the Government's decision to introduce strict exchange controls. Many techniques to evade controls were used, such as the under-invoicing of exports and over-invoicing of imports. Physical smuggling of currency and precious stones and metals were resorted to by many residents, determined to get their assets out of the country. The country was literally under siege, and found its reserves of foreign exchange being depleted or not growing at the pace required, in spite of the licensing of imports and stringent exchange controls and regulation of exports.

However, because of the tranquillity prevailing in the country, and the confidence with which national leaders approached official lenders and foreign corporations handling suppliers' credits, by 1969/70 the Government was able to embark on many new projects. Factories for manufacturing consumer items, especially textiles and garments, tourist hotels and lodges were built by the newly founded parastatal corporations. Most of the negotiations for compensation for nationalised assets were also completed by this time, and a measure of confidence returned to the extent that the exchange controls were relaxed. The new National Bank of Commerce and the National Insurance Corporation got off the ground fairly smoothly. State Trading had teething problems, and had to be reorganised into regional and sectoral national trading companies, although many ultimately failed because of mismanagement, corruption and/or lack of adequate capital.

A major construction project at this time was the Chinese-financed Tanzania-Zambia Railway (TAZARA), which had a significant impact on the economy. The construction started in earnest in 1970. The supply of Chinese consumer goods, for the generation of local currency for the building of TAZARA, disrupted some of the local industries and caused complaints from erstwhile Kenya suppliers of competitive items. The local population, however, welcomed the cheaper items from China, and the complaints were officially ignored.

The calm atmosphere was, however, disturbed in 1971, when all rented large residential and commercial buildings were nationalised, ushering in the third phase of the Nyerere era. The majority of the owners were members of the Asian urban community. The panic that ensued saw a large number of them emigrating, especially to India, Pakistan, Canada and the United Kingdom. A massive flight of capital, leading to a rapid depletion of our foreign exchange reserves, made the Government tighten exchange controls again. This time even payments to partners within the East African Common Market were subject to control. One can only imagine the futility of controlling the movement of money when there was supposed to be free movement of people and goods within the Community and the Common Market!

Incidentally, even people like myself were affected by the building nationalisation measures. The house in Mzinga Way was on the list of nationalised houses, although in line with the code of conduct for the leadership, I had surrendered it to my mother on moving into the Governor's official residence, once its construction was completed in 1969. My mother had then rented it out to cater for our extended family. So the house fell into the category of large houses to be nationalised. I made strong representations to the President, since I had consulted him prior to transferring it to my mother. Many other officials were similarly affected, and nationalised houses were restored to public employees, provided they moved back to live in them.

About 1973/74, the fourth phase of the evolution of the economy began, when the Government and Party embarked on serious and vigorous implementation of the Ujamaa Villages Programme. Practically the whole country was involved. Under this scheme, people were relocated from their traditional homesteads to new areas planned as communal villages. These ujamaa villages were designed to have basic social amenities, including schools, hospitals, social halls or community centres, water supply, and would, of course, be easily accessible, or located beside a main road. Each family was allotted a small parcel of land to grow food and/or other crops of their choice. But most important of all, there was a large piece of land earmarked for the whole village, for communal farming. This was a replication of the Chinese communes that had impressed Nyerere when he visited that country in the late 1960s.

The scheme had started in 1972 by persuading the population and explaining the advantages of relocation. However, when it came to moving people en-masse, those with perennial crops or permanent dwelling houses, showed reluctance. Over-enthusiastic officials, either in the Government or TANU, began to coerce the people, and some houses were even burnt down, in order to make residents move to the new locations. Some of those forcibly evicted from their homes were even attacked by wild beasts, as they had nowhere to stay other than in unsheltered, insecure temporary shacks.

A large proportion of the population of Tanzania, all of a sudden, found itself building shelters or houses in their new villages. In these new locations, it became necessary to feed the new arrivals, and a large amount of public funds was set aside for purchasing food for whole communities. The season for preparing the land for annual crops passed without a large proportion of the population performing their routine seasonal farming activities, because of their pre-occupation with building new houses or shelters. Large areas of farmland lay fallow, without their normal annual crops. In areas with perennial crops, especially cashew, farmers had moved so far away that they could not properly tend their crops. This was a sure prescription for future famine, and paucity of vital agricultural harvests, from which Tanzania has not fully recovered even today.

Unfortunately, the period of major relocation to the ujamaa villages coincided with the severe drought of 1973/74. The famine that resulted from these twin causes was devastating. Tanzania found itself with a large percentage of its population on the verge of starvation. Disproportionately large emergency food imports had to be secured, almost exhausting the foreign exchange reserves. We even had to import from unfriendly countries, such as Rhodesia and South Africa, when shipments from far-off overseas areas seemed likely to arrive late. The Government appealed to UN agencies and friendly countries for food aid in order to stave off widespread malnutrition and possible starvation. Our reserves of foreign exchange dropped to rock-bottom, and Tanzania began to experience difficulties in effecting the repayment of contractual debt on due dates. It was at this time that as a nation, we also started experiencing negative GDP growth.

The non-performance of many of the parastatal organisations established as a result of the Arusha Declaration also intensified at this period. Many were under-capitalised; others lacked proper management, whilst other failings, especially in those organisations involved in manufacture, were the result of the supply of faulty, over-valued, second-hand or inappropriate machinery. The Treasury found itself either giving huge loans to rescue management from irate workers, who had not been paid salaries for long periods; or repaying loans as guarantors, since the borrowing parastatals were not generating the necessary surpluses. Factories under construction were left uncompleted, equipment delivered for installation was either faulty or lay in building sites in their packing crates, rusting and rotting for lack of funds and/or experts to install them properly.

In spite of these bottlenecks, the Government was pressing on with new projects in many parts of the country. The international financial situation was awash with funds. This was the period of excessive petrol-dollars in the world money markets, following the escalation of prices for petroleum products and the massive accumulation of reserves by OPEC countries. A large number of potential creditors were ready to lend or provide equipment and machinery on suppliers' credit, as long as a Government guarantee was forthcoming. Many of these projects proved to be abortive, so that Tanzania was soon dotted with unfinished projects or white elephants all over the country, funded by loans which the Government has to repay as guarantor. Hence, the origin of the unsustainable foreign national debt, for which the Government still, pleads forgiveness today.

The fifth and final phase of the Nyerere era began afterI had left government. It saw Tanzania's inability to repay contractual loans and the accelerated accumulation of bad national debt from 1980. Our imports exceeded our exports in value by a wide margin, since agricultural production could not recover fast enough from the disruptive impact of the ujamaa village exercise. In addition, most parastatals were running at huge losses, unable to produce enough for export or to meet local demand. Others were closing down for lack of imported raw materials, or spare parts, or simply because they could not pay their workers when the National Bank of Commerce refused to allow further overdrafts. Huge borrowings by the Government from the banking system to finance the subsidies to the near-bankrupt parastatals excacerbated the inflation to double-digit figures Import of essential items was minimal, as foreign exchange allocated was inadequate.

The scarcity of consumer commodities caused by the failure of the parastatals, and our inability to import enough to close the gap, gripped the country. This led to a futile system of rationing, resulting in corruption and extreme hardships for sections of the public, especially those on a low income. Because of the petrol shortage, Sunday driving was banned. This was followed by actual rationing of petrol and diesel, according to what bureaucrats decided a vehicle owner should be allowed to do with his vehicle. Long queues of people at parastatal outlets, such as the Regional Trading Companies, with chits from Government officers authorising them to purchase normal household requisites, including soap, toilet paper, sugar, salt, *sembe* (maize flour), rice, cooking oil, matches and practically all normal household items, made living in Tanzania intolerable. Clothing was so scarce that some people resorted to using empty cement or fertiliser bags as normal wear. It was a pathetic situation.

The shelves of privately owned shops were literally empty. Whenever a shopkeeper was able to procure any item for sale, the price was very high. So-called luxury items were banned, and even those who could obtain foreign exchange lawfully, such as Tanzanians working abroad, were not allowed to come back with items like television sets or saloon cars.

It was at this time that I had been appointed Executive Director of the International Monetary Fund, and was living in Washington. When I came to East Africa for normal duties, I always made a point of seeing how my farm was being managed, and so would go to or through Nairobi, from where I drove to the border. A vehicle from my farm would then meet me at Namanga. Before driving to Namanga, I had to seek permission by telephone from the Government in Dar es Salaam to cross the border, since it was "closed". The government official I contacted, would give me permission to cross the border; otherwise I would have had to go by aeroplane to Addis Ababa in order to fly to Kilimanjaro International Airport. However, invariably the official, whatever his seniority, also requested me to buy him in Nairobi items like toilet soap, toothpaste and other normal household items impossible to get in Tanzanian shops. Many friends and relatives made similar requests, so that my car used to come loaded with cartons and cartons of these items to relieve, albeit temporarily, the hardships they were experiencing.

Because of the scarcity of goods and the ever-rising prices, those with money started to buy whatever was available, even though they might not need them immediately. If an official travelled to Mbeya, he would return to Dar es Salaam with two bags of rice in his official vehicle. If he saw a transistor radio in a shop, he would buy it even though he might possess several already at home. Similarly with furniture: houses occupied by well-to-do individuals were congested with items of furniture acquired simply to avoid the escalating inflation. Shopkeepers who chanced to find saleable goods would purchase them in bulk and stock them. Sometimes they would not sell them immediately, knowing that they would make even more of a killing if they waited for a while. They guessed that in a month's time the price could rise by as much as fifty per cent.

It was at this time that Parliament enacted the Economic Crimes and Sabotage Act. The new law was aimed at controlling what the authorities considered to be people acquiring wealth illegally, and curbing the activities of the shopkeepers hoarding goods in order to make windfall profits when they were released. Under this law, many citizens and non-citizens who appeared to have substantial assets were rounded up and detained and required to explain how those assets were acquired. A number of the movable assets were seized by unscrupulous officials, and many of them were never recovered. Few of those recovered were serviceable and there have been interminable claims for compensation ever since.

Most of those who were detained were released after appearing before a special Tribunal set up under the Act. Some were freed because of intervention by relatives or friends who had direct access to President Nyerere. But because the Tribunal had to go round the whole country to hear their "cases", it took a long time for most detainees to be released.

To many of the victims it was a real shock that they were detained, for they were honest hardworking, shrewd businessmen and traders who were able to make money in a very hostile official environment. In many cases, people were detained for petty reasons, such as selling goods to a friend, or even to a partner in the firm, without the specific required chit from the government officer in charge of allocation. Others seem to have been detained on the instructions of jealous, vindictive senior officials, intent on settling old scores.

A prominent businessman in my neighbourhood was detained following his request to the Government to purchase a personal aircraft in order to assist his travels between his business operation centre (Mererani) and Dar es Salaam. Apparently, the authorities were surprised that he could have so much money, and therefore detained him in order for him to give an account of how he had built up his assets. They appear to have ignored or conveniently forgotten the fact that he regularly submitted his accounts to the Income Tax Department every year, where they could easily have checked his worth. The shock of detention debilitated him, and he died soon after release.

I know a number of such people who similarly never recovered from the shock of detention, either in terms of their health or their business. The Economic Crimes and Sabotage Act as originally conceived and passed by Parliament was clearly a measure which dealt with the symptoms of the economic disease rather than its causes. Its initial administration exposed rulers who were mean-minded, often carrying out personal vendettas and lacking the essential rudiments of business sense. In its original form, it was bound to fail, as Tanzania transited from the Nyerere to the Ali Hassan Mwinyi regime.

CHAPTER 19

Public Financier turned Farmer

As I said before, immediately after I tendered my resignation as Minister, I arranged to implement my plans to acquire Ogaden Estate. At that time, I had a premonition that the Government might refuse to give, or might deliberately delay, permission for me to acquire a title to the land. In order not to go through the motions of seeking formal government approval, I decided to have the shares of the company that owned the Ogaden farm transferred to my wife and me. This procedure needed the approval of no other party apart from the shareholders and ourselves. After all, I was no longer part of the executive, bound by the Arusha Declaration code that prohibited owning shares in a company.

There was no problem in transferring my house at Mzinga Way to Mrs Herman Steyn, provided the necessary stamp duties were paid. The transactions were completed so that exactly on New Years Day 1980, we moved into the farm-house at Ogaden Estate. I had consigned all my personal effects from Dar es Salaam to Arusha by Railway, and we spent the next few days moving them from a warehouse in town to our new home.

Settling down as a farmer was unexciting. Ogaden Estate had about thirty fulltime employees and all except the Farm Manager and a Supervisor were willing to continue working with us. The Farm Manager, a Tanzanian of Arab extraction had moved from the house specifically allotted to him into the vacant owner's main house in the last few months and felt humiliated by "an African" when I asked him to return to his own house. Apparently, he was also uncertain about our ability to finance the operations of the farm and to pay him. So he had applied for a similar position in another coffee estate in Oldeani. After his resignation he stayed in Arusha town for some time, and then moved to Oldeani with the Supervisor, whom he had highly valued at Ogaden. Nevertheless, I was able to recruit a new Farm Manager, and I learnt a great deal about the details of coffee growing and processing in working him. Indeed, he ran the farm during my sojourn of four years in Washington.

The first coffee crop year (1980/81) was a lean one. But during the harvesting season it was somewhat hectic for us learners. During this season we had to have a minimum of a hundred casual employees to work as coffee pickers every day, to ensure that ripe coffee was brought in for pulping at the right time. As neighbouring smallholder farmers also had ripe coffee berries to pick, we had to go as far as Karangai, sixteen kilometres away, to get pickers every morning. For this, the pick-up vehicle acquired from Steyn proved handy, and I would go early at 5.00 a.m and make three trips before 8.30. In the evening I would also return these workers to their homes, making a minimum of two trips. At the peak of the picking season, I had to hire another vehicle to fetch workers from as far as Doli Sisal Estate in Usa River, more than twenty kilometres away. Msafiri Ally, the tractor driver, had to assist in this exercise.

Financing the operations of Ogaden Estate was facilitated by the fact that as a company we were members of the Tanganyika Coffee Growers' Association (TGGA), a co-operative established in 1945. The supply of inputs such as fertilisers, insecticides, fungicides and herbicides was financed by credit obtained from a bank by TCGA. Even equipment like pumps and knapsack sprayers were financed through the co-operative. The co-operative would buy in bulk, using credit, and members would take what they required from the TCGA warehouse. The value of such inputs and equipment, plus accrued interest of the advance, would then be deducted from the coffee sales proceeds when the member sold his product. All the coffee was sold at an auction organised by the Tanzania Coffee Board and payment to members of TCGA had to pass through the co-operative's bank account.

In addition to the procurement arrangements, TCGA secured credit from the National Bank of Commerce (NBC) for financing farm operations during the harvest season. The terms of this credit facility were negotiated between the bank and the Managing Committee every year. The Annual General Meeting of the Association approved the credit and agreed to pledge its assets as collateral. In addition, the AGM required each individual member utilising the credit to hypothecate to the bank and TCGA the coffee he delivered to the curing company during the period his credit remained outstanding. As credit to facilitate the operations of the TCGA estates was very large, the NBC welcomed us as customers. Since the overdraft was always liquidated at the end of the crop season, TCGA was able to get more favourable terms in terms of interest than individual company borrowers. When we sold our coffee, funds advanced for the picking season as well as the cost of inputs procured through TCGA, plus any interest charges, were deducted from the proceeds before we were paid.

I found membership of the Tanganyika Coffee Growers' Association very useful. All members were coffee growers of repute and had large plantations, although as a result of the nationalisations of 1973, their number was small. Even at the time I joined their ranks, there was still unease amongst them that more take-overs could occur at any time. Indeed, I discovered that some farmers were preparing to leave, and a few actually abandoned their farms, when they could not sell them. In spite of this, I became a very active member of TCGA. I could not, however, take the opportunity of rather "cheap" estates to acquire a larger farm than Ogaden because I knew that the current CCM (the ruling party) policy was to limit the size of individual farms to fifty acres. I preferred to supplement the coffee income by doing other things.

TCGA's Managing Committee utilised my contacts in Government and my knowledge of government policies and procedures in making their casesfrom time to time, and I found myself being elected Chairman of the Association in 1981/82. The decision to elect me initially was so that I could represent the Association on the Boards of Directors of the Coffee Authority of Tanzania and the Tanganyika Coffee Curing Company. The boards of these two vital organs in the coffee industry had recently changed their regulations in order to conduct all their deliberations at board meetings in Kiswahili rather than English. The Chairman of TCGA was automatically a member on both boards, and the Association considered that by electing me, I could provide effective representation for them. My predecessor, Chris Bannister, became Vice-Chairman so that he could "run me in smoothly' about the intricacies of TCGA and the two boards. Membership of the two boards also helped me to keep abreast with developments in government policies regarding coffee, crop boards and agriculture generally. Because of these contacts, I have been active ever since in many for relating to Tanzanian coffee and agriculture generally, to the extent that many coffee farmers regard me as their spokesman.

Although President Nyerere never specifically made any further statement relating to my resignation, in spite of what he implied when accepting it, the international press continued to speculate on it, even when I was already settled at Ogaden Estate. However, early in the New Year, he made a major policy statement when he was addressing a rally at Kigoma. In this, he was very critical of the International Monetary Fund and the World Bank. He asserted that he rejected their attempts to pressurise him to devalue the Tanzania Shilling and privatise the publicly owned corporations. He explained that he disagreed with them on the question of devaluation because past actions along such lines had not benefited the people of Tanzania. He declared that he would never abandon socialism and the public ownership of the major corporations. Referring to the Old Testament, he declared that he would never look back on socialism for he did not want to turn into a pillar of salt like Lot's wife, when she defied the angel's instruction and turned to see Sodom and Gomorrah burning. This reference to "Lot's wife turning into a pillar of salt" became a famous admonition to those of us who doubted the wisdom of applying doctrinaire socialism in Tanzania.

The Kigoma speech unleashed a spate of demonstrations by the people of Tanzania, led by the Youth Wing of CCM, expressing solidarity with the President and against Western exploitative capitalists. Demonstrations all over the country, blazoned in all the local newspapers and broadcasts over the radio, occupied the population for months. Although I was not specifically singled out for criticism for siding with the IMF, the foreign press often referred to me as a supporter of Fund policies. They made frequent references to the fact that I had resigned from the Government because of differences with my boss over his policies.

At this time, I was often in contact with Hon. Amir Jamal, who had taken over as Minister for Finance. When we were discussing the Kigoma statement and "Lot's wife turning into a pillar of salt", I remarked that I hoped that those in Government could use mirrors to see the burning of Tanzania behind them as they marched forward into socialism. He paused for some time and then quipped: "The world is round, Edwin, and if they march on fast enough they will definitely come back to the spot where they started, and so witness the burning without using mirrors". We both laughed; and I ended by saying that I hoped God would allow us enough time to realise who was right or wrong among us. Both Nyerere and Jamal are no more, but they did live to witness indications of a U-turn with the promulgation of the Zanzibar Declaration and the initial implementation of the Structural Adjustment Programmes from 1986 onwards. It is a pity for Tanzanians that the U-turn has been so haphazard, unleashing a pent-up craving for wealth on the part of Nyerere's successors and supporters, leading to rampant corruption.

As the demonstrations continued, a number of foreign media reporters came to see me, either at my home or when I happened to be in Dar es Salaam. I was determined to avoid any confrontation with the authorities, but even if I refused to answer a question, the publication of 'no reply' could imply anything a reporter wanted to write. I remember the Editor of "The Africa Confidential", a biweekly bulletin published in London, coming to interview me and being very insistent on writing about my last encounters with the President. David Martin, who had left "The Daily News", also came to see me and I was only able to talk briefly with him. The East African Standard of Nairobi even had a news item published on its front page, announcing that I had been arrested and detained by the Government. The newspaper alleged that I was popular with the Tanzania People's Defence Forces, and so I had been detained under the Preventive Detention Act as there was some restlessness in the army. This was shocking news to me and arose purely out of their imagination.

A friend in Nairobi telephoned me and read the paper to me the very morning it was published. He was, of course, checking if the story were true. When I later contacted the Editor of The Standard to enquire how he could have published such a serious allegation without verifying its authenticity, he apologised, but added that it was done without malice and with good intention. He explained that if it had been true, my friends and other well-wishers would have intervened for my release. I told him that I found his explanation totally ridiculous since he himself could be reported as detained so that, if true, he would be swiftly released by his friends intervening!

This 'news' item was soon afterwards published by a Tanzanian English daily newspaper in a popular column called "What They Say About Us". As this was embarrassing both to the Government and myself, I consulted my lawyer and we agreed that the East African Standard should be sued for libel. However, after they published an apology, an agreement was reached to drop the court case, and I was paid damages and awarded costs.

I should mention that about this time, I became increasingly aware of the fact that many of the senior Government officials, including ministers, who were visiting me as friends at my farm, were assessing my views and plans and were meticulously reporting back to their superiors in Dar es Salaam. A great friend and an admirer of my stance on national issues, who happened to hold a senior position in the National Security Service, sent an emissary and warned me that I should be very cautious. He said that my visitors could, wittingly or unwittingly, misreport what I said to them and that under the current law, my freedom could be in jeopardy. With that warning, I might have become somewhat circumspect; but I think I maintained my frank and dispassionate assessment of issues throughout this uneasy period.

About September 1980, the Government asked me to be Chairman of the Board of Directors of the Tanganyika Development Finance Company Limited. TDFL was a joint venture, owned by the Governments of Tanzania and those of the United Kingdom, Federal Republic of Germany and the Netherlands. I accepted the appointment. So after only about ten months, I was again contributing, albeit modestly, by way of ideas about the financing of development in my country.

Without a pension worth the name (my pension for government services rendered until I retired in 1966 as Principal Secretary to the Treasury was a mere TShs. 480.00 per month i.e. 24.00 Pounds Sterling), and an uncertain income as a coffee farmer, we had to live modestly. My wife had a chicken run in Dar es Salaam, which she had transferred to Ogaden. I also embarked on a joint business venture with some friends, but with this I could expect only Directors' fees or dividends at the end of the trading year, since I was basically a "sleeping" partner. We had five children to educate, three of them boarding in secondary schools. As I said above, I was lucky to have the credit facilities through TCGA to run the farm and we carried on praying that the harvest would produce enough surplus to enable us to feel more comfortable financially.

The year 1981/82 produced a bumper crop, and coffee prices were reasonably good. I was able to repay the input and harvest credits and remained with enough money to liquidate a loan I had secured for the purchase of an Isuzu lorry. We obtained the services of a good lorry driver, who not only brought the coffee pickers to ensure the bumper crop was properly brought in for timely processing, but was also hired to transport produce from as far as Mang'ola in Karatu District and Babati. During this time I visited Dar es Salaam frequently in my capacity as chairman of TDFL Board of Directors and sometimes as a Board Member of the Coffee Authority of Tanzania. In this way I believe I avoided the possibility of 'rusting".

I should also mention that, probably because of the views I was known to hold, a number of the Word Bank and IMF staff who visited Arusha wrote or telephoned to ask for interview with me. These included Executive Directors like Timothy Thahane of the World Bank and Semyano Kiyingi of IMF. (Timothy Thahane was subsequently appointed to the staff of the World Bank as Vice-President and Secretary to the Executive Board. On retiring from the Bank he was for a period Deputy Governor of the Reserve Bank of South Africa, before becoming Minister of Finance in his native Lesotho.) I had known these two personalities during my tenure as Minister, when I served as Governor of the IMF and World Bank for Tanzania. Indeed, it was they who had brought forward my name for the proposal at the Belgrade Annual Meetings for Tanzania to be elected Chair of the Boards of Governors for 1979/80 fiscal year. Little did I realise that these contacts would soon lead to my career as a farmer being interrupted for four years.

Chapter 20

Appointment to the Executive Board of the IMF

The Executive Board of the International Monetary Fund at this time was made up of twenty Executive Directors. Each of the seven Members with the largest votes appointed an Executive Director. The other countries grouped themselves into thirteen constituencies, each electing one Executive Director. The English-speaking African countries, excluding Ghana and South Africa, but including Guinea Conakry, Rwanda and Burundi, formed the constituency to which Tanzania belonged. Each of the Executive Directors had an Alternate Executive Director who attended all Board meetings, and participated but voted only when the substantive Executive Director was not present. Our constituency had an arrangement whereby each Member in turn provided a candidate, who served first as an Alternate Executive director for two years, after which he was elected Executive Director for another two years. It happened that in October 1982 it was Tanzania's turn to propose a candidate for Alternate Executive Director, and my name was put forward by the Government and accepted by the Governors of the Constituency.

Before the Annual Meetings of the Boards of Governors, the Prime Minister, Mr Cleopa Msuya, had telephoned me to enquire whether I would be interested in the appointment. Apparently, some very senior officials in the financial sector in Tanzania had expressed their interest to be considered for this assignment, and the President felt that my taking it would save him looking for a replacement. In view of the current economic situation, and the problems relating to the education of our children, this offer came as a godsend and a great relief to my family, and I readily accepted. By the end of October, I had arranged for the proper management of Ogaden Estate, as well as all the visas and the transfer of the children from their respective educational institutions. In order to report for duty on 1 November, I left a few matters to be completed by my wife. I expected the family to join me by the end of November, by which time I hoped I would have fixed up the necessary accommodation.

The family joined me at the beginning of December, and we moved into a house in Bethesda, Maryland on the outskirts of Washington D.C. On the advice of Daudi Ballali, my friend and former staff of the Bank of Tanzania who was then a staff member of IMF, I had purchased the house with a mortgage arrangement facilitated by an advance of salary from my new employers, and a loan I arranged with an insurance company. Regarding the family, Nora, our eldest daughter had just been admitted as an undergraduate at the University of Dar es Salaam, and I was able to arrange for her to transfer to Carlton University in Ottawa so that she could be near. Lillian had completed her secondary schooling and qualified for admission into Maryland University, College Park Campus, as a day student. The boys, Mashinda and Melyi, went to a neighbouring High School, Walter Johnson's; and our little girl, Kineneko, was admitted to the Ashburton Elementary School, next door to our newly acquired house.

Joining the Executive Board of the International Monetary Fund was an exhilarating learning experience. The economy of every member country of the Fund is analysed by the staff each year, and a report written for consideration by the Board. This report analyses the impact of the economic, financial and payments policies pursued by the Member's government on the domestic as well as the external economic environment. The Executive Board deliberates the Reports and makes decisions, which are passed on to Members as advice regarding how matters can be improved, for better performance or to minimise adverse impacts on other economies. Many countries, I discovered, treated the discussions by the Board very seriously and sent senior officers to listen to the Board's deliberations and/or answer questions.

Executive Directors or their Alternates representing member countries whose reports were under discussion, were the spokesmen for those countries during such debates. In cases where Members were using or requesting to use resources of the Fund, the staff prepared special reports making proposals regarding the conditions under which the resources would be drawn down and repaid. These reports spelt out the so-called "'conditionalities" for specific members to access Fund facilities, and it was indeed on such conditionalities that I had differed in November 1979 with my boss, the President, leading to my resignation as Minister for Finance and Planning.

Sitting on the Executive Board enables one to observe the good performance of Members, as well as those of the unsatisfactory performers. It was during this period that many developing member countries of the Fund began to accumulate large overdue debts, to commercial creditors as well as to bilateral and multilateral lenders. Many of the countries in our constituency were either already heavily indebted to the Fund, or needed to negotiate with it in order to obtain credits to finance their balance-of-payments deficits. From the date I joined the Fund, I found myself making trips to Africa almost every other month in order to consult with these members on such matters.

Initially, I was Alternate Executive Director to N'Faly Sangare, a national of Guinea Conakry, and we made arrangements so that when he was away in Africa consulting, I would be in Washington in order that I could participate in Board discussions, and where necessary present papers concerning our Members. Similarly, if I was absent from Washington, he would almost invariably be available, so that our constituency was always represented by one of us at every meeting. The Executive Board met at least once every week, normally on a Wednesday.

I should recall that once, when there was a change of regime in Guinea Conakry, N'Faly Sangare went home for official consultation. The new regime, however, would not let him return to Washington as scheduled. We were unable to establish contact with him for about a fortnight and the Guinea Embassy in Washington was unwilling to reveal or explain what was going on. We therefore became very concerned. After I consulted with the Managing Director, the IMF formally intervened and the Guinean authorities allowed Mr Sangare to return to Washington to resume his duties. His term as Executive Director expired at the end of October, and I took over formally from him in November 1984. My Alternate then was Ahmed Abdallah, a Kenyan national, whom I had known for many years, especially as Deputy Governor of the Central Bank of Kenya.

The IMF and its sister institution, the World Bank, have assembled probably the most highly respected groups of professional economists anywhere in the world. Their analyses and assessment of economic and financial issues and problems, and proposals for solutions, are taken seriously by many authorities. They participate in numerous economic forums, national as well as international, and produce analytical and policy proposal papers on all sorts of subjects relating to economic and financial development. Many Executive Directors attend such meetings and conferences, where papers are presented by the staff, and I found myself at many of these gatherings, intervening wherever possible to give a political or social touch in the proposals for solutions, especially where they related to countries in our constituency.

Every third year, the IMF and the World Bank Boards of Governors Annual Meetings are held outside Washington. The Annual Meetings of 1984 were held in Seoul, Republic of Korea. I arranged to travel to Seoul a little early, via San Francisco, Honolulu and Tokyo, so that I could relax a little and see these places. San Francisco, Honolulu and Japan were much as I had expected, but I was highly impressed by what South Korea had achieved in recent years. The annual meetings were uneventful, and my appointment as Executive Director was formally approved by the Governors of my constituency. After the Meetings, I travelled back to Washington via Hong Kong, Singapore, Bombay, Dubai and Nairobi. I had not been in Singapore since my study tour of 1961 and so noticed the extraordinary progress made by that city-state in those twenty-five years. It was with this trip that I was able to satisfy my ambitions as a globetrotter.

From Nairobi, I was able cross the border to see how our farm was being managed, and visit a number of friends and relatives. I spent a few days discussing the rehabilitation and remodelling of our farmhouse, before leaving for Washington.

As far as my own country, Tanzania, was concerned, my assignment to the Fund enabled me to follow very intimately its financial and economic developments and the policy decisions pertaining to those developments. For four years, from November 1982 to November 1986, I was in Dar es Salaam almost every other month. I would either visit alone, or with a Mission from the Fund. Whether as Executive Director or Alternate, I had access to the highest ranking decision-makers including Presidents, Prime Ministers, Ministers of Finance and their Permanent Secretaries, or Chief Economic Advisers; as well as the Governor of the Bank of Tanzania and his senior advisors. All of them knew me well, and I could discuss and argue with them boldly and dispassionately regarding the policies they were pursuing, revealing to them my views and the attitude of the Fund towards these policies and the performance of other countries.

I recall a visit I made to Tanzania a few months after the Economic Crimes and Sabotage Act was passed. Parliament was in session, and I had to go to Dodoma to meet the Minister of Finance. After discussion with the Minister, I went for an audience I had sought with the Prime Minister, Hon. Edward Moringe Sokoine. As there was not much time, he invited me for lunch at his official residence so that we could have a discussion during the afternoon break of Parliament. Edward had been Prime Minister during my tenure as Minister, but had gone abroad briefly for studies soon after I left the Treasury. He had been re-appointed Prime Minister on his return. He was a very dedicated, patriotic politician and was genuinely committed to tackling the poverty and other social problems confronting the people he was participating in leading. One could see in him a passion for finding solutions and he listened very carefully to advice, taking notes and seeking clarification if necessary.

During my discussion with Edward during that luncheon, I did not mince my words regarding my views on the policies being pursued by the Government. I was particularly concerned regarding the Exchange Rate policy. I pointed out that as a result of the over-valuation of the Tanzania Shilling, production for exports had severely suffered, and our lack of earned foreign exchange had starved our market of imported goods, including essential raw materials and spare parts. Strengthened by my stay at the IMF and my contacts with other African Governments for the previous fifteen months, I talked confidently. I explained that the inflation caused by the fiscal deficits and the huge government borrowing from the central bank meant that people had a substantial amount of money in an environment of extreme scarcity of goods. I pointed out that most of the parastatal corporations borrowing from the National Bank of Commerce were running at such large losses that they would be unable to repay the Bank, and so make it insolvent. Prices were bound to continue to sky-rocket, whatever control measures the Government imposed. In a situation of runaway inflation, as the country was currently experiencing, individuals inevitably hoarded goods since these were liable to become unaffordable as time passes. Similarly, traders hoarded stocks in order to make windfall profits by postponing their sale.

I joked with him that if he were free to window-shop in Independence Avenue (now renamed "Samora Machel Avenue"), and he chanced to notice a Transistor Radio displayed, he would probably walk into the shop and buy it, in spite of the fact that he had several already at home. Thus he himself would be "hoarding", and in breach of the recently passed legislation. I explained that because of the inflation, people with money tended to avoid banking their earnings and cramped their residences with furniture and other equipment they did not immediately need. I noticed that he was nodding and looking at his own sitting room which was rather overcrowded with sofa sets.

When he asked what I thought the solution might be, I replied candidly that the answer lay in removing the causes of the escalating prices by ensuring that production in agriculture and industry was substantially increased, so that goods would be available in the shops. We had to have enough foreign exchange to import essential goods as raw materials and for consumption. Production for export in order to earn foreign exchange was diminishing because exporters were unable to make a profit while the TSh was so highly overvalued. In addition, the non-performing parastatals that were siphoning huge subsidies from the Treasury and overdrafts from the NBC must either be wound up or sold to people capable of rehabilitating them. I capped my advice by pointing out that Government was itself too large for Tanzania's current resources, and that some posts had to be abolished and staff redeployed.

I had talked so much that I had almost ignored the food. The Prime Minister took notes as he asked for clarifications. At the end, I felt that I had delivered the message to the right person. He said he would discuss my points with the Finance Minister and others in the Government, and that definitely they would be in touch with me and the Fund to see how the deep problems of Tanzania could be solved.

I thanked the Prime Minister for his hospitality and for the audience, and left to fly to Dar es Salaam from where I caught a plane for Lusaka, Zambia. In Lusaka I had interviews with senior officials in the Ministry of Finance and the Bank of Zambia, who were actively pursuing negotiations with the Fund. The negotiations went well, and President Kenneth Kaunda even invited us to have breakfast with him at State House so that he could be fully briefed regarding the Fund proposals.

The economic and financial situation in Zambia was also bad, but the authorities were flexible and willing to discuss with the Fund, unlike their counterparts in Tanzania. President Kaunda knew me from earlier visits; especially those connected with TAZARA, and enquired whether I had seen his friend, President Nyerere, when I was last in Dar. I replied I had not, but that I would go through Dar es Salaam on my way back to Washington and would try to see him then. He remarked that they both had problems in managing their economies when commodity prices had fallen in the world market, and asked me to tell him he wished him well. I thanked him and said I would do so.

I was able to see President Nyerere in Dar es Salaam on my way back to Washington. I found that Parliament had ended its session in Dodoma and that the Prime Minister had already talked with the President about matters touched upon in our luncheon conversation. President Nyerere's first remark after welcoming me to sit was: 'Edwin, I understand from Edward that you consider that all of us are guilty of hoarding'.

I was taken aback a little. But I replied slowly by saying, 'Well, Mwalimu, I have been to several homes of my friends here in Dar es Salaam, and the impression one gets is that they have rather an excess of movable assets like furniture and similar equipment in those houses. Of course, those without money have barely anything to hoard'. He was nodding his head, and I went on to say that I fully understood the predicament of those hoarders, since money left in bank deposits was losing value everyday and whenever they could buy something which did not lose value, they did so. He continued to nod and I added that since prices were rising because of the shortage of goods, even shopkeepers would try to hoard whatever goods they were able to procure. This was not only for their own personal consumption in an unpredictable market, but also so that they might make windfall profits when they later slowly released them for sale.

He asked me what I thought the solution was. Again I was very candid in my reply, and repeated what I had said during my discussion with the Prime Minister. I stressed that the long-term solution lay in ensuring that our exports grew in volume and value in order to import what was required, including the necessary raw materials and spare parts for our factories. In the medium or short term, we had to secure financing to facilitate the bridging of the gap between our meagre foreign exchange and the value of urgent requirements. I ended by saying that producers for export must find it profitable to continue producing, and our exports have to be competitive. Therefore, I saw no alternative to making the necessary adjustment to the exchange rate for the Shilling. In addition, I said that the Government must ensure that the publicly owned corporations operated profitably, because to finance them from Treasury subsidies or from bank overdrafts which might not be repaid, was unsustainable.

I knew that I was touching a raw nerve of the President. But he sighed and after a moment I was surprised when he reacted by saying, "Well, Edwin it is more than four and a half years since you and I last discussed this subject. My advisors have now convinced me that the exchange rate must be used as a tool for managing the economy. There are, however, so many other things that have to be done that it appears we will take some time before we reach agreement with you fellows in Washington". I said that it was good to hear him talk about the exchange rate being a tool. I added that it was also true that many other decisions had to be made to accompany any exchange rate change. Some of those decisions would require study and might take place after we would be able to inject resources into the system to relieve the current shortage of commodities in the market. An early decision on the exchange rate to facilitate such an injection of resources might therefore be advisable. He kept nodding as I talked. Before I left, I told him that President Kaunda had asked me to pass on his good wishes; and we briefly discussed the tentative agreement the Fund Mission had reached with the Zambian authorities.

I did not realise that the President's remarks signified a fundamental shift in his policy until I was back in my hotel room scribbling notes regarding the interview for follow- up when back in my office in Washington. However, after a few weeks, I got news from Tanzania that the Prime Minister had given instructions that parastatal firms were to use their staff buses to carry public passengers, when they were not required to carry their own workerforce. This was a most welcome decision and would ease the transport bottle-necks in the city of Dar es Salaam. Public transport in the city had been severely strangled by the fact that most of the buses owned by the state-owned monopolist transport company were unserviceable due to the lack of spare parts. Tragically, soon afterwards, Edward Sokoine was involved in a fatal road accident and this new trend of bold pragmatism stalled.

In line with the new pragmatic approach, however, President Nyerere was quoted in *The Daily News* with the remark that he was 'not wedded to no devaluation' and that the Exchange Rate must be used 'as a tool for managing the economy'! These may appear innocuous statements, but the Fund management and staff at this period were very sensitive to what was happening in Tanzania, and used to bring to my attention anything that appeared to indicate a softening of attitude. Because of this statement, the Managing Director asked whether I could arrange to return to Dar es Salaam for more consultations. I did so and I found Mr Msuya, the newly reappointed Minister for Finance, very keen to resume negotiations with the Fund. After discussion, we agreed that on my return to Washington I would write him a full brief on what I thought a Structural Adjustment Programme would entail. This would cover the minimum prior actions that had to be taken by the Government, and the likely resources that would be made available by the Fund.

I knew that these resources would be related to Tanzania's current Quota in the Fund, which was somewhat modest. But I stressed to Mr Msuya that resources from the Fund would open up channels for flows from the World Bank, and many other bilateral donors who were anxious to assist Tanzania once an agreement was reached with the IMF. Mr Msuya was aware of the tentative offers made by donors who predicated their assistance on Tanzania concluding an agreement with the Fund. I therefore left Dar es Salaam with the understanding that I would arrange for the IMF staff to start preparing a draft for a Structural Adjustment Programme (SAP) for Tanzania. I knew that this had to be preceded by a Mission to carry out an in-depth study of the current under-lying economic and financial situation.

1985 was an election year for Tanzania, and the discussions and negotiations for a SAP with the Fund had to be conducted within that environment. Early in the first quarter of that year, President Nyerere had announced that he would not run for re-election, although some prominent Tanzanians for various reasons were campaigning and urging him to do so. In my case, I was preoccupied with developing a SAP which would be workable and beneficial to my country in the long-run. I believed that President Nyerere had such prestige in the country and was so lucid and persuasive in explaining issues once he was convinced, that I felt he was the right person to be in charge when the country was accepting such a programme. I feared that a successor might be unable to explain Tanzania's U-turn on policies Nyerere had so categorically and eloquently opposed. A hesitant successor, in my assessment, might therefore delay the reaching of an agreement. On this basis, I actually found myself joining the group of people trying to argue with Mwalimu that he should indeed run for the presidency in 1985. I talked with him on the subject when I called on him in March. I reasoned that he was the only person who could accept and fully explain the proposed SAP agreement to the people of Tanzania, having regard to the stands he had taken earlier. He brushed my argument aside, and told me that he did not see why agreement could not be reached before October.

In the end, of course, Tanzania was unable to reach an agreement with the Fund in 1985. Few of President Nyerere's advisors either saw the logic of accepting the agreement or had the courage to confront him with the points contained in the proposed agreement, which they thought were still anathema to him. So, in spite of the fact that I spent most of 1985 shuttling between Dar es Salaam and Washington, the negotiations did not materialise into concrete and mutually acceptable proposals. And as the delay in reaching an agreement persisted, the economic difficulties in the country intensified.

President Ali Hassan Mwinyi took over in November 1985. He found discussions still going on with the Fund. I believe he was much more conscious of the plight of the people, in terms of their suffering from the scarcity of goods and difficulties in transportation and other essential services. Immediately on taking over, for example, he directed that an oil tanker carrying crude oil that was docked in Dar es Salaam harbour should discharge her cargo to enable the refinery to restart operations and process it, thus relieving the oil shortage in the country. The ship had threatened to sail away with its cargo, as it appeared that the suppliers had not been paid for a previous delivery. To solve this problem, Mwinyi accepted an offer of credit from a German buyer of coffee (Bernhardt Rothfoss) in order to pay for the oil consignment. The German agreed that he would be repaid by the proceeds of coffee, which would be harvested, processed and delivered to him, later in that coffee season. Although this arrangement interfered to some extent with the normal operations of the international coffee auctions at Moshi, it was worthwhile, since the immediate availability of oil in the country eased the transport bottlenecks and enabled factories to start functioning again.

The enhanced pragmatism displayed by the new government gave me a lot of reasons for optimism. By the end of May 1986 it was possible to present an agreed programme to the IMF Executive Board of Directors. The Government agreed to devalue the Tanzania Shilling to TShs. 47.00 = US$ 1.00. The Fund had been pressing for a larger devaluation, but I argued with the staff and my colleagues on the Board, that this would be only the beginning, and that further steps would be taken once the benefits started to be felt. I feared that a too radical devaluation might trigger a reaction from retired President Nyerere to oppose it. He was still very powerful as Chairman of CCM, the ruling party.

Subsequent devaluations of the Tanzania Shilling are a matter of history. Currently, it stands at TShs 1,250 = US$ 1.00, a rate which I find very difficult to defend, in spite of the stand I took in the mid-1980s. Other steps taken within the context of reform, although not exactly of the magnitude that precipitated my resignation in November 1979, have generally been in the same direction. For instance, most of the public corporations have been privatised, others wound up or retained as joint ventures with the private sector. The dependence of Government on bank financing has been considerably scaled down with financial intermediation improved following the opening up.

It is significant to state that I had opportunity in August 1992, when launching Chama cha Demokrasia na Maendeleo (CHADEMA) "The Party for Democracy and Development", to publicly explain why the IMF agreed measures failed to produce instant success in Tanzania. I explained that at that time Tanzania was like a sick man who refused to take medicines prescribed by his doctor until he fell into a coma. Fortunately, countries do not die, but Tanzania was now in the intensive care unit (ICU) of the economic hospital. Although the patient had been in coma and in the hospital's ICU since 1986, he was still being attended by the same nurses and general medical practitioners, who, like the sick man, did not have full confidence in themselves or in the consultant doctor or in his prescriptions.

I went on to say that Tanzania would continue to be in the ICU until we were able to trust consultant doctors and new nurses. I was, of course, campaigning for my party. CHADEMA was the consultant doctor, conceived to adopt market economy forces and to approach national issues in an objective, scientific and pragmatic manner; maximising the use of local resources, including our own talent, and purging the country of corrupt elements. Looking at the situation as it is in 2007, as I write, I am afraid my predictions were correct.

We have not made much headway in poverty eradication, although the exploitation of natural resources, the building of some new infrastructures and facilation of more tourism have added to growth somewhat. The wholesale divestiture of the post Arusha Declaration public corporations and many of the preceding ones, in the spirit of implementing the SAP has been haphazard and extremely costly to Tanzania.

As implied in this narrative, Tanzania having found herself in the economic and financial crisis of the mid-1980s, had no option but to accept the terms that the SAP demanded in order for her to access and utilize the resources that IMF, the Word Bank and other donors offered. But in order to reach the intended goals, we ought to have had our own serious experts capable of following up implementation. Such experts would be arguing continuously with these "donors" for necessary amendments or changes to suit our environment and any evolving problems. Indeed we ought to have involved our own experts more intimately in the actual preparation of the programme. Properly trained, committed and patriotic staff, adequately remunarated should have been assigned to examine each project or corporation for financing or for restructuring, including those for winding up so that we would minimize losses and maximize benefits to ourselves. My rating for Mwalimu Nyerere was that he would have been the best leader to accept the U turn that was implied in the SAP.

I apologise to the reader for jumping to examining events and the situaion, almost nineteen years after the Structural Adjustment Programme was initially launched. But I believe that what is happening now is the result of entrusting responsibilities to people who are not sure of their roles or who are more preoccupied with their individual concerns.

After the Executive Board gave formal approval for the SAP, and Tanzania started to draw resources from the Fund and the World Bank, I felt a great relief that the direction of development in my country would proceed in a more realistic and pragmatic manner. After this, I was able to devote my time to my role as Executive Director without too many parochial or nationalist distractions.

The following months were spent in preparation for the Annual Meetings of the Board of Governors, after which my term would expire. I therefore also started to prepare to wind up my affairs in Washington, focusing especially on arrangements to continue the education of our two sons, who were undergraduates at the University of Maryland, College Park Campus. Nora had married late in 1984, and was completing her studies together with her husband at Carlton University in Canada. Lillian had returned to Tanzania in 1985 and was at the Medical School of the University of Dar es Salaam, studying to be a doctor. Our little Kine would return with us to Tanzania, as she still had to complete her secondary schooling.

There was no problem in selling the house I had acquired on mortgage, as demand for real estate, especially residential properties, during that season was high. We were lucky to get a buyer who paid a price good enough to enable us to discharge the mortgage, with a worthwhile sum left over.

As Executive Director: leading an IMF Delegation to the ECA Ministerial Meeting, Addis Ababa, 1985.

The Annual Meetings had been uneventful as far as I was concerned, and at the end of October 1986, I handed over to Ahmed Abdallah. On our way back home, we spent a week in London with my brother-in-law, Colonel Geoffrey Marealle, who was serving as Military attache at the Tanzania High Commission. We were glad to resume life as farmers at Ogaden Estate in the second week of November.

Chapter 21

Mixing Farming with Public Service

Adjusting to the normal life of a farmer after four years in metropolitan Washington, brushing shoulders with personalities in high finance and international payment systems was a little awkward for me. As I said earlier, we had arranged for substantial renovations to our farmhouse during our last two years of our absence, and following its refurbishment and the arrival of our furniture and equipment from Washington about the second week of December, I started to consider other possible avenues of activity.

I made several trips to Dar es Salaam and Nairobi, where I met a number of old friends and acquaintances. I rented offices in the Arusha International Conference Centre, which we had built when I was Secretary General of the EAC, and tried to set up as a Financial and Business Consultancy. A few large companies offered me directorships on their boards. These only paid out-of-pocket expenses during board meetings, plus directors' fees at the end of the trading year; they met very infrequently, thus providing very little intellectual challenge. In the end, I declined offers of directorships when I discovered that my name was being used to drum up official support where it would not otherwise be forthcoming.

I tried to be more active in the building and contracting company I had jointly founded with friends, in 1976, when I was Secretary General of the EAC. Being neither an architect nor an engineer, I sometimes felt my fellow directors on the company's board considered my high finance queries about their activities irritating. In any case, the building industry was operating very sluggishly during this period and clients often failed to meet their contractual obligations to enable us complete projects on schedule. I should, however, stress that these efforts were made to keep me active rather than to earn a living. We have always pursued, as a family, a life of moderation and with the income from our farm and the IMF pension I started drawing when I turned 55, we were able to pay for the education of the children without worrying about money.

I should mention that immediately after I had returned to Tanzania, I had gone for formal debriefing with the President, the Prime Minister and the Minister for Finance. I think it was because of this trip to Dar es Salaam that a few months later I was approached to take over again as Chairman of the Board of Directors of the Tanganyika Development Finance Company Limited (TDFL). This appointment made it possible for me to fly to Dar es Salaam frequently on TDFL business, and it was on these occasions that I also took the opportunity to pursue some of the tasks described above. I was also able to follow up fairly closely, on the implementation of the SAP.

In December 1987 the Tanganyika Coffee Growers' Association re-elected me as Chairman for the same reasons they had done so in 1981. This enabled me to return to the boards of directors of the Coffee Board and the Tanganyika Coffee Curing Company. I have subsequently been very active in coffee sub-sector forums. Indeed, since 2001 I have served as chairman of the Board of Directors of the Tanzania Coffee Research Institute, which is currently spear-heading a national scientific renovation and rehabilitation of the industry, geared towards addressing the most urgent needs and demands of stakeholders in the industry, as identified by themselves. The development and distribution of new coffee hybrid varieties has been a major pre-occupation if the Institute's board during this time.

During my various assignments, I had made useful contacts not only in Tanzania and within East Africa, but also throughout Africa, especially during my time as Executive Director of the International Monetary Fund. Because of this, I have found myself being invited to a number of forums discussing social, political and economic developments in Africa. Of special mention were those initiated by the Africa Leadership Forum (ALF), then led by General Olusegun Obasanjo, who had distinguished himself by relinquishing voluntarily the presidency of Nigeria to a civilian president. After attending several of these ALF conferences, I was co-opted as the Tanzania Representative on to the Steering Committee of the Forum.

The ALF conferences and symposia at this time mainly discussed sustainable development, and the problems of corruption and good governance in Africa. I was able to act partly as host when the venues for these gatherings were held in

Tanzania. General Obasanjo visited our farm at Ogaden Estate when he was attending one of these conferences, and we were able to entertain him with a Chagga dish. This was just before he decided to re-enter Nigerian politics. His party subsequently won the General Election, enabling him to become a civilian president of Nigeria for two consecutive terms.

Playing host to General Olusegun Obasanjo on his visit to Tanzania as Chair of the Africa Leadership Forum.

In pursuance of the undertaking to implement structural reform of the economic and financial system implied in the 1986 SAP and its successors, the Government of Tanzania set up, in July 1988, a Presidential Commission of Enquiry into the Monetary and Banking System. The Commission was to be chaired by the Governor of the Bank of Tanzania, Mr Charles Nyirabu, and I accepted an invitation to serve as one of its sixteen Members. These Members included another ex-Minister, former Deputy Ministers, the Permanent Secretaries to the Ministries of Finance of the Union Government and Zanzibar, prominent businessmen, and senior managers of public corporations. Its terms of reference were wide-ranging and covered the reform of the whole financial and monetary sector.

In the second half of 1989, whilst I was still participating as a Member of this Commission, the Government set up another one: the Presidential Commission of Enquiry into Public

Revenues, Taxation and Expenditure; and I was asked to be its chairman. This was a Commission with twenty Members. But the remarkable aspect of its membership was the number of ex-Cabinet Ministers on it —seven of them. There were also four serving Permanent Secretaries, one former Deputy Minister, two serving Members of Parliament, three tax experts from the University of Dar es Salaam, an expert on local government financing, a prominent co-operator and a Chief Executive Officer of a public corporation. The Honourable Members were so many that when we first assembled, one of them quipped that we were the "other Cabinet".

The Nyirabu Commission produced its final report in October 1990. As it will be recalled, its recommendations resulted in the ending of the National Bank of Commerce's monopoly of the banking business in Tanzania. The role of the Central Bank was spelt out and clarified in the anticipated environment of competitive banking. State monopolies in other financial services and insurance were reviewed, and the whole parastatal system of corporations was to be restructured. Although the subsequent handling of individual non-performing public corporations in the restructuring exercise might have left much to be desired, the basic approach recommended by the Commission was in the right direction. Government must withdraw from direct commercial enterprises except those providing essential socio-economic infrastructure; its main functions remaining to maintain law and order, engendering peace and stability, and to create the enabling environment for private sector initiative. I feel proud that I played a part in the Commission that formally and boldly incorporated this approach to national economic and social policies.

The Commission that I chaired on taxation, revenue and public expenditures approached its task in a practical way. Because of the vastness of the task before us, we knew that it would take at least two years before we would be able to submit a final report. As we wanted to influence Government policy in the field of our assignment as quickly as possible, we issued two interim reports. The first was presented in May 1990 in order to influence the 1990/91 budget. One of its recommendations was that the Threshold for Income Tax, determined arbitrarily every year by the Minister for Finance, depending on the need for revenue, should be related to the Statutory Minimum Wage. It was argued that to fix the threshold such that minimum wage earners suffered PAYE deductions was irrational, since even the Government acknowledged that the statutory minimum wage was the bare subsistence level of payment. The Government accepted the proposal.

The second major recommendation in our interim report related to the Road Toll. The Toll had been introduced two or three years before, and entailed the collection of a levy from vehicles using public roads. Since the collection points had to be constructed in order to enforce payment, only certain roads were selected for the initial imposition. From the moment the Commission was set up, it received strong representations that this tax was unfair since it affected only the users of particular roads in this vast country. Another omplaint was that it was very easy to evade the Road Toll, since the officials collecting it could let vehicles pass without paying, either because of favouritism or corruption. Those paying did not demand receipts, especially when many were in a hurry, and unscrupulous collectors started to amass wealth. The Commission noted that the Road Toll in Dar es Salaam was paid by motorists at the time they purchased fuel at petrol stations. It therefore recommended that an extra charge per litre of fuel should be imposed as Road Toll in addition to the customs or excise duty on petrol or diesel. In this way, all road users had to pay, whether they were in Dar es Salaam or any other part of the country. The Government accepted this recommendation also, and thus made savings by abandoning the construction of planned Road Toll stations and the subsequent reduction in staff costs, with effect from the new financial year 1990/91.

The single disadvantage of paying for the Road Toll through fuel levy was that it applied even to fuel not meant for motor vehicles. It would have been possible, of course, for the Government to devise mechanisms for refunding those sectors on which it did not want to impose this particular tax. Nevertheless, this tax has since become a major source of revenue in the Government Budget, and it has the advantage of being a tax that can be allocated for the specific function it is expected to finance — namely, the building and maintenance of roads. Eventually, it became the base on which the Government' road agency, TANROADS, was established.

The second Interim Report of the Commission was issued in May 1991. By this time the Commission had firmed up its views on many aspects of its terms of reference. It was therefore considered that the Government should be apprised of these views so that, if possible, the forthcoming budget due to be presented to Parliament in June would take them into account, or at least, not impose measures that would conflict with the intended recommendations. Government welcomed the second Interim Report and implemented a number of the proposals, so that the final report issued in December 1991 did not conflict with the preceding budget.

The Report of the Presidential Commission of Enquiry into Public Revenues, Taxation and Expenditures that was presented to President Ali Hassan Mwinyi on 19 December 1991 is a matter of history. It is not intended in this narrative to set out in detail what it contained. Suffice it to observe that as Chairman of the Commission, I played a major role in guiding the Members to reach those views, and participated in writing the main conclusions.

Rationalisation of tax measures, such as those in respect of the Threshold of Income Tax and the Road Toll mentioned above, was only part of the recommendations. The proposal to replace Sales Tax with Value Added Tax, and other modifications, including changes to Property Tax were also among our recommendations.. There were also proposals for the integration and co-ordination of the Revenue Departments to form an independent Tanzania Revenue Board, which eventually evolved into the Tanzania Revenue Authority. Finally, the Commission was categorical that the expenditures then being incurred on the non-performing public corporations were unsustainable, and that the Government must either let them die, sell them to the private sector, or enter into joint ventures for their rehabilitation and operation.

Looking back at what has transpired, I feel proud to have led the Commission that made suggestions, which, in the circumstances, were particularly bold, and to have played a part in laying the foundations for sound financial management in my country, in spite of the setbacks I had endured earlier.

CHAPTER 22

Multiparty Politics and Nurturing a Political Party

As the Tax Commission was giving the final touches to its Report, the Nyalali Commission, which had been appointed to study and recommend whether and how Tanzania could revert to multiparty politics, submitted its own historic report. I warmly welcomed the recommendation that the Constitution of Tanzania be amended to allow for multiparty politics.

Whilst the amendments to the Tanzania Constitution were being deliberated by the public and in Parliament, several groups emerged planning to found political parties. A number of people, who knew my stand on national issues and shared my views, discussed with me the possibility of launching a political party. I was then frequently in Dar es Salaam on Tax Commission business and we formed a group, which I chaired, to prepare aims, basic policies and a party constitution. Indeed, it is possible that I might have hastened the completion the Report of the Presidential Commission on Revenue, Taxation and Public Expenditures in order that I could participate more freely in this new, largely self-imposed task.

The discussions for the launching of our party started casually at the Legion Club, and most of the founder members were Club members. As the discussions got more serious and started to require notetaking, we shifted the venue to my hotel, and later to Geoffrey Marealle's house where I was a guest when my stay in Dar es Salaam became indefinite, and rather too costly for me on the completion of the Tax Commission work. If it was necessary to meet during the day, we used the Chairman's office in the TDFL building.

Information started to spread that I was involved in serious preparations for a political party to be launched immediately the law allowed, and I started to receive visitors. Many were current or former ministers or deputy ministers in the Government or senior functionaries of the single ruling party (Chama cha Mapinduzi). I was quite candid with them, and in many cases we discussed the possibility of their joining our party. At this time I also became aware of the fact that the National Security Service was following my movements closely, and especially trying to identify those who were visiting me – either at home in Arusha, or in my hotel if I happened to be in Dar es Salaam. This surveillance did not bother me, or any of my friends. We were determined to observe the law strictly; and we openly and candidly explained what our intentions were, even if this were a handicap to our fast growth and success.

The amendments to the Constitution and the new law relating to the launching and operation of political parties were passed by Parliament in April 1992. It was announced that the new Constitution would be operative from 1 July 1992, and that new political parties could be provisionally registered from that date.

At about this time, Edward Barongo, who had been a prominent politician since the early TANU days and had served as a Deputy Minister and Regional Commissioner during the Nyerere era, came forward and declared his intention to join us. He held bitter feelings against the CCM government, having suffered detention under the Economic Crimes and Sabotage Act, and we welcomed him. Indeed, when the day for submission of our formal application for provisional registration came, he and I were chosen by the preparatory committee as the joint signatories for that application.

Later, Edward was somewhat disappointed when he did not become Vice-Chairman at the first formal elections of office bearers for CHADEMA. But he served well as our first National Publicity Secretary. Before the 1995 General Elections, however, he resigned from CHADEMA and rejoined CCM, claiming that the party was too élitist, and falsely alleging that only university graduates were treated seriously by the leadership.

The people who came forward to discuss the possibility of launching the party were convinced that doctrinaire socialism would not work in Tanzania. We wanted to design a society in which the state would create conditions for all able-bodied citizens to apply themselves fully to earn a decent living. We would allow market forces to operate in our country, and would put in place regulations so that the exploitation of national resources would benefit all citizens, particularly indigenous ones, whilst ensuring that there were adequate incentives for foreigners with capital, including technology, to come forward and invest in Tanzania. Under this policy, which we called "Indigenisation", we agreed that it was necessary to discriminate positively in favour of the native population because they had suffered prejudice under colonialism; and it was vital to correct the imbalance as early as possible, if Tanzania were to avoid instability in the long run. We considered that the Government would have to withdraw from purely commercial activities, whilst retaining control of basic social and economic infrastructures.

We needed to think of a name for our party. In view of the recent history of the country, especially the economic hardships and the curtailment of individual freedoms entailed, some thought we should call it the Social Democratic Party. Others suggested it should be the Progressive Party of Tanzania. Another thought was that we should simply be Liberal Democrats. In the end we agreed that the name of our party should reflect democracy, both within its own structure and for the country, and development. We believed that by maximising participatory democracy in our country, we would attain genuine sustainable development by and for our people. We therefore resolved to name the party *Chama cha Demokrasia na Maendeleo*, which literally translates as "The Party for Democracy and Development" (CHADEMA).

Immediately CHADEMA was provisionally registered, we embarked on a membership recruitment drive throughout the country in order to attain the necessary legal requirements for full registration. These included a minimum of two hundred members in each of at least ten regions, two of which had to be in Zanzibar (one in Unguja and another in Pemba). A party had to satisfy these conditions within six months of the date of provisional registration; otherwise its registration would lapse.

We had no problem at all in getting two hundred members in each of the twenty regions of Tanzania Mainland, and indeed many prospective members came on their own initiative to Dar es Salaam and were duly enrolled. They were then issued with membership cards and returned up-country to enrol those in their own areas wishing to join CHADEMA. As interim Chairman, I myself toured Zanzibar and held rallies in Unguja and Pemba. Before the end of September 1992, we had the required number of party members.

In October we submitted our formal application for full registration. This had to be accompanied with lists of members in each region, showing their personal particulars and addresses so that the Registrar of Political Parties could verify their existence during visits to the respective regions. Due to the delay in verification, CHADEMA was not issued with the Certificate of permanent registration until the second half of January 1993. The Union for Multi-party Democracy (UMD) and National Coalition for Construction and Reform (NCCR) were also fully registered on the same date. The Political Parties Act had been framed in such a way that Chama cha Mapinduzi (CCM), the ruling party, did not have to be provisionally registered.

The membership recruitment drive gathered momentum after CHADEMA's permanent registration as a political party. In order to strengthen the party, we needed to mobilise resources to be able to have offices at least in all regional headquarters. As soon as possible, we wanted branches in each of the district headquarters and every ward and village, all over the country. We planned to ensure that the leaders in those up-country offices were mobile for purposes of outreach and dialogue with the people. There was a great deal of public support and we received donations of money, equipment and rental space from our members and other sympathisers. We were able to purchase a number of second-hand vehicles to enable us to travel widely in our publicity effort. In addition, many of the national and a number of regional leaders used their personal vehicles to carry out party functions. In August 1993 we held the First National Party Conference at which I was confirmed Chairman for the next five years. Similarly, the other office bearers were duly elected at the conference.

As recruitment and consolidation intensified, we started to make contact with like-minded foreign parties and institutions, and soon we were receiving invitations to visit their countries or to attend conferences and seminars relevant to our vision and declared intentions. I had ceased to perform in a paid job, but was completely engrossed in the party effort and was enjoying the assignment. I had to stay in Dar es Salaam for most of this period and Geoffrey Mareatle, who had a large residence, continued to play host to me. I accepted this because the Party could not have afforded to provide housing for me.

Campaigning with Mary Kabigi, who headed the Women's Section, to recruit members for Chadema, 1994.

The opportunity to gauge the impact of multiparty politics in Tanzania came with a bye-election in Ileje constituency late in 1993, where the incumbent Member of Parliament, who happened to be the Minister for Finance, had died. CHADEMA tried to persuade the other parties to agree to field a single candidate against that of the CCM. When we failed, we proposed to the NCCR that we would support them in Ileje if they would support us in the Kigoma-Ujiji constituency bye-election due less than two months later. The CCM candidate won at Ileje, but NCCR came second, probably because of our support.

The real test came at Kigoma-Ujiji. CHADEMA put up Dr Aman Walid Kabourou, whom we had brought back from a teaching assignment in an American university. CCM had a local trader of Asian origin, Azim Premji, as their candidate. A few other parties also put up candidates. The entire CHADEMA national leadership moved to Kigoma for the bye-election campaign, which was so intense and threatening, that CCM responded by placing all their arsenals into the fight. Their national leadership also came, including their chairman, President Ali Hassan Mwinyi, who flew into Kigoma, surprisingly in a Government aircraft. All the paraphernalia of the state were placed at the disposal of CCM in support of Premji. As a result he scraped in by a small margin of votes, but Kabourou, assisted by CHADEMA, challenged the validity of the results in the High Court. Our grounds were partly that there were irregularities in the counting of the votes and partly that government equipment and services were used in favour of Premji, contrary to the provisions of the Elections Act. We also submitted that Premji's Tanzanian citizenship had been irregularly and illegally obtained.

The High Court case dragged on for months, whilst Premji went on attending Parliament as an "elected" Member! In the end the High Court upheld Kabourou's submissions that there were unlawful uses of Government resources and facilities, and that Premji's citizenship was invalid. The High Court therefore annulled the results and ordered another bye-election. CHADEMA celebrated, confident that we would trounce them in the next round.

However, CCM, in spite of their apparent acceptance of the multiparty political system, were determined not to have an opposition MP sitting with them before the next general elections. They went to the Court of Appeal, but the date for the hearing kept being postponed for months and months, until some of the members of our Party and the public started to question the neutrality of the Appeal Court. By the time the Court of Appeal reached its verdict upholding the High Court ruling, the provisions of the Elections Act requiring that bye-elections cannot be held within six months of the next general election took effect. Kigoma-Ujiji was therefore without a representative in Parliament until after the 1995 General Elections when CHADEMA's Kabourou resoundingly defeated Azim Premji, who had in the meantime regularised his Tanzanian citizenship.

I spent the three years between 1993 and 1995 touring the whole of Tanzania. I visited all districts except Ngara, Ukerewe and Makete. In each district we were able to set up at least one or two branches of the party. Branches at the ward and village levels were established by the new leaders, elected at district level during these visits. I had been able to procure a brand new four-wheel drive Landcruiser Hardtop in June 1993 which carried me over some of the toughest roads anyone can imagine. That we were able to get through that gruelling experience without a slipped disc or serious accident was due to the care and expertise of Franco Kabigi and Teo Oswald, the dedicated drivers CHADEMA had enlisted and put at my service.

During this period I was able to visit the United Kingdom and America on CHADEMA business, where I talked with and recruited Tanzanians working or studying in those countries. I also renewed contacts with various institutions, which proved most useful in the evolution of our future relationship.

One incident that demonstrated that the CCM government was unprepared for political multipartysm was when my lifelong friend Anthony Nyakyi, our Ambassador to the United Nations, entertained me during my New York visit. Another lifelong friend, Felix Mosha, an employee of the UN was my host and Tony invited both of us for dinner at the Ambassador's residence. Apparently an embassy official thought I was *persona non grata* and reported to Dar es Salaam regarding the dinner. Strangely enough, the Ministry of Foreign Affairs, promptly recalled Anthony Nyakyi from his posting in New York.

There were a number of angry reactions in the local and international press because of this incident, sympathetic both to Nyakyi and me. Tony was a true Tanzanian patriot and an accomplished diplomat. He was soon afterwards appointed by the Secretary General of the United Nations as the UN Delegate to war-torn Liberia, where he performed a marvellous job. He also subsequently worked with Mwalimu Nyerere in the efforts to reconcile the Burundi warring political factions before he went into private business.

As chairman of CHADEMA, I was also invited several times to tour the Federal Republic of Germany and a number of other EU countries, even after the 1995 General Elections. On all these occasions we tried to avoid the Tanzanian embassies in order not to embarrass embassy staff in the manner Tony Nyakyi had suffered. It is a pity that the stance of the Ministry of Foreign Affairs' on opposition political parties can lead to our representatives abroad not being conversant with the true political climate in the country.

Chapter 23

The 1995 General Elections

The General Elections of 1995 were the first real test for multiparty democracy in Tanzania. While CHADEMA was preparing for them by consolidating our membership throughout the country, Augustine Lyatonga Mrema resigned from CCM. Mrema had been Minister for Home Affairs in the second term of President Mwinyi, and because of his tough handling of criminal elements in the country, the President had designated him Deputy Prime Minister, although this post did not actually exist in the constitution. Towards the end of President Mwinyi's tenure, Mrema, however seemed to have overreached himself in his publicity drive and the President removed him from this crucial ministry, appointing him Minister for Labour instead. Mrema's penchant for bold approach to national issues however, continued and led him to attack some government measure in Parliament. He was therefore promptly relieved of his ministerial portfolio for breaching the principle of collective cabinet responsibility. Soon after this, Mrema announced that he had resigned from CCM.

Parliament was about to be dissolved pending the elections, and Mrema, who was very popular with the masses, was being courted by a number of political parties to join them. CHADEMA sent a delegation to discuss with him the possibility of his joining us. His conditions, which he spelt out, were that CHADEMA should nominate him as the Presidential candidate for the next election, as well as appoint him national Party Chairman. The National Conference of the party had already been held and had mandated the National Executive Committee to decide on a presidential candidate in collaboration with other opposition parties willing to co-operate with CHADEMA. As for party chairmanship, our constitution specifically required that the chairman be elected by the national conference. So even if I personally had been willing to resign to make way for Mrema, logistics and cost meant it was impossible to reconvene such a conference. CHADEMA was, therefore, prepared to nominate Mrema as its presidential candidate, but not as its national Party Chairman. As a result,

Mrema decided to join NCCR, taking over from Mabere Marando as chairman, and also standing as their presidential candidate.

CHADEMA stated that it would be ready to campaign for Mrema on the understanding that together with NCCR we would form a coalition government if we won. The central committees of the two parties would sit together and determine how to apportion the constituencies to ensure that whichever of the NCCR or CHADEMA candidates were stronger would stand to challenge the CCM or other party candidates. However, as it turned out, CHADEMA appeared to have been too enthusiastic in promising to support Mrema before an agreement in writing had been thrashed out and signed.

In spite of treating Mrema as also our party's presidential candidate, CHADEMA found itself being opposed in the constituencies by NCCR candidates. The Central Committee of NCCR argued that it had no mandate from its national conference to force their -candidates not to stand against ours. With Mrema as their presidential candidate they seemed to have suddenly become confident that they would win without the support of any other party.

The campaign turned into a farce. Mrema was attracting such large crowds of unregistered unemployed youngsters, pushing his motor vehicle and women spreading their *khanga* for him to walk on, that he appeared to think he was already in State House. He started making reckless, vitriolic attacks on CCM stalwarts, threatening that if elected President he would summarily arrest some of them for crimes they had perpetrated and covered up. He brushed aside advice I gave him that he should be cautious and tone down his threats. Instead, he even stated that within twenty-one days of his entering State House, Ali Hassan Mwinyi would be in the high security prison of Ukonga, "drinking water from a '*karai*', the large metal basin used by masons for carrying concrete mix.

When Mrema and his NCCR campaign team paid a courtesy call on Mwalimu Nyerere at his Butiama residence, during their tour of the Mara Region, Mwalimu is reputed to have bluntly told them that he would never allow his country to be thrown to the dogs. Perhaps because of the reckless statements by Mrema,

Mwalimu Nyerere now fully entered the campaign in support of his favourite, Benjamin Mkapa, whom he rated as "clean and incorruptible"! One prominent CCM member recently told me that from the day I announced that my party, CHADEMA, would support Mrema, he lost confidence in me. In retrospect, I must confess that this was one of my major errors in life. But it was the majority view of CHADEMA that I was trying to respect. Perhaps I ought to have been bolder in-opposing it more vigorously.

Campaigning in the Arusha Urban Constituency for a Parliamentary seat, October, 1995.

The results of the Tanzania presidential and parliamentary elections of 1995 are now a matter of history. Benjamin Mkapa won the presidency, and Augustine Mrema came second. In the parliamentary votes, CHADEMA, which prior to Mrema entering the scene had been rated as the second largest party after CCM, came third after NCCR. I myself had stood for the parliamentary seat of the Arusha Urban constituency. As I said earlier, in spite of my party pledging full support for Mrema throughout the whole country, he decided to sponsor Makongoro Nyerere to stand against me. Makongoro had caused a national stir by resigning from his father's party (CCM), and people were curious to hear what he would say. In my naïve enthusiasm for NCCR, and my belief in the need for the smaller parties to unite, I had even partly financed the public address system for their Arusha district office. At the time, of course, I was expecting them to use it to campaign for me, whilst Makongoro would continue to be in Mrema's national campaign team. However, on obtaining the backing of Mrema, Makongoro returned to the Arusha Urban constituency to campaign on an NCCR ticket, and won the seat. I came third, after the CCM candidate, another Mrema (Felix).

After the 1995 elections, I concentrated as Chairman on trying to build up the party. However, I was by then 63 years old, and felt that younger blood would be more suitable for the gruelling journeys up-country. I was, therefore, determined that at the end of my term as chairman in 1998, a younger CHADEMA member, preferably one of the elected Members of Parliament, would take up the challenge for leading a political party designed and committed to the evolution of genuine democracy and equitable, sustainable development for our country. With this in mind, I initiated an amendment to the Party's constitution to make membership of the Party's Executive Committee automatic for the few MPs who were not already members. This also made them Members of the National Governing Council, as well as Delegates to the National Conference of the Party.

Opposition Party leaders on tour in the Federal Republic of Germany.

At this time, CHADEMA had strong relations with the Liberal Party of the Federal Republic of Germany, and the Friedrich Naumann Foundation representative in Tanzania arranged several trips for our cadres, including myself, to attend seminars and tours of Germany. The Foundation also strongly supported the Association for Regional Integration for Eastern and Southern Africa (ARIESA), a local NGO dedicated to strengthening democratic evolution in this sub-region in order to facilitate genuine regional political and economic integration.

ARIESA supported many of our early efforts in civic education. Many seminars and short courses involving young CHADEMA enthusiasts and other cadres of the budding political parties were locally organised and paid for by ARIESA. Because of these activities, and the fact that we were able to maintain enthusiasm for CHADEMA in spite of the small number of MPs we had secured, the impression was gained that the leadership was receiving large donations. At one of our Governing Council meetings, there were even demands that I should list all donors from the party's inception and the type of assistance that had been granted.

I was able to explain the sources of many of the gifts and assistance we had been given as a party. However, in some cases it would have been a breach of faith and confidence to reveal the identity of the benefactors. Indeed, in some instances, I did not even myself know the names of people who had given money to CHADEMA as they insisted on strict anonymity.

I cited the example of a businessman I had found in the office of a bank manager where he had been admitted in order to count the cash he was depositing. The bank manager had found out that I was sitting in his waiting room and had asked me to go into the office, requesting the businessman to continue counting his money. I was quietly explaining to the bank manager at his desk the reason for my visit. When the businessman had finished counting and was writing the pay-in-slip, the bank manager raised his voice and asked him if he knew me. He looked at me and replied that my face was familiar, but he did not know my name. The manager explained that I had been governor of the Bank, Minister of Finance, had resigned from Nyerere's government and had now formed an opposition party. The businessman stood up and we shook hands.

I apologised to the businessman for interrupting him in his transaction at the bank, but I explained that I was trying to mobilise funds in order to purchase a new vehicle for the party. He said he had read about CHADEMA and – there and then agreed to contribute one million shillings by re-writing the bank pay-in-slip and giving the sum in cash to me. He insisted that his name should not appear in any party records, and I wrote him a receipt in the name of "Kobe". I explained that "*Kobe*" which means "'tortoise"' in Kiswahili, was a sign of good fortune in my tribal tradition, and that if one meets a tortoise when going on an errand, it portends success and good fortune. I never knew the name of that Asian businessman, although the bank manager later told me the company's name. In view of this explanation, the majority of the Governing Council members were satisfied, many noting that, in any case, the Chairman had made enormous personal sacrifices in terms of money, use of his assets, including his time, for which CHADEMA did not compensate him.

Other than the junior staff such as clerks, cashier, drivers and office attendants, all workers at CHADEMA's headquarters were volunteers and received no monthly salaries. The national chairman and all the other members of the Executive Committee who spearheaded the campaign for the recruitment of party members did so as volunteers. Initially, we travelled at our own expense,s using our personal vehicles. Later, as party funds started trickling in, we were able to get some reimbursements for hotel accommodation if we travelled up-country. On most of these journeys, however, friends put us up, or we were accommodated by new members in remote villages, who were joining the party in their masses. There were no hotels in those villages, in any case.

At party headquarters, initially we found it difficult to pay regularly the monthly wages to junior staff, due to inadequate party funds. As party chairman I would, under these circumstances, convene an emergency meeting of the Executive Committee so that those members who were able to do so could, make contributions to enable the party to pay its staff. On many occasions, when contributions from Members of the Executive Committee were not enough, the Party Treasurer, Colonel Geoffrey Marealle, and I would visit a number of friendly businessmen in town to solicit funds. It was very disheartening, therefore, to note the non-recognition of all these efforts by a number of senior members of the party, imputing in 1997 that funds had been misappropriated by the chairman. I resolved then that I would not put my name forward for re-election in 1998.

Brown Ngwilulupi had been Vice-Chairman since the inception of CHADEMA. He also was unwilling to offer himself for election to any office when the National Conference was convened. Bob Makani, who had served as Secretary General from the beginning, was elected Chairman, with the Vice-Chairmanship going to Willibroad Slaa, the MP for Karatu. Dr Aman Walid Kabourou, MP for Kigoma-Ujiji, was elected Secretary General.

Another major decision at the 1998 National Conference of CHADEMA which affected me personally was that the Party's Constitution was amended to provide for past national chairmen to be life Members of the Executive Committee (now renamed Central Committee), and therefore automatically members of the National Executive Committee and Delegates to the National Conference. Since retiring from formal office, I have therefore followed very closely activities and developments within CHADEMA. Having devoted six years of my working life in the non-remunerative service of CHADEMA, and spent a great deal of my personal fortune on it, the politics and progress of the party continues to be a major focus in this narrative of my life, even after relinquishing top leadersip role.

CHAPTER 24

Subsequent General Elections

The General Election of 2000 saw CHADEMA again trying to co-operate with other opposition political parties in order to put up a meaningful challenge to the ruling party. This time our collaboration was with the Civic United Front (CUF). CUF's Ibrahim Lipumba was the candidate we backed for the presidency, and it was further agreed that in the parliamentary and civic elections, the two parties would ensure that it was only the stronger of their two candidates who would go forward to stand in a constituency or ward to challenge the CCM or other party candidates.

However, as in 1995, very few of the contending CUF candidates agreed to observe the official party line. Each thought he was the stronger, and many exercised their constitutional rights to stand. The result was that the two parties found themselves opposing one another in most of the constituencies and wards, although they campaigned jointly for Lipumba as their presidential candidate. The opposition constituency votes were therefore split, and as a result CUF won only three seats on the Mainland, whilst CHADEMA won four. CHADEMA was able to control three local government district councils, whilst CUF won the majority of the parliamentary seats in Pemba Island. Once again, the presidential candidate we backed, Ibrahim Lipumba, came second after the incumbent CCM's Benjamin Mkapa.

At the subsequent review of CHADEMA's performance in these elections, it was clear that at each of our attempts to co-operate with other parties we had sacrificed the chance of coming second, losing the position to the party with which we had co-operated. It was further realised that there was a danger of atrophy, particularly as the official subsidy to political parties was based on the number of votes won in the election and the number of candidates who secured parliamentary seats. It was therefore resolved that whilst efforts would continue to encourage parties with a similar approach to national issues to join forces, and if possible, merge with us before the 2005 elections, CHADEMA must put up its own candidate for the presidency. In the meantime, the party should strengthen and widen its network from the grassroots level, reactivate the 1995 branches and establish as many new ones as possible, especially in the rural areas.

The publicity and membership recruitment drive that followed was spearheaded by the Members of Parliament who, by virtue of the amendments to the Party Constitution that I had initiated, were all Members of the Central Committee. At the National Conference of 2003, the most active of the MPs in this effort, Mr Freeman A. Mbowe and Dr Willibroad P. Slaa, were elected Chairman and Secretary General respectively. Dr Amani Walid Kabourou became Vice-Chairman and Mr Philemon Ndesamburo remained Chairman of Kilimanjaro Region. Together with Mrs Grace Kiwelu, who had won the parliamentary special seat for women, they covered almost the whole country and put CHADEMA firmly on the political map of Tanzania, in time for the General Election of 2005.

Preparations for the 2005 General Election were made with the aim of offering CHADEMA candidates in all wards and parliamentary constituencies. It had already been determined at the 2004 National Conference that we would field our own presidential candidate, if possible by inviting support for him from other opposition parties.

Determined to make the party as transparently democratic as possible, CHADEMA decided that the six candidates who had come forward to compete for the presidency should together tour the country to address zonal conventions of the Party. These conventions would hear them and cast votes indicating whom they would want to be their candidate. In this way CHADEMA hoped to avoid the irregularities and unethical politics—including but not limited to corruption—that had become part of Tanzania's political landscape. Many among the ruling party (CCM)'s candidates openly and liberally gave gifts in the form of party uniforms, food, alcohol and money, legally permitted under the so-called "*takrima*" (traditional hospitality), so much so that the whole country appeared to have been caught up in a frenzied fiesta with party members clad in black, yellow and green, the colours of CCM.

CHADEMA's innovation of preliminary zonal conventions proved a resounding success. The country was divided into six zones and a large number of party members assembled at each of the venues and voted for the candidates after a huge rally in which he or she would set out how they would implement the party manifesto if elected. The candidates included two women. Three of the male candidates dropped out from the contest before the final rally, so that only Mrs Anna Valerian Komu (née 'Maulida Abubakar), Mrs Chiku Abwao and Mr Freeman Mbowe appeared finally at the Special National Convention which received the Secretary General's report on the Primary Elections.

During the primaries, Freeman Mbowe had received an average of 84 per cent of the votes of the zonal party conventions,. so the Special National Conference endorsed him as CHADEMA presidential candidate. Indeed, the other two candidates voluntarily withdrew their names during the Conference, offering to campaign for him once formally nominated. Hence Mbowe was the unanimous presidential candidate for CHADEMA. The National Conference also nominated Jumbe Rajabu Jumbe as his running mate.

The Conference took place on 12 August 2005 and the formal submission of party nominations to the National Electoral Commission was set for 20 August 2005 to enable the national campaigns to begin formally the next day. The required endorsement of Mbowe and his running mate by at least two hundred and fifty registered voters from each of ten regions, including two from Zanzibar, was easily obtained in those nine days. All the other political parties had already nominated their candidates and were, for all intents and purposes, campaigning in spite of the provisions of the Elections Act which proscribed electioneering prior to nomination day, 21 August.

CCM had nominated Jakaya Mrisho Kikwete on 4 May 2005, and since that date he had been touring the country, meeting and addressing multitudes of people "to thank Members of CCM and to introduce himself to them", while asserting that he was not campaigning! The CHADEMA campaign committee determined that the formal launch its national campaign would be in the Municipality of Shinyanga on 15 September 2005. This gave me an opportunity to visit that town again after those gruelling journeys of the mid-1990s.

The launch was a marvellous performance on the part of our presidential candidate, and almost the entire population of Shinyanga Municipality came out to witness it. It began about ten in the morning, when a huge crowd gathered at Shinyanga Airport to welcome and receive the candidate flying in from Dar es Salaam. The long convoy of vehicles from the airport (which is about twelve miles from centre of town) almost came to a halt at Maganzo, seven miles from Shinyanga, when the villagers surged on to the road to have a glimpse of Freeman Mbowe.

The candidate obliged by getting out of his car to shake hands with the multitude. He and his wife, who had accompanied him, then decided to walk the remaining seven miles to town, gathering almost the entire population in a march to their hotel in the centre of Shinyanga. The rally was scheduled for two-thirty in the afternoon and the candidate had only a few minutes to clean up and sign the visitor's book at the CHADEMA regional office, before appearing at the by now tumultuous gathering, anxiously awaiting his message.

I was very excited that at last it was possible to bring forcefully to the people of Tanzania, the message of national redemption, conceived in 1992 by CHADEMA, without its being adulterated by compromises with other political parties. Our original platform and basic policies for national development as envisioned in 1992 had, of course, been partly adopted by several parties, including the ruling party, CCM, which implemented aspects of it with partial success. Events since then had, in any case, altered the political scenery somewhat. CHADEMA had subsequently modified its approach to national issues, and this was spelt out in the Party Manifesto for the period 2005-10 and elaborated by our presidential candidate at the formal launch. Freeman Mbowe articulated the CHADEMA message so succinctly and clearly that I almost shed tears with pleasure. I felt that at last we were on the brink of success.

CHADEMA presidential candidate, accompanied by his wife and two retired National Chairmen marching to the launch of the campaign on 15 September, 2005.

As retired Founder Chairman Mtei greets the multitude at the launch in Shinyanga.

After the formal launch, the candidate accompanied by his running mate continued to run intensive district by district campaigns, first starting in the Lake Zone, where his charisma and eloquence attracted huge crowds. At the end of the month CHADEMA was able to hire a helicopter, which was put at the candidate's disposal so that he could cover the whole country in the remaining thirty days of campaigning. This innovation increased the size of the crowds and Freeman Mbowe was able to address more than six rallies a day in some of the remotest areas of the country, with the new slogan *Hakuna kulala mpaka kieleweke*, meaning "no sleeping until it is understood." He visited and addressed large crowds in some areas where no presidential candidate or even a ruling president had ever visited in the forty-five years of the nation's history.

CHADEMA's was a simple and clear message: to give the people of Tanzania the courage to choose an alternative party after forty-four years of failed experiments. Freeman Mbowe argued candidly and persuasively that the CCM of Mwalimu Julius Kambarage

Nyerere had undergone complete metamorphosis, and that under Ali Hassan Mwinyi and Benjamin Mkapa it was no longer the party of the downtrodden. It was now a Party of the 'filthy rich', backed by unscrupulous, corrupt international capitalist tycoons, masquerading as pro-development envoys under the umbrella of globalisation. He quoted Nyerere and his bequeathal and writings extensively and liberally, and his sincerity touched the hearts of many Tanzanians who flocked in their thousands to his rallies to hear his message.

Freeman Mbowe, addressing the multitude at the launch of his presidencial campaign.

In a tragic turn of events, Jumbe Rajabu Jumbe, Freeman Mbowe's running mate, fell ill in the first few weeks of the campaign and had to be rushed to a hospital in Dar es Salaam for intensive care. Efforts to save his life, however, failed and he died five days before the declared official polling day of 30 October 2005.

In accordance with the provisions of the Tanzania Constitution and the Elections Act, the National Electoral Commission suspended the presidential campaigns on 27 October, and gave CHADEMA twenty-one days in which to select and submit a new name as candidate for the vice-presidency.

Mbowe continued to attract huge crowds right up to the end, seen here in Moshi.

In order to minimise costs and inconvenience to voters, the Commission also decided to postpone the polling for the parliamentary seats and the civic elections, so that all would be held on 14 December, together with the presidential poll. Although the parliamentary and civic election campaigns continued, the presidential contest in respect of all parties, did not resume until 19 November 2005, when CHADEMA was able to include Anna Valerian Komu (née Maulida Abubakar) as its candidate for the vice-presidency.

Anna Komu was a stalwart founder member of CHADEMA and had held senior positions in the party hierarchy, including serving as Party National Publicity Secretary, and rising to head the Women's Department at Headquarters. During the CHADEMA Primary Election Campaigns, as noted earlier, she had sought the presidential candidacy, and had, indeed, come second to Freeman Mbowe. Her talent for debate and lucid exposition of national issues was a real asset for CHADEMA in the final phase of the 2005 campaigns. She accompanied the Presidential candidate in some of the initial rallies after 19 November, but in many of the later meetings she stood on her own, carrying the CHADEMA flag and message to the people. A few die-hard conservative elements in Zanzibar, probably alarmed by their perception of being swept under by the CHADEMA tidal wave, tried in vain to block Anna Maulida Komu's candidacy. They protested on the grounds that she was married to a non-Zanzibari Tanzanian and that one of her parents was a Comorian. This delayed her fully-fledged entry into the campaign for a short time; but once in, her performance was superb.

In the second and final lap of the Campaign, it was again possible to place the helicopter at the disposal of the CHADEMA presidential candidate. There had been complaints by some of our parliamentary and ward candidates that CHADEMA was using excessive resources for the presidential candidate, and so denying much-needed help to them. This complaint was fanned by an exaggerated estimate of the helicopter's cost, a rumour spread by a minister who was desperately defending his parliamentary seat. CHADEMA had in any case decided to concentrate on the most promising of the constituencies, where Freeman Mbowe specifically appealed to the electorate to vote for the CHADEMA parliamentary and ward candidates if Tanzanians genuinely wanted an effective government that would genuinely care for their interest.

Nevertheless, a few of our parliamentary candidates did withdraw from the contest, protesting that they had not been given sufficient material support by the party. As one or two of them promptly joined the ruling party and started campaigning for Jakaya Kikwete, it seemed obvious that all this was part of the machinations of CCM, a party determined to cling to power by hook or by crook. Indeed, there were other allegations that offers of substantial amounts of money were being made by CCM agents to CHADEMA's candidates to withdraw from the contest, but most of our candidates persisted in fight on to the end.

So much money was spent by the ruling party on clothing almost the entire Tanzanian population in CCM colours and Jakaya Kikwete T-shirts, *khangas*, *vitenge*, as well as providing them liberally with food and drinks to ensure victory, that it began to seem futile for the other parties to remain in the race. As I have noted already, before the campaign started, the ruling party had initiated legislation to legalise the anticipated 'gifts' as traditional hospitality, christening them *takrima*, so that even if the National Electoral Commission might have considered them as corruption, they were legally silenced and unable to query the practice.

The High Court ruling that *takrima* is illegal and unconstitutional was received with great relief, although other provisions in our Constitution still make it impossible to nullify the election of a President who may have benefited from its practice. As bribery or corruption is a crime the world over whichever way it is looked at, the next question to be put on the political agenda is a call to amend the Tanzania Constitution so that the election of a President, like that of a Member of Parliament, can be challenged and annulled even if the National Electoral Commission has declared him or her elected. If it can be proven in a court of law that his or her victory was secured through corrupt and other unethical practices, then it should be annulled and a fresh election organised.

Before polling on 14 December 2005, CHADEMA faced the formidable task of identifying reliable polling agents for our candidates in every polling station. Under the CCM arrangements and practice, polling agents were paid a *per diem* allowance either by the candidate or their party, which none of the other political parties could afford. Because of this, many of the people who came forward to assist our candidates expected similar payment. As we could not afford such expenses, it was suggested that in the wards we were contesting, each of our candidates should try to get relatives and trusted friends to act as polling agents. There were, on average, around twenty-five polling stations in a ward, so a candidate should be able to find enough friends and relatives to cover them. It was assumed that these agents would not only faithfully take care of the interests of the ward candidate but also all the votes cast for the CHADEMA presidential and parliamentary candidates. As relatives and friends of the ward candidate, they would not expect too much pay. Indeed, it was assumed that the ward candidate's family would arrange for the delivery of a packed lunch and dinner to the respective agents if they were to be as vigilant as we expected them to be.

The problem that arose was how to ensure fair play where there was no CHADEMA candidate in a ward. There were also constituencies where we had no parliamentary candidates; and, worst of all, there were constituencies and wards in which CCM was unopposed, so the only contest was for the presidential candidate. In these constituencies CCM was obviously very strong and even if we had succeeded in arranging for polling agents to be at these polling stations, we knew that unruly CCM supporters would be booing and harassing them. In view of the alleged history of rigging of elections and vote-stealing in the past, the absence of any agents other than CCM's may have given the ruling party a field day. The fact that all the other political parties had competing presidential candidates, made it impossible for them to co-operate to put up a joint polling agent to watch over their interests as opposed to those of CCM.

The odds against CHADEMA and the other parties were only too obvious. Against this background of a party not fully established at grass-root level in all regions, of lack of adequate resources in terms of personnel, money and equipment; of a party not fully established at grass-roots level in all the regions; of a National Electoral Commission not much concerned in creating a level playing field; and of a ruling party, determined to hold on to power at all costs despite its claims to accepting the need for democracy, clean and above board electral processes; the odds against CHADEMA and the other parties were insurmountable.

Nevertheless, CHADEMA put up a spirited challenge right to the end, our presidential candidate pulling in huge crowds with the Party's message of *Mabadiliko ya Kweli, Uhuru wa Kweli* (Real Change, Real Freedom). He reminded Tanzanians again and again that forty-four years of leadership by the same party espousing the same policies had reduced Tanzania to a beggarly nation of destitute people. There was no hope of reviving the economy by entrusting our destiny to that same party, however eloquent the enunciation of policies by the new leaders in CCM might be, with their slogan of *Nguvu mpya, Ari mpya na Kasi mpya*. (New energy, new enthusiasm and new speed).

In spite of the postponement of the Union elections, the Zanzibar Electoral Commission had persisted in holding theirs, for the Zanzibar President and House of Representatives, on the original set date of 30 November, 2005. As in the previous two general elections, voters in Zanzibar were more or less evenly divided between CCM and CUF. However, it was evident that the security forces harassed people who appeared likely to be CUF supporters, and there were allegations of manipulation in the counting of votes after the poll was closed. Even some international observers publicly noted the irregularities after the results were announced.

Nevertheless, in Pemba CUF had a clean sweep, winning every seat in the the House of Representatives. In Unguja, CUF managed to win one seat, whilst several others were won only narrowly by CCM, after some dispute. Incumbent President Amani Abeid Karume defeated Seif Shariff Hamad of CUF by a small margin of votes that remains a matter of dispute upto now. A re-count of the votes was refused by the Zanzibar Electoral Commission and, as a result, the political impasse in Zanzibar persists. Although CUF Representatives have not boycotted sittings of the House of Representatives, their party has refused to recognise the election of Karume as President of Zanzibar! Tanzanians anxiously await the results of the apparent determination of Jakaya Kikwete, in his capacity as Union President, in tackling this seemingly intractable problem.

Casting the ballot in respect of the Union Elections on 14 December was generally uneventful. However, when it came to the counting of the votes, there were inordinate delays, especially in the constituencies where opposition candidates had posed a serious challenge to the CCM candidates. Many Returning Officers seemed unable to believe or accept that any opposition candidate could win in any ward or constituency. Many re-counts were ordered, and in numerous areas delays occurred in the delivery of ballot boxes, which raised doubts as to the neutrality of the National Electoral Commission officials.

In the Moshi Urban constituency, for example, allegations of manipulations and attempts by the NEC officials to favour the CCM candidate nearly turned into a farce; and the three-day vigil, which the CHADEMA candidate and his supporters mounted to prevent tempering with the ballot papers, almost caused a riot. In the end, Philemon Ndesamburo, of course, recaptured his seat. Similar attempts by the NEC officials in the Karatu stronghold of CHADEMA to frustrate the winning candidate, Willibrod Slaa, only highlighted the shameful efforts of a party unwilling to accept the verdict of history. The ruling party's candidate accepted defeat, but it appears that CCM cadres have fabricated stories to challenge Slaa's victory in the High Court, apparently simply to maintain the harassment and divert his efforts to work with the people of his constituency for the development and benefit of all. Fortunately the High Court dismissed this case with costs.

The absence of polling agents at many of the stations left an open field for our opponents, allowing returning officers to make declarations of victory for the ruling party that were absurd. For example, at many polling stations in Dar es Salaam, Hai, Arumeru and Shinyanga constituencies, where conspicuous supporters of Freeman Mbowe had cast their votes in his favour, the returning officers announced that he had no votes at all! If this could happen in constituencies where CCM was publicly opposed, it is not difficult to imagine that where the CCM parliamentary candidates were unopposed, the practice was probably to give 100 per cent of the votes to their candidate disregarding the usual protest vote that had been cast even during the one-party regime.

Many of us were aware of these manipulations and machinations, and took note of the bias in favour of CCM on the part of NEC officials and the extent of public corruption, as well as of the weakness in terms of resources and manpower on the part of the opposition parties. We were not, therefore, much impressed or even surprised by the so-called 'landslide' victory of 80 per cent on the part of their candidate. Neither did we take too seriously the fact that CUF had won no constituency seat on the Mainland even though it had obtained 11 per cent of the votes. CHADEMA won five constituency seats on securing 7 per cent of the national votes.

What is important to note, for genuine Tanzanian patriots and committed democrats is that in spite of the rampant abuse of national resources to bribe an unsophisticated, poverty-stricken and starving electorate, and all the other manoeuvres and manipulations, at least 20 per cent of the people of Tanzania spoke out and said NO. And I urge all genuine patriotic democrats to rise to the challenge of these courageous, intrepid stalwarts, and to organise ourselves so that victory can be ours in 2010.

To conclude on the outcome of the General Elections of 2005: when the special seats reserved for women were counted, CHADEMA had won an additional six seats, making a total of eleven MPs. CUF, which had won nineteen constituency seats in Zanzibar (eighteen of them in Pemba), had an additional eleven special seats making a total of thirty. UDP had won one seat and so did TLP.

CHAPTER 25

Epilogue

This story of my life has turned out to be not strictly about me, but about my times and the major events that impacted on our country and people. It has also been about the institutions in which I played some role in running or founding. It is my hope that those who read it will not treat it as presumptuous, but will see it as an attempt to record what happened, the people who were involved, why they acted as they did and my own personal involvement in, and assessment of the major events of these times, and of some of the main actors. I hope that the revelations of my own modest, humble beginnings will also give hope and inspiration to many of our increasingly disadvantaged youngsters: that in spite of any hardships confronting them now, perseverance, hard work, honesty, rectitude and boldness may eventually place them on a plane of relief and lead them to a more fulfilling and better life

Looking back over the years, I consider that a combination of salutary lessons, dogged application, good luck, courage and pride in myself have contributed to making me what I am. Before I was in my teens, my mother told me repeatedly that she was a widow and that there were only the two of us who must exert ourselves in order to survive. During week-ends or school holidays she insisted that I accompany her to the shambas, several miles from our homestead where she grew maize, finger millet or beans. As I revealed at the beginning of this story, I was born at one of these shambas. We woke up an hour or more before dawn and walked those miles to the shamba, to hoe, to weed or to harvest, depending on the season. In the afternoon, we would be ready to walk back home. If it was harvest time, we would return with a load of crops. The lessons of this time toughened me up and became a permanent reminder that I must continuously apply myself. I have therefore always enjoyed waking up early and working hard and late.

There used to hang in my Dar es Salaam office a plaque inscribed in Latin, presented to me by a Catholic ex-seminarian friend who had noted my commitment to hard work. He had written it himself quoting a Spanish scholar he admired and it read: *Virtus, vigor et divitia labor est* meaning "Work is virtue, vigour and riches". Certainly concentrating on the major tasks before me has meant that I have avoided many indulgences which could have tainted my character; and in these days of incurable ailments and afflictions, excessive indulgences could have ended my life earlier. As for riches, I may not have succeeded extravagantly, but coupled with the modest demands from a devoted and loving wife, we have led a contented life and have responsibly paid for our essential requirements, including the education of our children.

Looking back to those early days and my contemporaries, I feel that I have probably always been 'the odd man out' in the sense that as a teenager and as a young man, I was often inclined to enjoy the company of persons older than myself. At more than fifty years of age, I am now inclined to enjoy arguments with and the company of those younger than myself. My youthful discussions and arguments with people senior to me in age in a sense helped me to mature early. Unlike our youth of today, we did not ignore advice and counselling from our elders as outmoded and unfashionable. Indeed, I believe that as parents of today we have failed to instill in the new generation, the benefits of the traditions of our society.

Partly as a result of this lapse on our part, a large percentage of our children are now afflicted by drug abuse and the devastating HIV/AIDS pandemic. Although those in authority are now spending many millions of shillings in organising seminars, debates, workshops and conferences on how to arrest the spread of the pandemic, we seem to turn a blind eye on shows and displays on television and other media which to our parents would have been rated as vulgar or obscene. These are obviously counter productive. In Western countries certain sex films are censored or banned, but here those of us who object to such displays are branded as outmoded and unfashionable.

Unfortunately, in Africa, south of the Sahara in particular, this deadly disease is spreading like wild fire, decimating the youth. With this trend unchecked, I fear that economic growth and even the survival of its inhabitants are threatened. In areas of dense rural population, the homesteads are being turned into graveyards for the younger generations at such speed that soon there will be no space to bury the older generations when they pass on. The situation is alarming, especially in the region of my origin, Kilimanjaro, where every weekend vehicles and aeroplanes bring in caskets containing bodies of victims, mostly young ones, from all corners of Tanzania and beyond, for final internment. There are alarming reports from areas like Makete that over 40 per cent of the population is HIV positive. Governments and everyone in positions of leadership must urgently and effectively rise to this challenge.

Returning to a more personal note, I should point out that many of the circumstances that led to what might be considered as my successes in life, have been mere coincidences, not of my planning or even expectation. The fact that immediately after my graduation from Makerere University College, the avenues for local staff promotion in the public service suddenly widened had nothing to do with my personal effort or planning. During that time, vacancies applied for candidates, rather than candidates applying to fill vacant posts. Very early in that period, again by coincidence, an enthusiastic and unbiased British public servant, David Anderson, joined our Establishments Department as Staff Development Advisor, and literally became my mentor. That I met bosses like A. L. Adu, the Ghanaian Secretary General of EACSO, who took such personal interest in my performance and promoted me so rapidly, was another pure coincidence.

Even my initial encounter with Mwalimu Julius Nyerere, which led to his valuing my performance and candid assessment of events, was fortuitous. The encounter could have been with another equally eligible Tanzanian. He favoured me with such fast promotions that when I was Secretary General of the East African Community in 1974 (when I was only 42 years old), a number of Kenyans and Ugandans thought that I was from the same tribe as Nyerere. They could not imagine that a non-tribesman could enjoy such high and frequent rises whilst so young. I was lucky to belong to Tanzania where Nyerere was president.

As to boldness, I look back to those sessions with my superiors, or in plenary discussions in conferences, in Cabinet meetings, in the Committee of Twenty Deputies on International Monetary Reform, in Executive Board meetings of the International Monetary Fund or the Tanzania Coffee Board, with nostalgic feelings. Once convinced, I used to say what I believed without fear or hesitation. In some cases, my conservative listeners thought I was naïve. In other cases, they thought I was rash. On many occasions there were claps of applause, when as I proved to be the spokesman of the fearful or down-trodden, and later of the poor unsure coffee farmer. Sometimes I was a minority or a lonely arguer, but as time passed on, I have on many instances, been proved right. Especially with my most important boss, President Julius Nyerere, I regret that I was not persuasive enough: The extent of our differences led to our parting. Had I succeeded in convincing him, my country's economic fortunes and history would have been different. Successor governments have, of course, embraced many of my views and approach to national economic and social issues, but it has been too late and our people have thus endured untold sufferings.

When I started writing this story in 2004, I intended to complete it by the middle of 2005. As the year rolled on, however, I found myself engrossed in the manner in which the political situation of my country was evolving. I noted especially that the political party I had participated in founding was heading for a confrontation, the results of which I thought I should witness, before concluding my story. In retrospect, I might have made a mistake, for if I had published this story, including my knowledge of the background to CHADEMA and its ethos, I may have enlisted the support of some of those who doubted our stance on national issues and so denied us their votes in December 2005. Nevertheless, if the release of my account this time helps to elucidate our approach to national issues and our patriotic commitment to resolving them, it may not be too late. A country never dies.

Three generations: rare group photograph of ourselves, our children, their spouses and all our grandchildren, at Ogaden Estate, December 2002.

However, as we stand looking towards the future, there is no gainsaying that the Tanzania political situation is on a dangerous trend. The tolerance for non-performing regimes, which has been shown for decades by the Tanzania people is fast wearing out. It lasted this long because the people believed that matters would in the long run, be sorted out satisfactorily because their leaders were clean, incorruptible, committed and dedicated patriots. Today in increasing numbers, they have come to realise that those virtues they counted upon in the leadership of the nation have been seriously eroded. Instead, selfishness and disregard for the pitiable plight of the poor have become the norm rather than the exception.

Revelations of corrupt deals of monumental proportions have rocked the nation, as have reports of gross abuse of power by individuals at top echelons of national leadership. More disturbing still, leadership displays an almost casual and disdainful attitude to demands by opposition parties for investigation of the allegations and where proven, for government to take corrective measures.

Even where obvious misdeeds have come to light, culprits are spared, and action against them postponed unnecessarily.

Lest I am accused of ignoring genuine achievements, let me conclude by stating that since the latter half of the 1980s, Tanzania has taken steps, albeit haltingly, to cover lost ground. At Independence we were neck-and-neck with our East African neighbours, Kenya and Uganda, in terms of progress in education and social services. We fell behind in the first twenty-five years because of the ill-fated *ujamaa* policies and also due to our delayed action in putting in place corrective measures when the 'socialist apparatus' started malfunctioning.

Since then, we have made strides to catch up, and I believe if, as a nation, we can properly utilise the huge resources at our disposal, by genuine hard work and application, whilst rooting out corrupt and self-serving leadership, the sky is the limit. It is therefore my prayers that the current opening up by the expansion and deepening of East African integration will propel the Tanzanian leadership into taking deliberate positive action to rekindle the confidence and trust of the people. Only such action can ameliorate the situation and lead to genuine sustainable political and social progress.

END

GLOSSARY OF NON-ENGLISH WORDS USED IN THE TEXT

Ari	-	Enthusiasm
Chama	-	Party
Kasi	-	Speed
Irutsa Mana	-	A ceremony of removing bones of the dead from their graves in order to place them with those of the ancestors at a shrine.
Kazi	-	Work
Khanga	-	A popular cotton printed cloth won by women
Kihamba	-	A farm plot
Mageuzi	-	Reform
Mapfundo	-	Initiation
Maendeleo	-	Development
Mapinduzi	-	Revolution
Mpango	-	Plan
Mpya	-	New
Mkara o Shima	-	Match maker
Mraru	-	Path
Kitenge/Vitenge	-	Cotton printed cloth that is heavier than Khanga
Shamba	-	Farm
Nguvu	-	Strength
Hakuna Kulala	-	No sleeping
Uhuru	-	Freedom
Ujamaa	-	Socialism
Takrima	-	Hospitality

www.ingramcontent.com/pod-product-compliance
Lightning Source LLC
Chambersburg PA
CBHW011139290426
44108CB00020B/2688